12

CLAMP

TRANSLATED AND ADAPTED BY
William Flanagan

LETTERED BY
Dana Hayward

BALLANTINE BOOKS · NEW YORK

A Del Rey Manga/Kodansha Trade Paperback Original

xxxHOLiC, volume 12 copyright © 2007 by CLAMP
English translation copyright © 2008 by CLAMP

Published in the United States by Del Rey Books, an imprint of The Random House Publishing Group, a division of Random House, Inc., New York.

DEL REY is a registered trademark and the Del Rey colophon is a trademark of Random House, Inc.

Publication rights arranged through Kodansha Ltd.

First published in Japan in 2007 by Kodansha Ltd., Tokyo

ISBN 978-0-345-50565-1

Printed in the United States of America

www.delreymanga.com

9 8 7 6 5 4 3 2 1

Translator and Adapter—William Flanagan
Lettering—Dana Hayward

xxxHOLiC crosses over with *Tsubasa*. Although it isn't necessary to read *Tsubasa* to understand the events in *xxxHOLiC*, you'll get to see the same events from different perspectives if you read both series!

Contents

Honorifics Explained

Throughout the Del Rey Manga books, you will find Japanese honorifics left intact in the translations. For those not familiar with how the Japanese use honorifics and, more important, how they differ from American honorifics, we present this brief overview.

Politeness has always been a critical facet of Japanese culture. Ever since the feudal era, when Japan was a highly stratified society, use of honorifics—which can be defined as polite speech that indicates relationship or status—has played an essential role in the Japanese language. When you address someone in Japanese, an honorific usually takes the form of a suffix attached to one's name (example: "Asuna-san"), is used as a title at the end of one's name, or appears in place of the name itself (example: "Negi-sensei," or simply "Sensei!").

Honorifics can be expressions of respect or endearment. In the context of manga and anime, honorifics give insight into the nature of the relationship between characters. Many English translations leave out these important honorifics and therefore distort the feel of the original Japanese. Because Japanese honorifics contain nuances that English honorifics lack, it is our policy at Del Rey not to translate them. Here, instead, is a guide to some of the honorifics you may encounter in Del Rey Manga.

-san: This is the most common honorific and is equivalent to Mr., Miss, Ms., or Mrs. It is the all-purpose honorific and can be used in any situation where politeness is required.

-sama: This is one level higher than "-san" and is used to confer great respect.

-dono: This comes from the word "tono," which means "lord." It is an even higher level than "-sama" and confers utmost respect.

-kun: This suffix is used at the end of boys' names to express familiarity or endearment. It is also sometimes used by men among friends, or when addressing someone younger or of a lower station.

-chan: This is used to express endearment, mostly toward girls. It is also used for little boys, pets, and even among lovers. It gives a sense of childish cuteness.

Bozu: This is an informal way to refer to a boy, similar to the English terms "kid" and "squirt."

Sempai/Senpai: This title suggests that the addressee is one's senior in a group or organization. It is most often used in a school setting, where underclassmen refer to their upperclassmen as "sempai." It can also be used in the workplace, such as when a newer employee addresses an employee who has seniority in the company.

Kohai: This is the opposite of "sempai" and is used toward underclassmen in school or newcomers in the workplace. It connotes that the addressee is of a lower station.

Sensei: Literally meaning "one who has come before," this title is used for teachers, doctors, or masters of any profession or art.

-[blank]: This is usually forgotten in these lists, but it is perhaps the most significant difference between Japanese and English. The lack of honorific means that the speaker has permission to address the person in a very intimate way. Usually, only family, spouses, or very close friends have this kind of permission. Known as *yobisute*, it can be gratifying when someone who has earned the intimacy starts to call one by one's name without an honorific. But when that intimacy hasn't been earned, it can be very insulting.

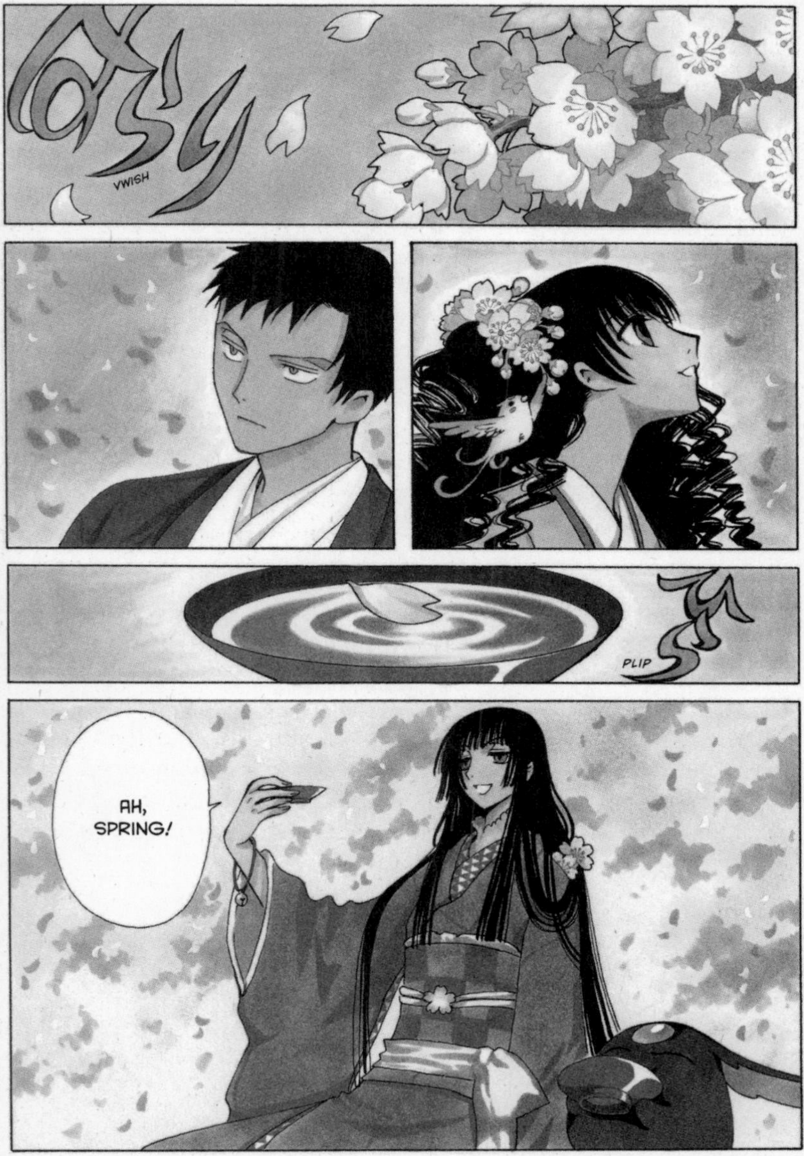
VWISH
PLIP
AH, SPRING!

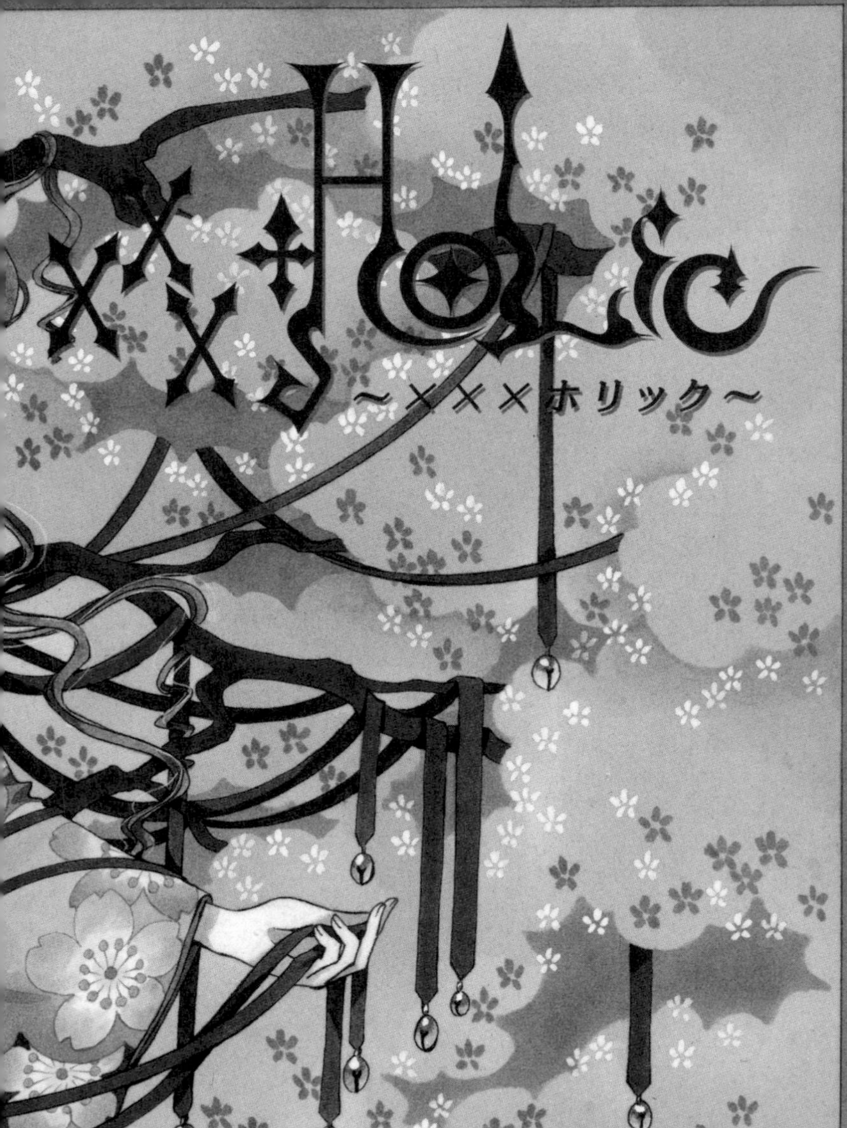
xxxHOLiC
~×××ホリック~

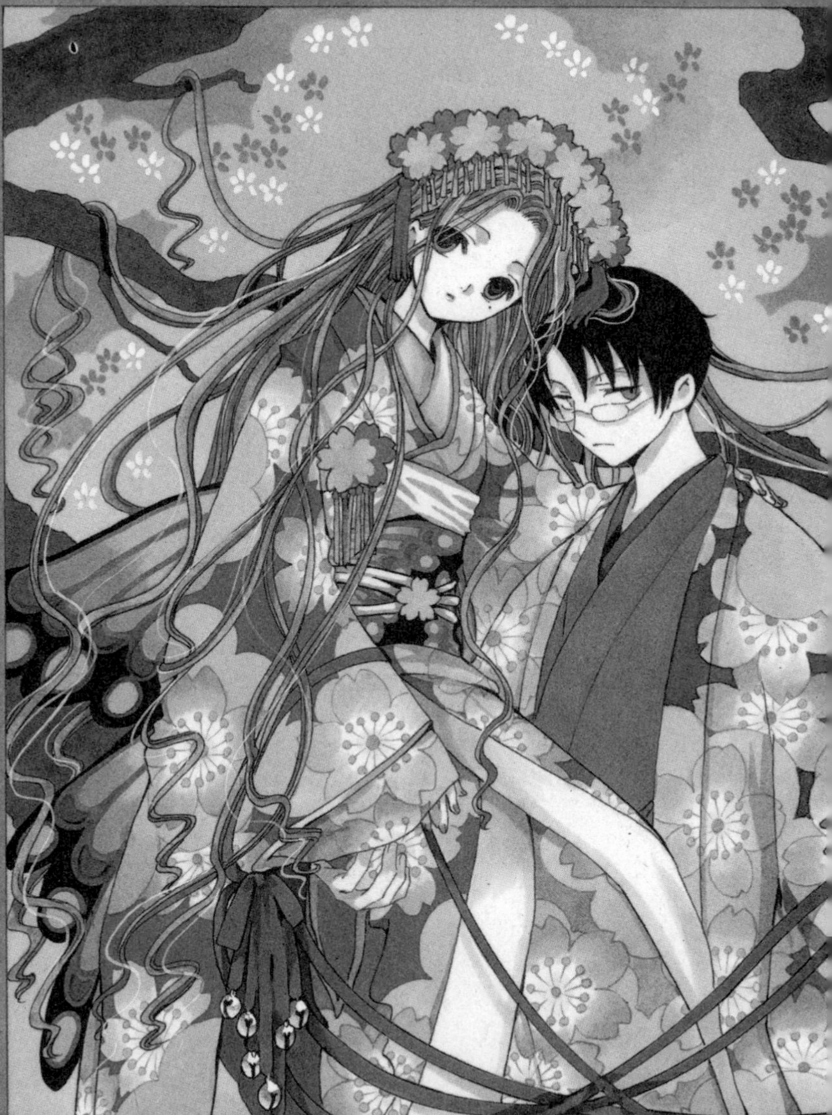

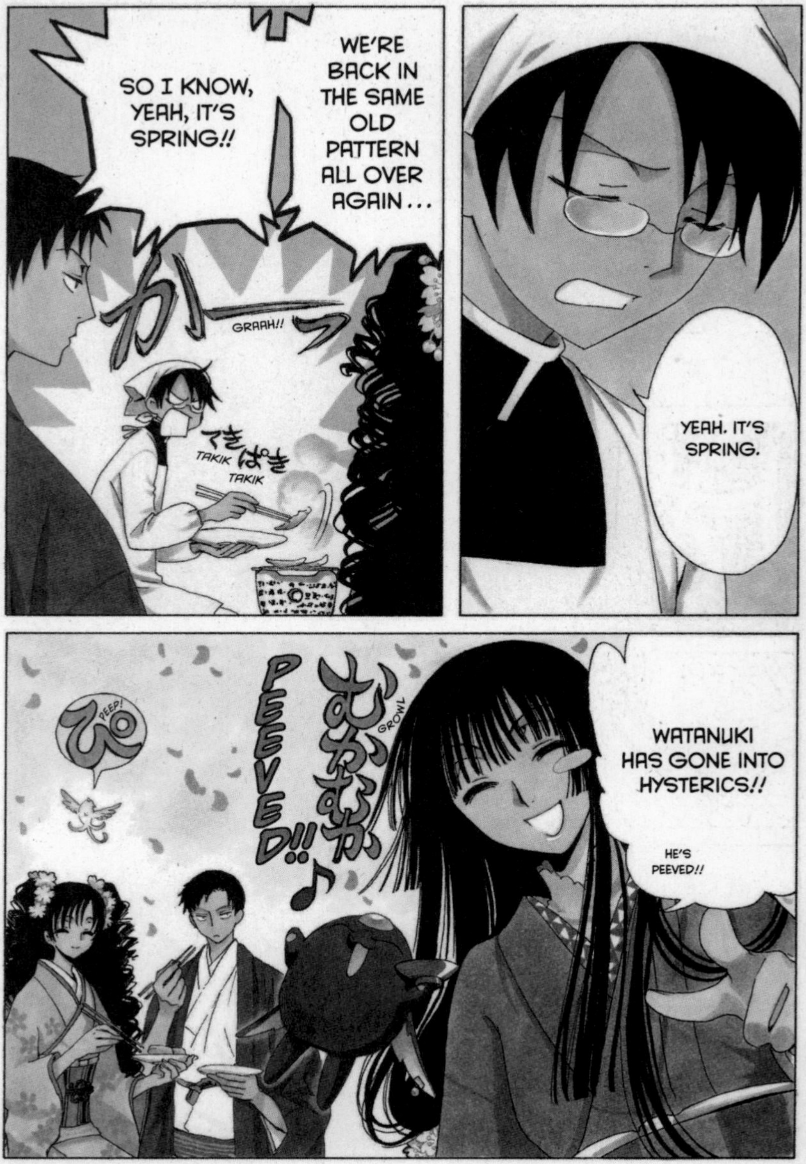
YEAH. IT'S SPRING.
WE'RE BACK IN THE SAME OLD PATTERN ALL OVER AGAIN...
SO I KNOW, YEAH, IT'S SPRING!!
かーっ
GRAAH!!
てきぱき
TAKIK TAKIK
WATANUKI HAS GONE INTO HYSTERICS!!
HE'S PEEVED!!
むかむか♪
GROWL
PEEVED!!
ぴ
PEEP!

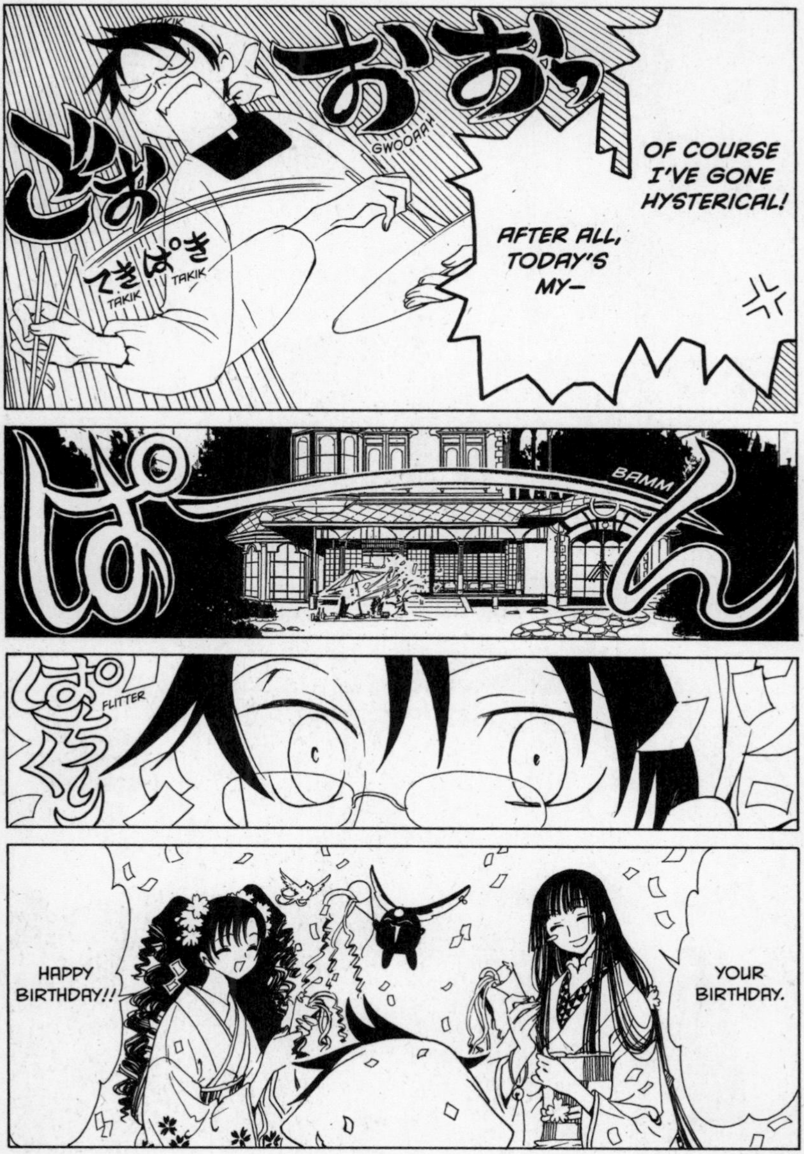

OF COURSE I'VE GONE HYSTERICAL!
AFTER ALL, TODAY'S MY—
GWOOARRH
TAKIK
てきぱき
TAKIK TAKIK
BAMM
FLITTER
YOUR BIRTHDAY.
HAPPY BIRTHDAY!!

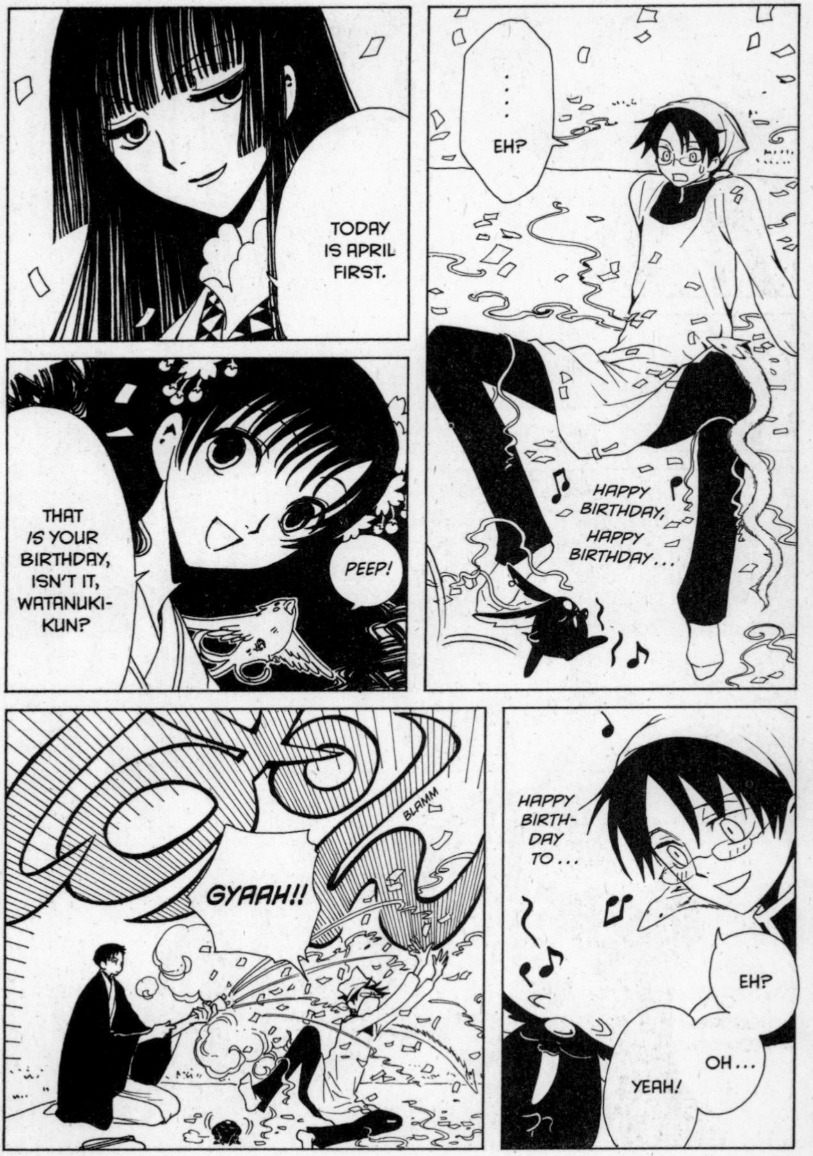

......
EH?
HAPPY BIRTHDAY, HAPPY BIRTHDAY...
TODAY IS APRIL FIRST.
THAT *IS* YOUR BIRTHDAY, ISN'T IT, WATANUKI-KUN?
PEEP!
HAPPY BIRTH-DAY TO...
EH?
OH... YEAH!
BLAMM
GYAAH!!

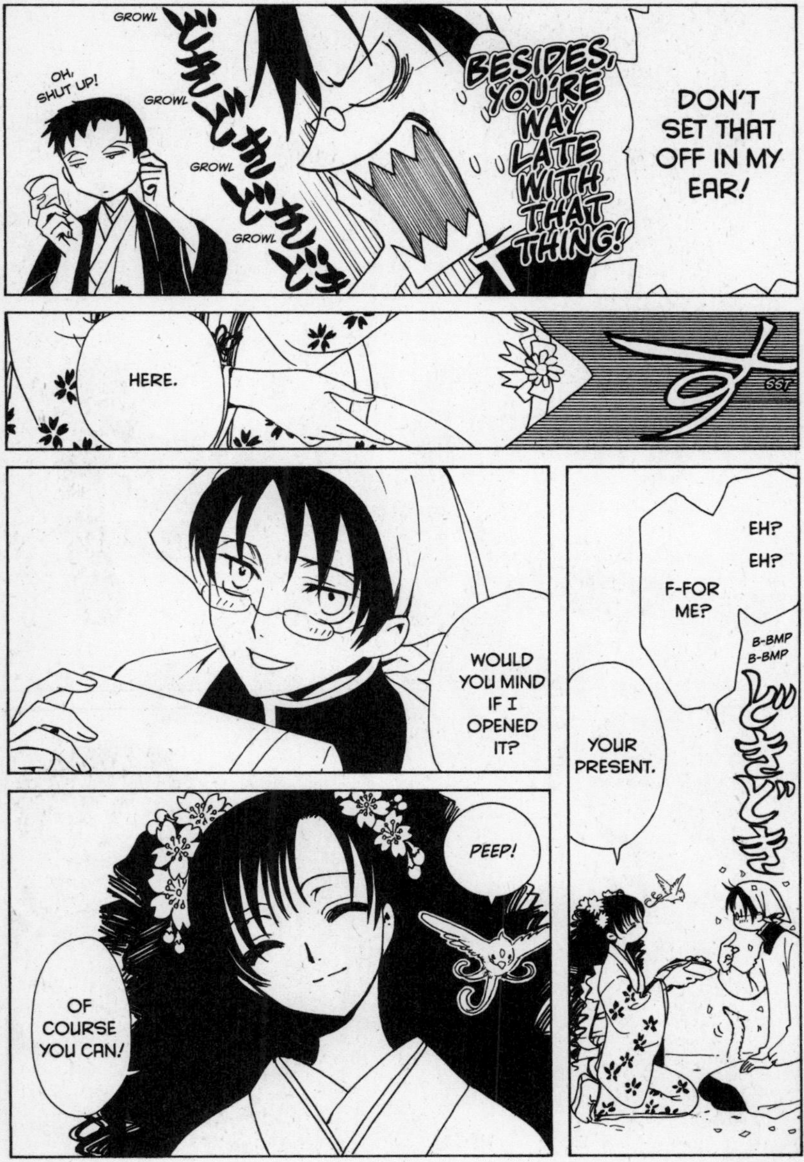
DON'T SET THAT OFF IN MY EAR!
BESIDES, YOU'RE WAY LATE WITH THAT THING!
どきどきどきどき
GROWL
GROWL
GROWL
GROWL
OH, SHUT UP!
す
SST
HERE.
EH?
EH?
F-FOR ME?
B-BMP B-BMP
どきどき
YOUR PRESENT.
WOULD YOU MIND IF I OPENED IT?
PEEP!
OF COURSE YOU CAN!

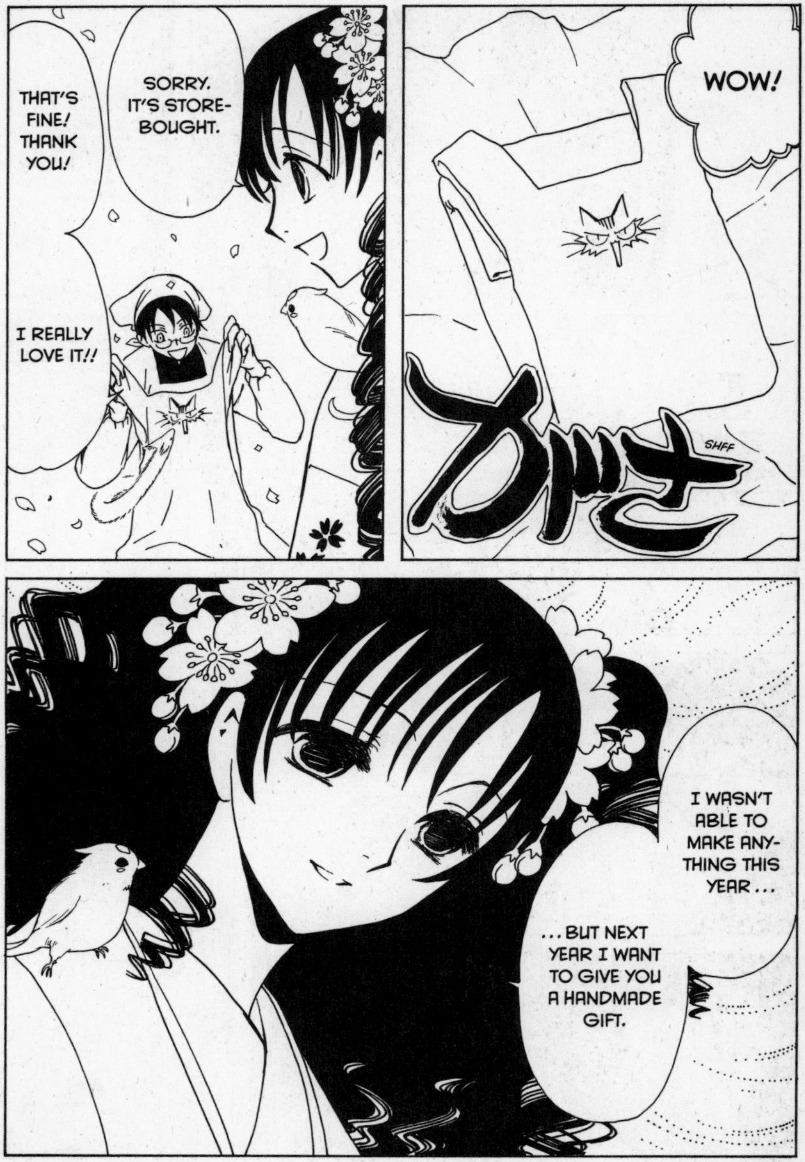
WOW!
SHFF
SORRY. IT'S STORE-BOUGHT.
THAT'S FINE! THANK YOU!
I REALLY LOVE IT!!
I WASN'T ABLE TO MAKE ANY-THING THIS YEAR...
...BUT NEXT YEAR I WANT TO GIVE YOU A HANDMADE GIFT.

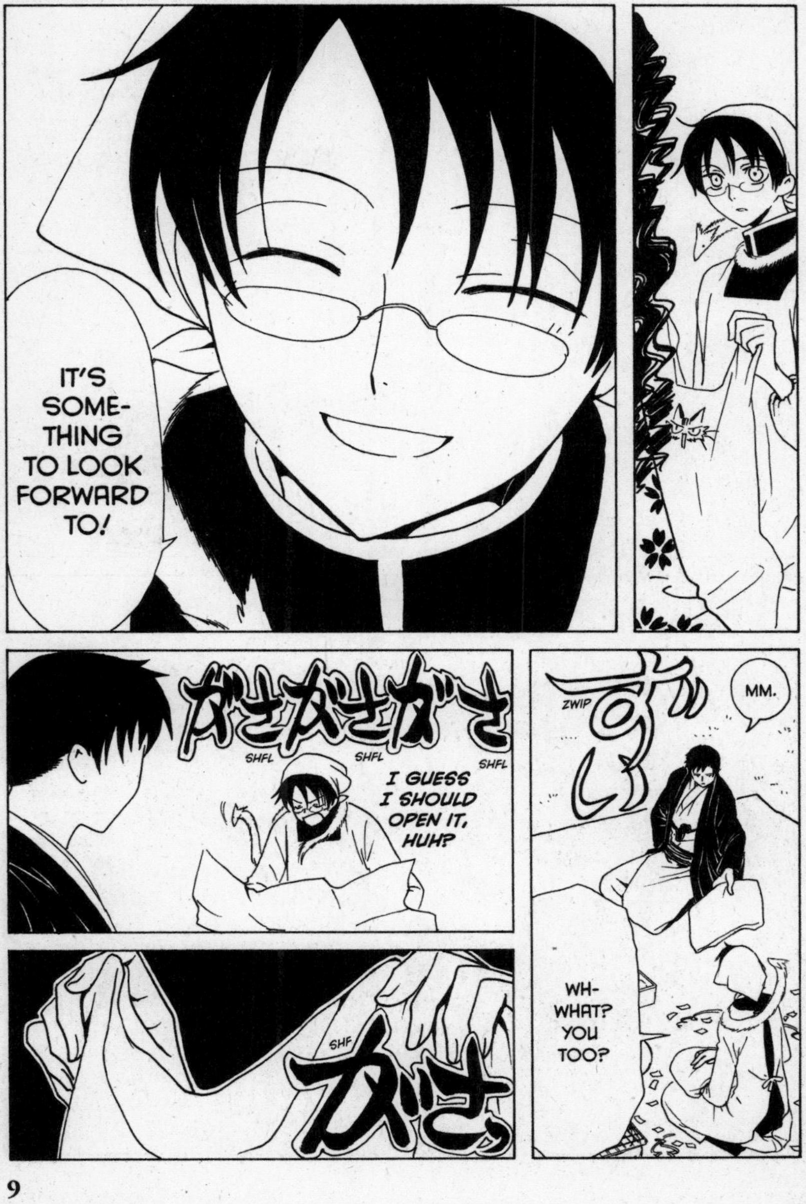

IT'S SOMETHING TO LOOK FORWARD TO!
ZWIP
MM.
WH-WHAT? YOU TOO?
がさがさがさ
SHFL
SHFL
SHFL
I GUESS I SHOULD OPEN IT, HUH?
SHF
がさ

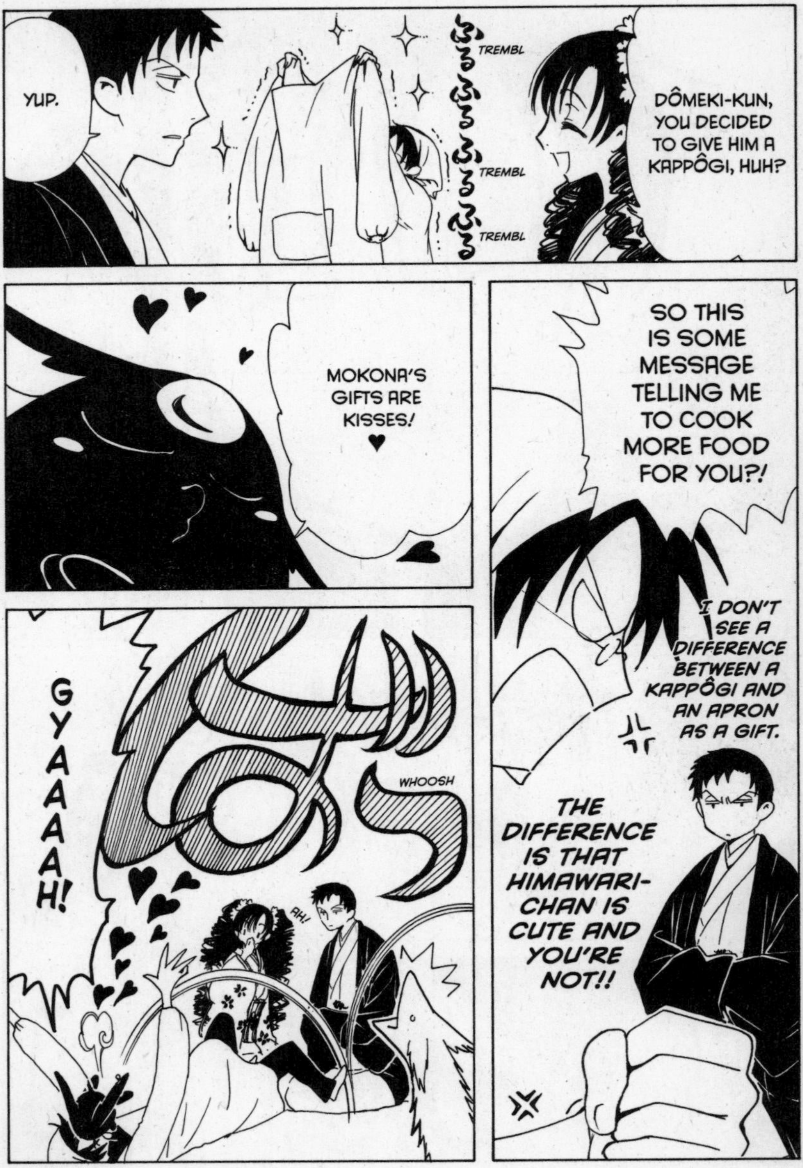
DÔMEKI-KUN, YOU DECIDED TO GIVE HIM A KAPPÔGI, HUH?
TREMBL
TREMBL
TREMBL
YUP.
SO THIS IS SOME MESSAGE TELLING ME TO COOK MORE FOOD FOR YOU?!
I DON'T SEE A DIFFERENCE BETWEEN A KAPPÔGI AND AN APRON AS A GIFT.
THE DIFFERENCE IS THAT HIMAWARI-CHAN IS CUTE AND YOU'RE NOT!!
MOKONA'S GIFTS ARE KISSES! ♥
WHOOSH
GYAAAAAH!
AH!

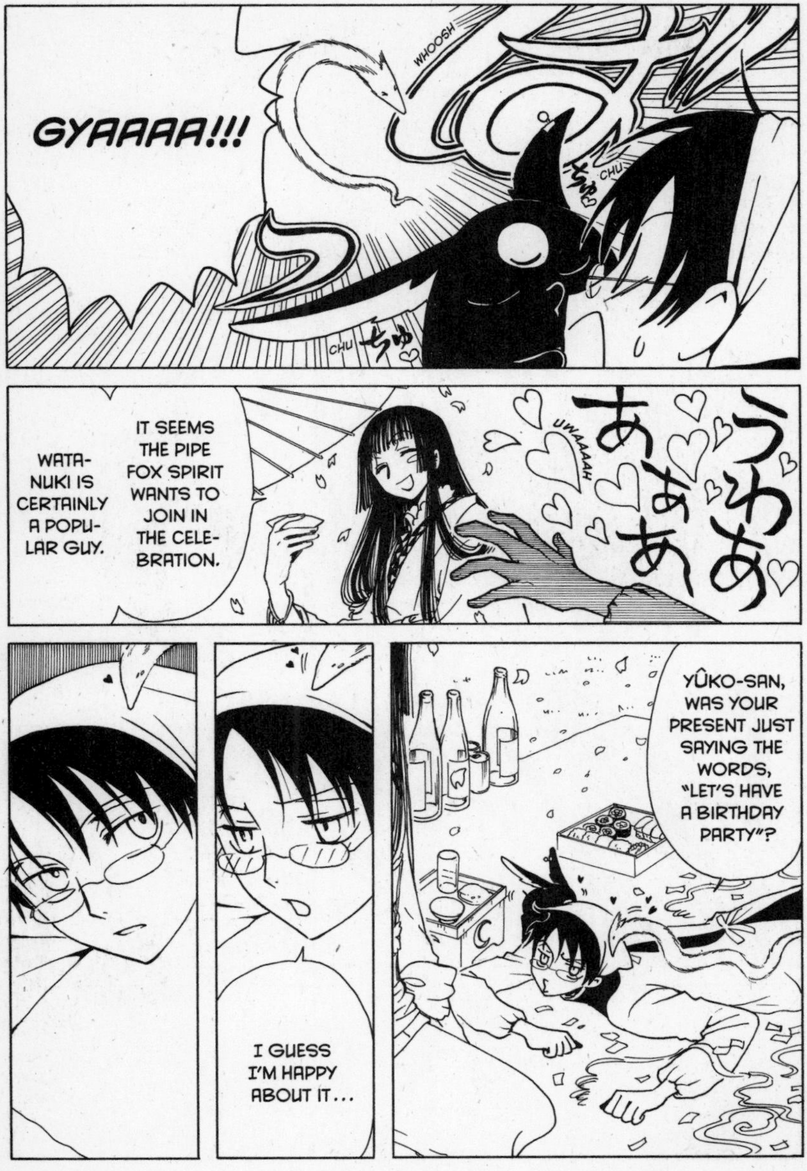
WHOOSH
GYAAAA!!!
ちゅ CHU
ちゅ CHU
うわああああ UWAAAAH
IT SEEMS THE PIPE FOX SPIRIT WANTS TO JOIN IN THE CELE-BRATION.
WATA-NUKI IS CERTAINLY A POPU-LAR GUY.
YÛKO-SAN, WAS YOUR PRESENT JUST SAYING THE WORDS, "LET'S HAVE A BIRTHDAY PARTY"?
I GUESS I'M HAPPY ABOUT IT...

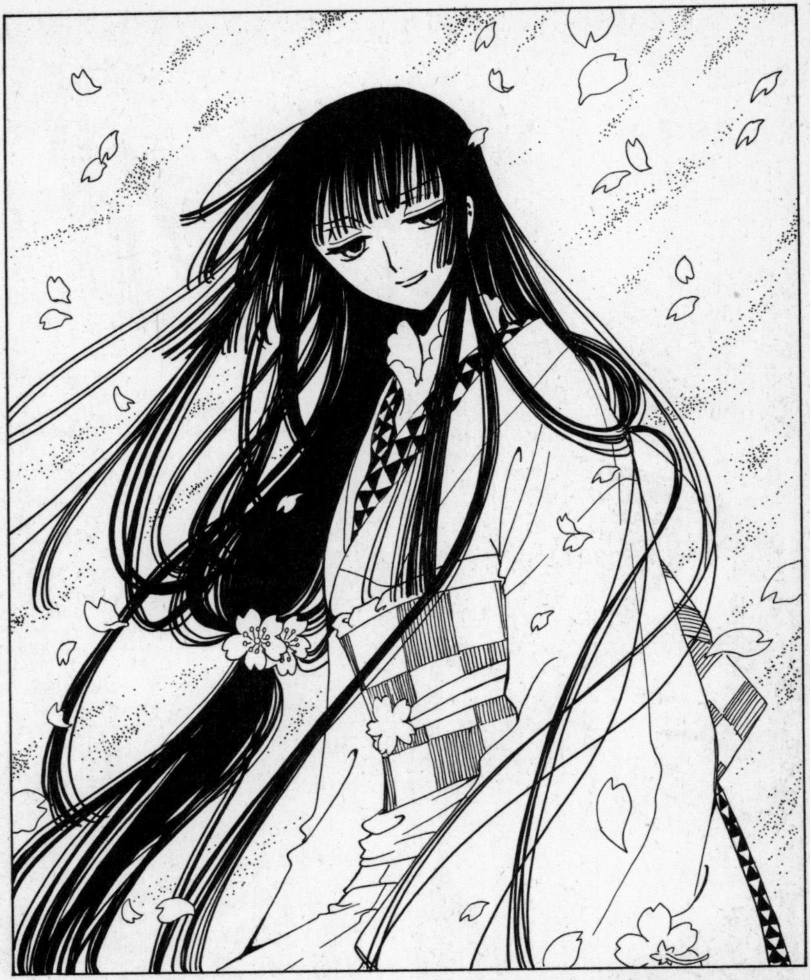

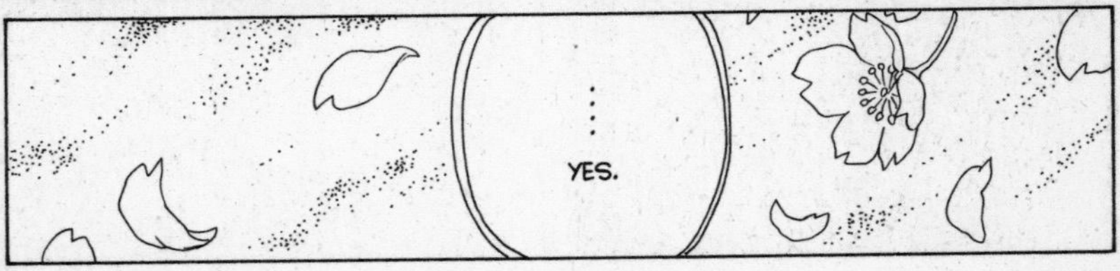
......
YES.

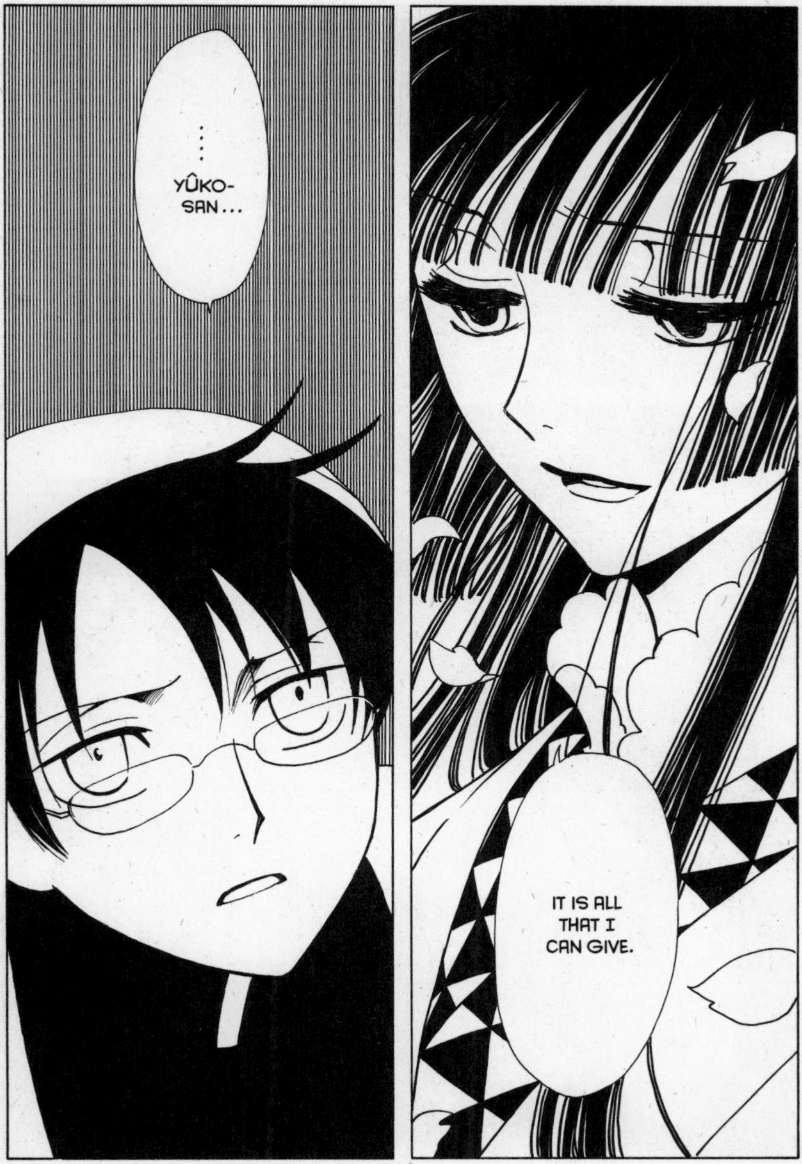
IT IS ALL THAT I CAN GIVE.
...
YÛKO-SAN...

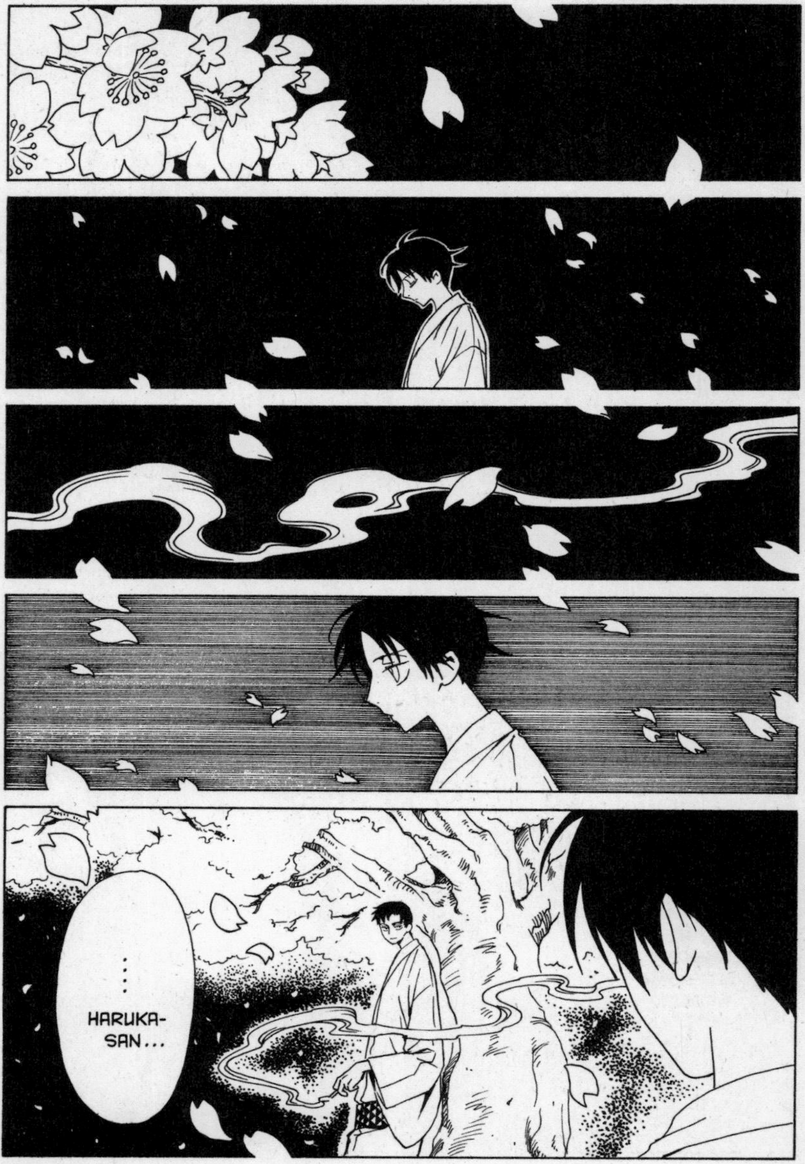
...
HARUKA-SAN...

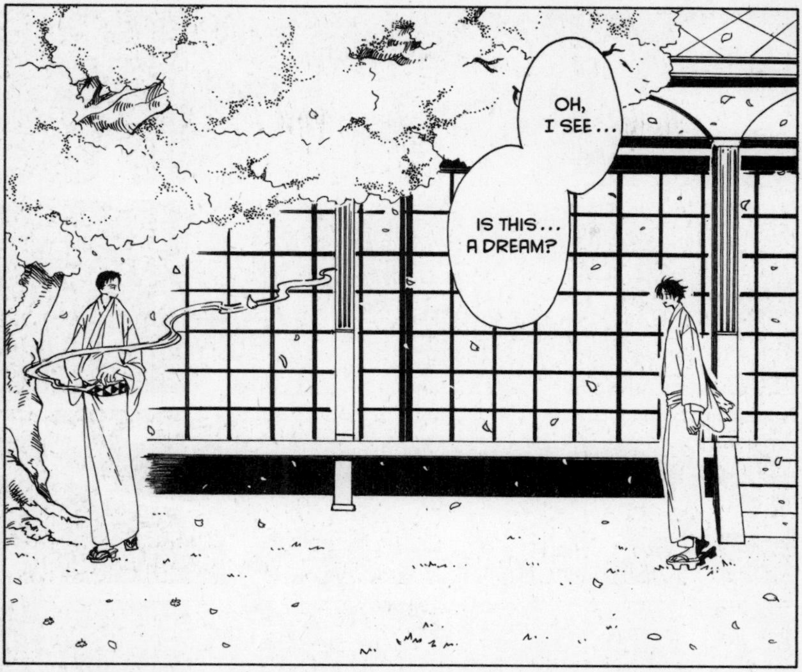
OH, I SEE...
IS THIS... A DREAM?

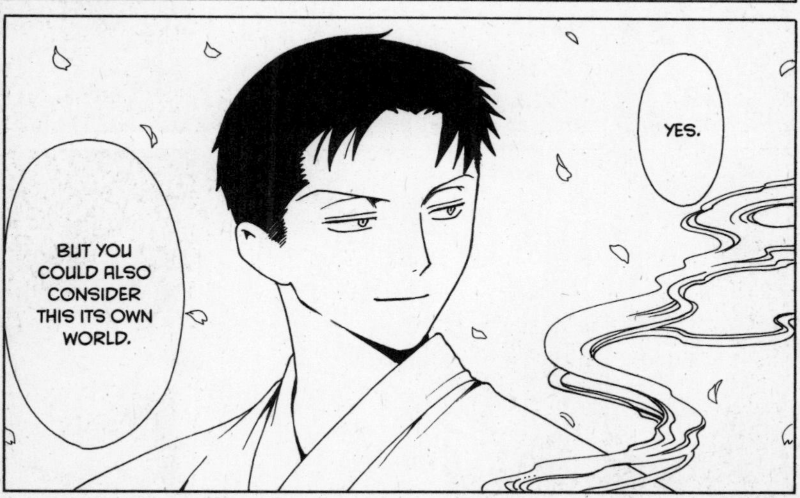
YES.
BUT YOU COULD ALSO CONSIDER THIS ITS OWN WORLD.

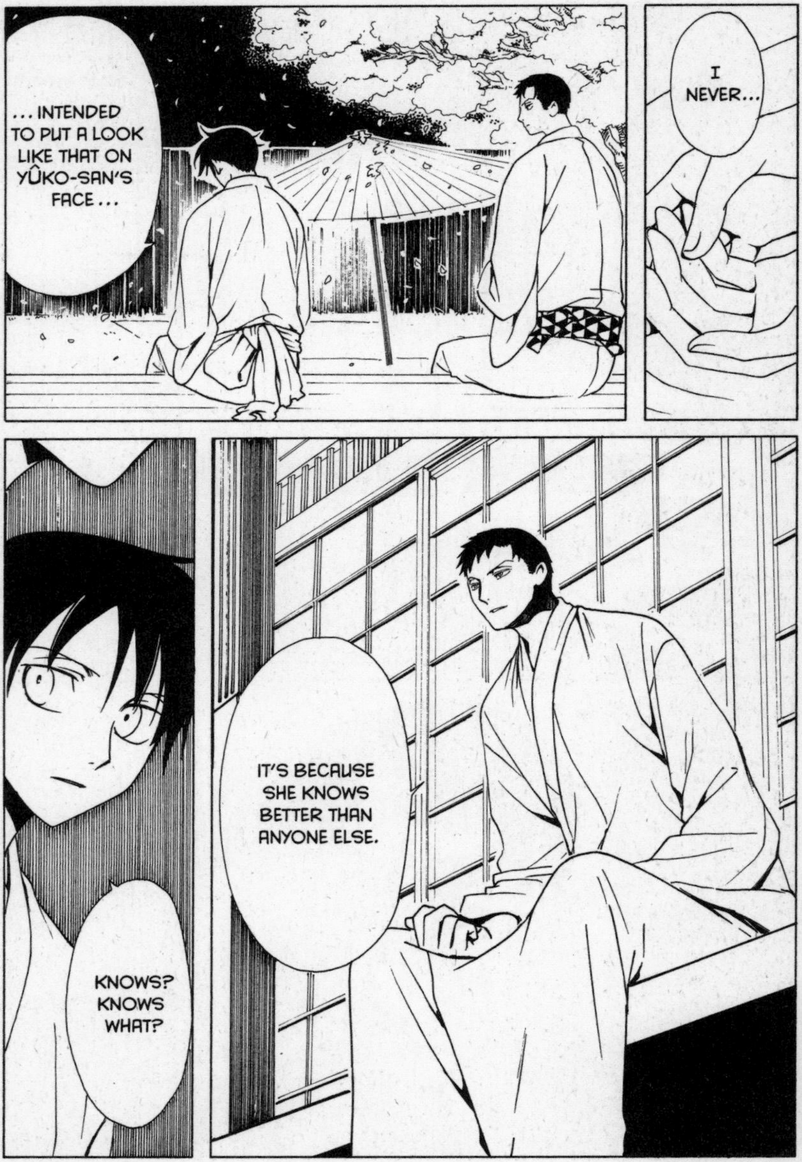
I NEVER...
...INTENDED TO PUT A LOOK LIKE THAT ON YÛKO-SAN'S FACE...
IT'S BECAUSE SHE KNOWS BETTER THAN ANYONE ELSE.
KNOWS? KNOWS WHAT?

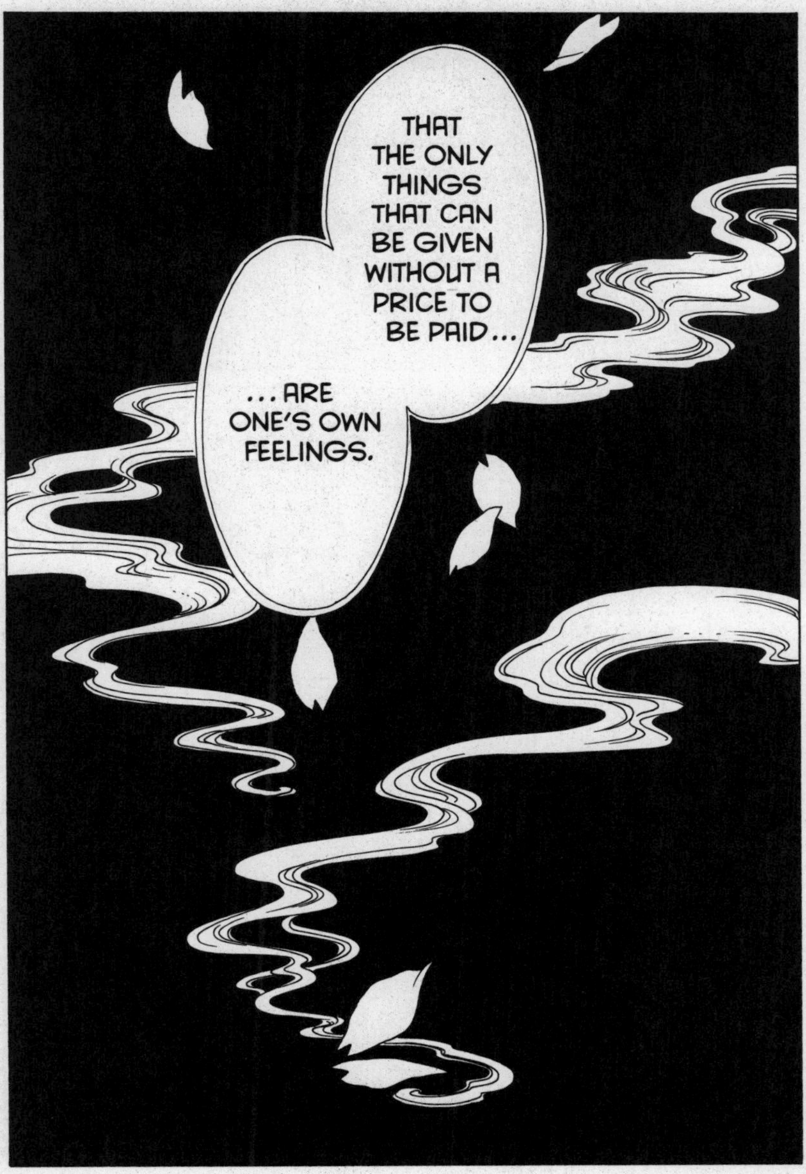
THAT THE ONLY THINGS THAT CAN BE GIVEN WITHOUT A PRICE TO BE PAID...
...ARE ONE'S OWN FEELINGS.

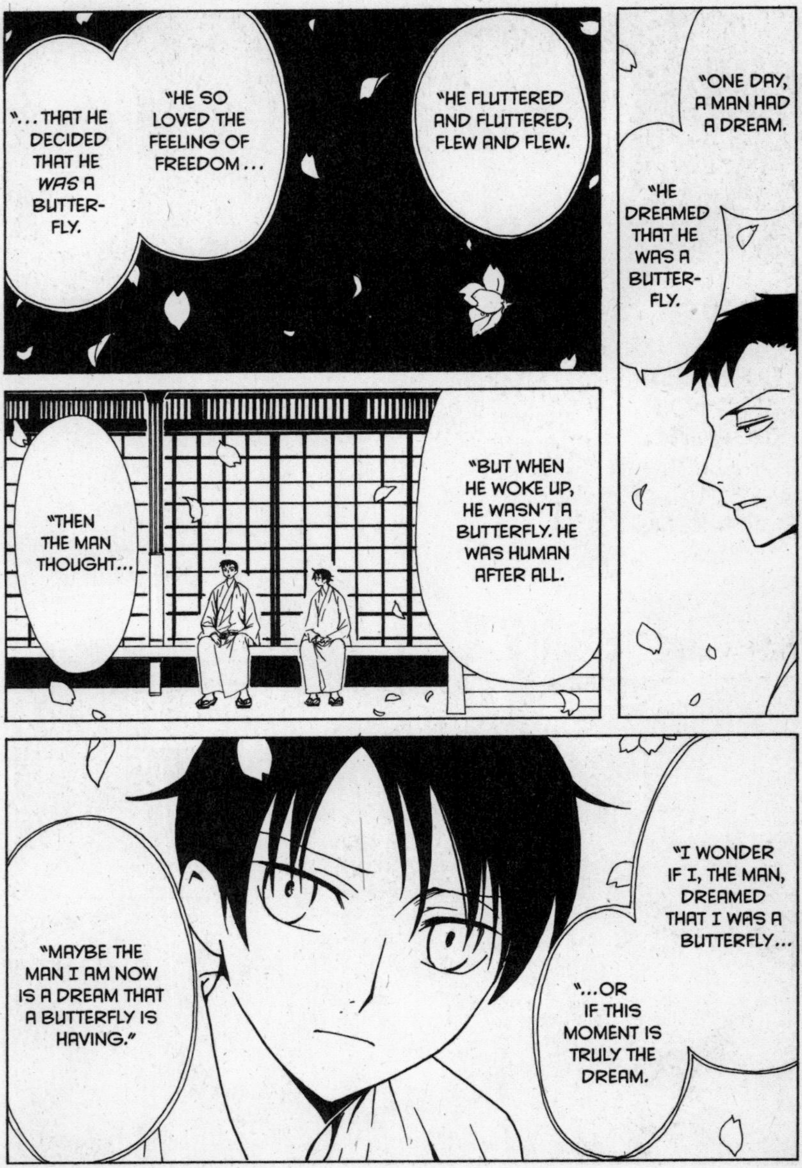
"ONE DAY, A MAN HAD A DREAM.
"HE DREAMED THAT HE WAS A BUTTER-FLY.
"HE FLUTTERED AND FLUTTERED, FLEW AND FLEW.
"HE SO LOVED THE FEELING OF FREEDOM...
"...THAT HE DECIDED THAT HE *WAS* A BUTTER-FLY.
"BUT WHEN HE WOKE UP, HE WASN'T A BUTTERFLY. HE WAS HUMAN AFTER ALL.
"THEN THE MAN THOUGHT...
"I WONDER IF I, THE MAN, DREAMED THAT I WAS A BUTTERFLY...
"...OR IF THIS MOMENT IS TRULY THE DREAM.
"MAYBE THE MAN I AM NOW IS A DREAM THAT A BUTTERFLY IS HAVING."

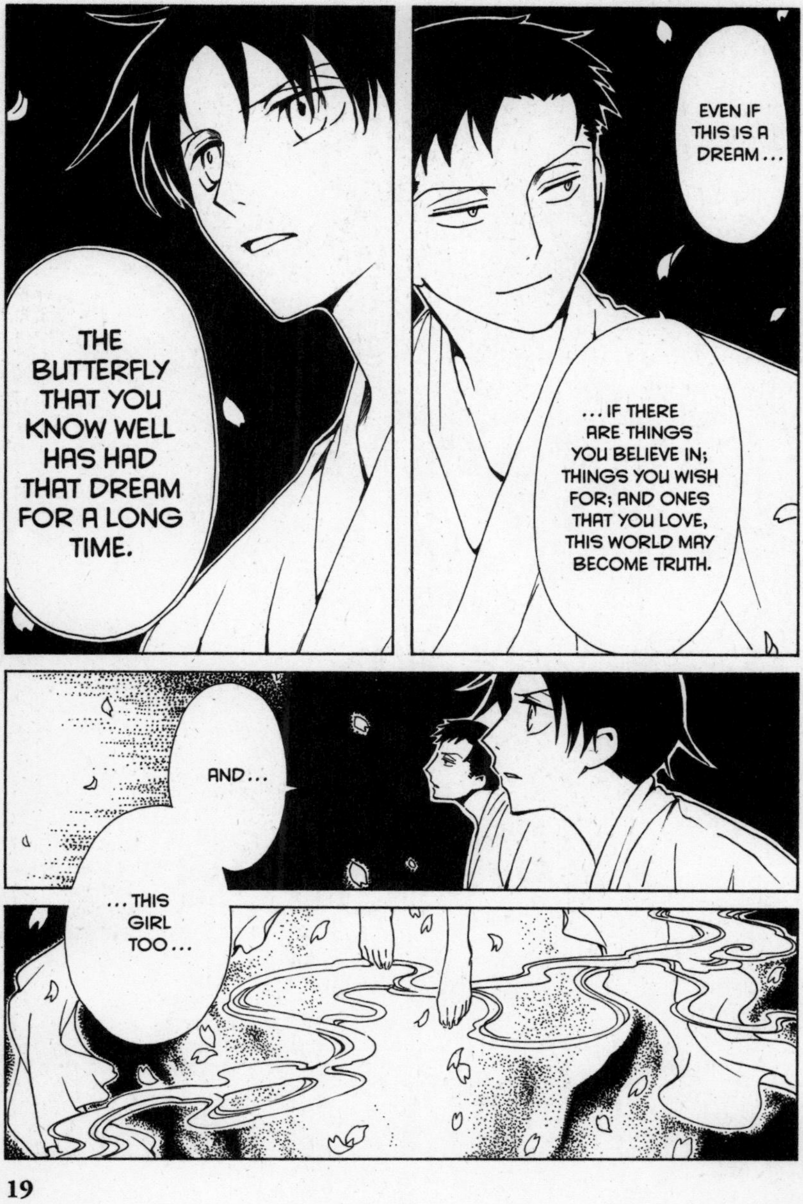
EVEN IF THIS IS A DREAM...
...IF THERE ARE THINGS YOU BELIEVE IN; THINGS YOU WISH FOR; AND ONES THAT YOU LOVE, THIS WORLD MAY BECOME TRUTH.
THE BUTTERFLY THAT YOU KNOW WELL HAS HAD THAT DREAM FOR A LONG TIME.
AND...
...THIS GIRL TOO...

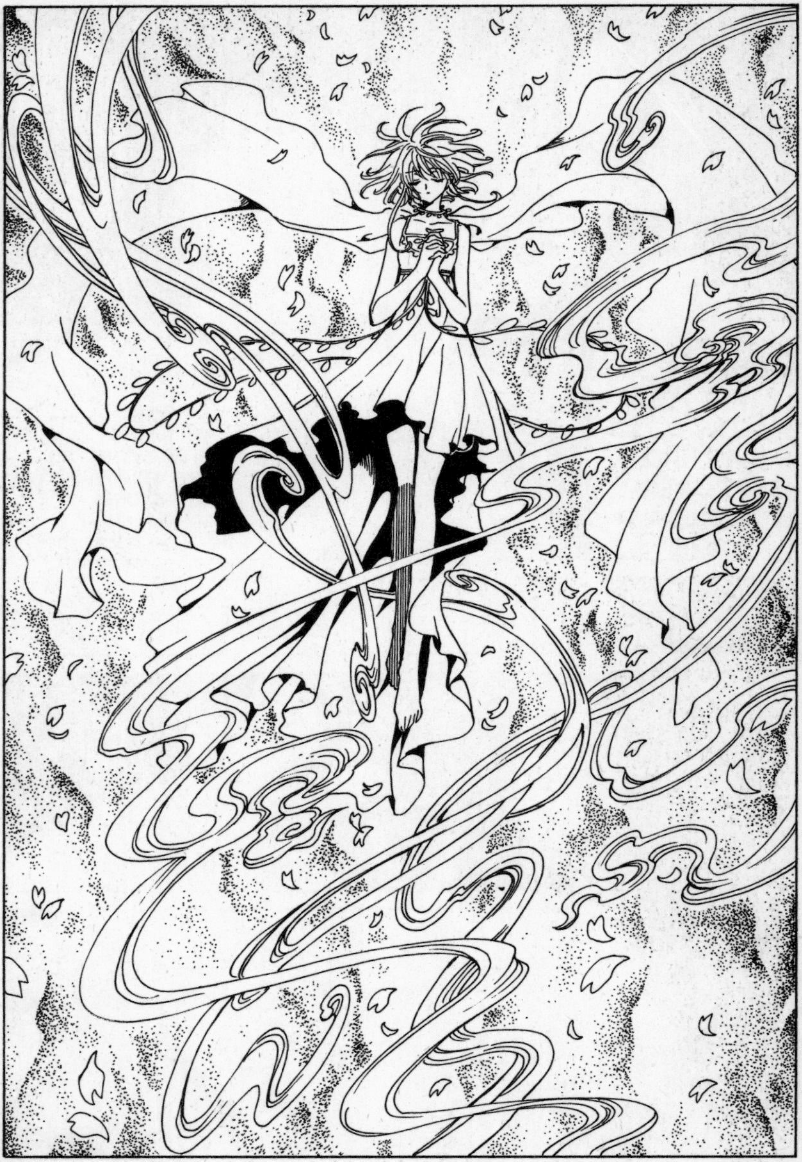

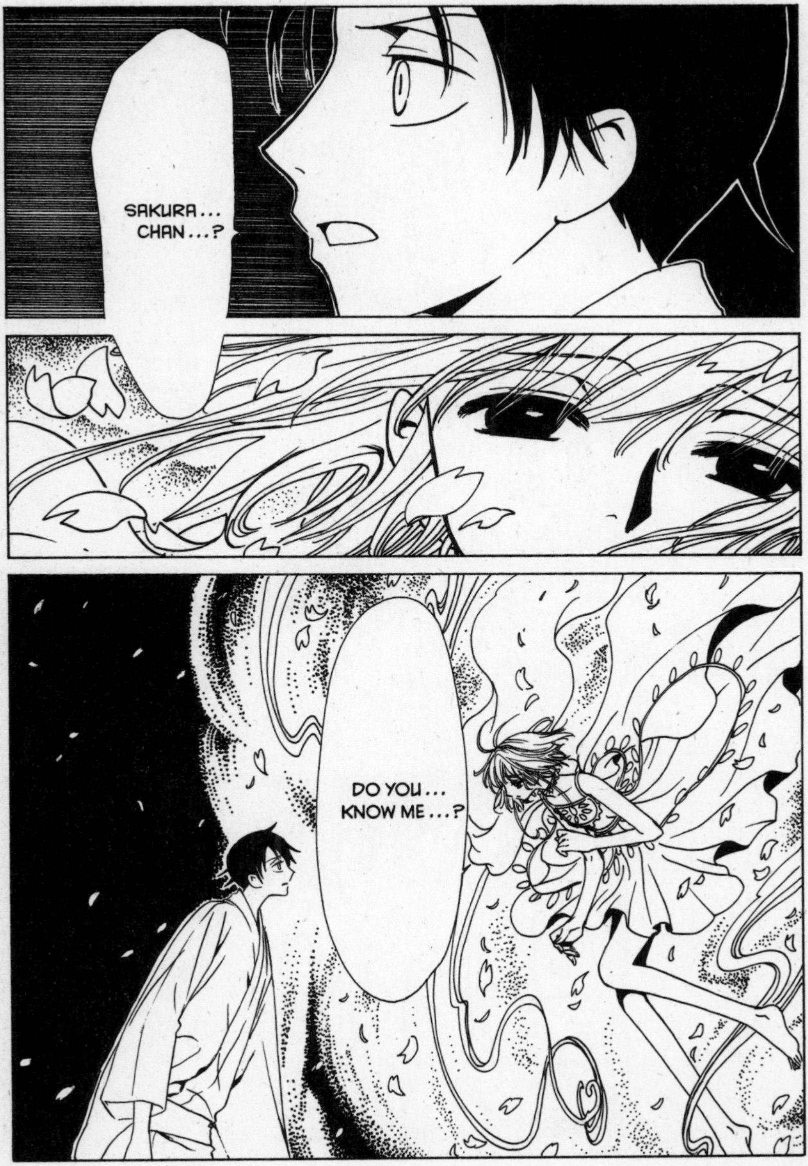
SAKURA...
CHAN...?
DO YOU...
KNOW ME...?

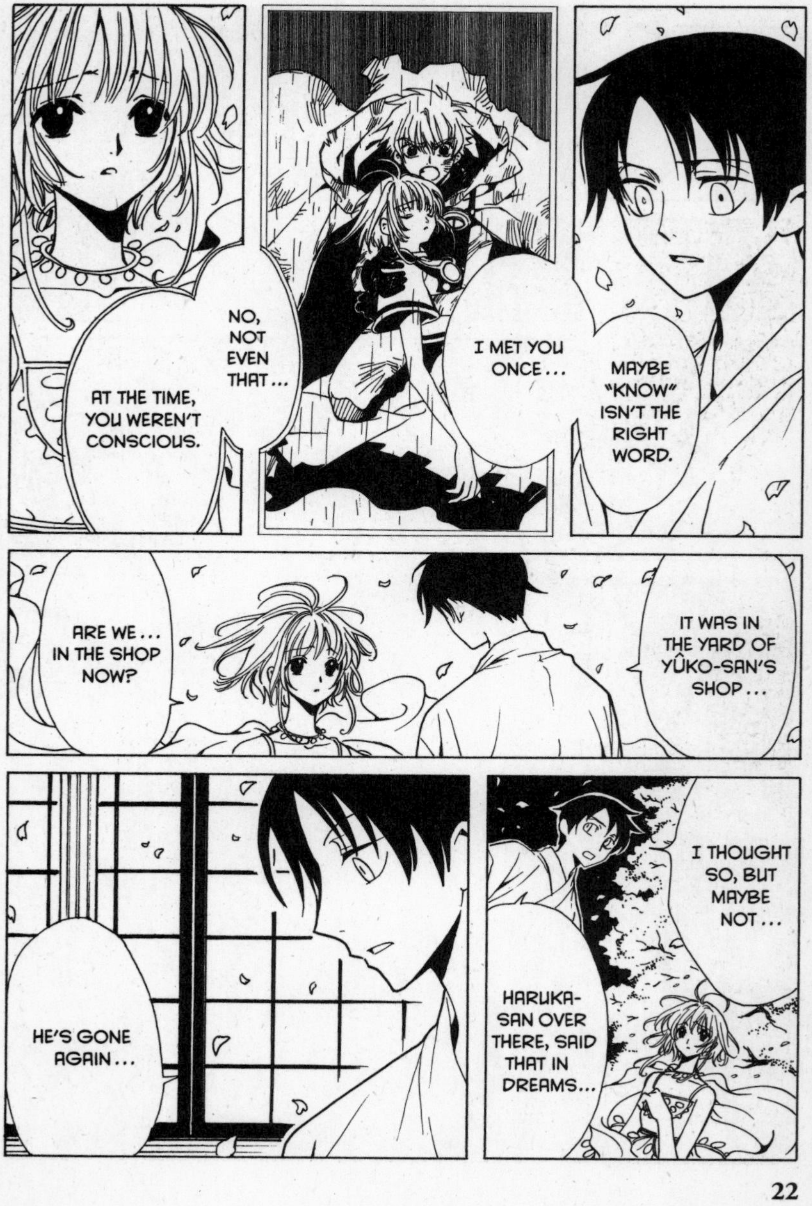
MAYBE "KNOW" ISN'T THE RIGHT WORD.
I MET YOU ONCE...
NO, NOT EVEN THAT...
AT THE TIME, YOU WEREN'T CONSCIOUS.
IT WAS IN THE YARD OF YÛKO-SAN'S SHOP...
ARE WE... IN THE SHOP NOW?
I THOUGHT SO, BUT MAYBE NOT...
HARUKA-SAN OVER THERE, SAID THAT IN DREAMS...
HE'S GONE AGAIN...

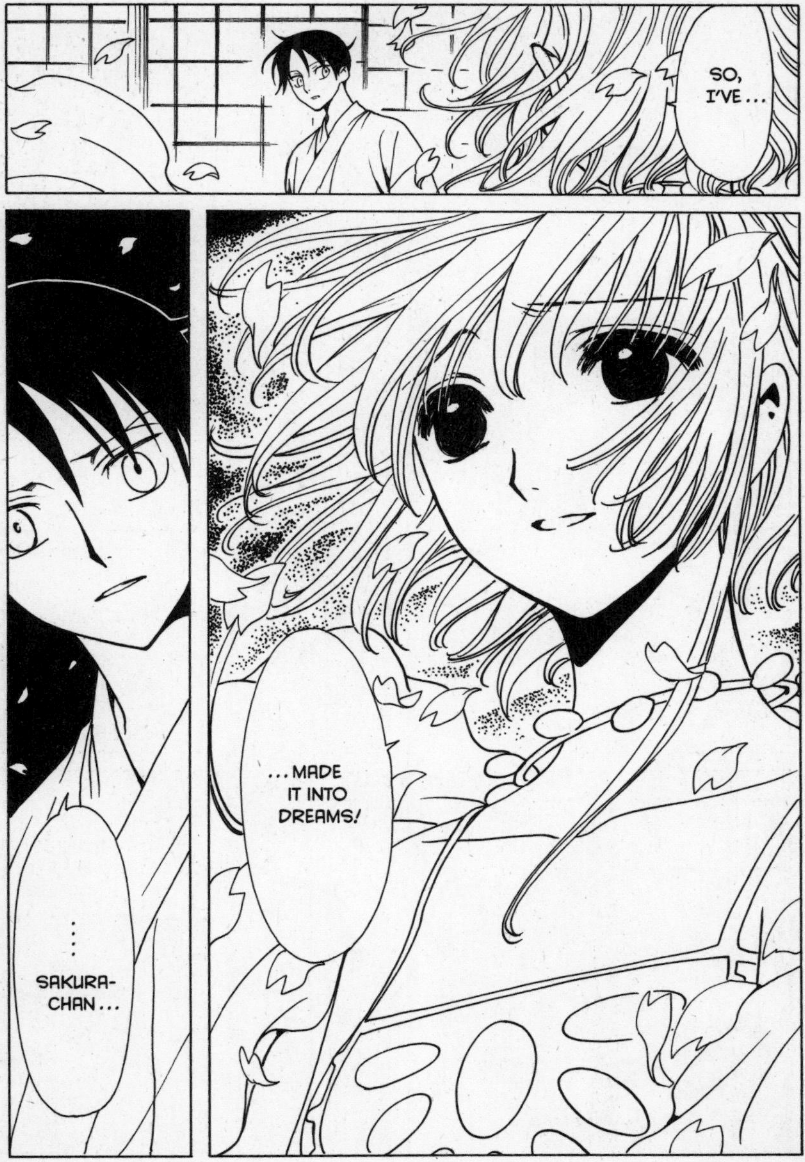
SO, I'VE...
...MADE IT INTO DREAMS!
....
SAKURA-CHAN...

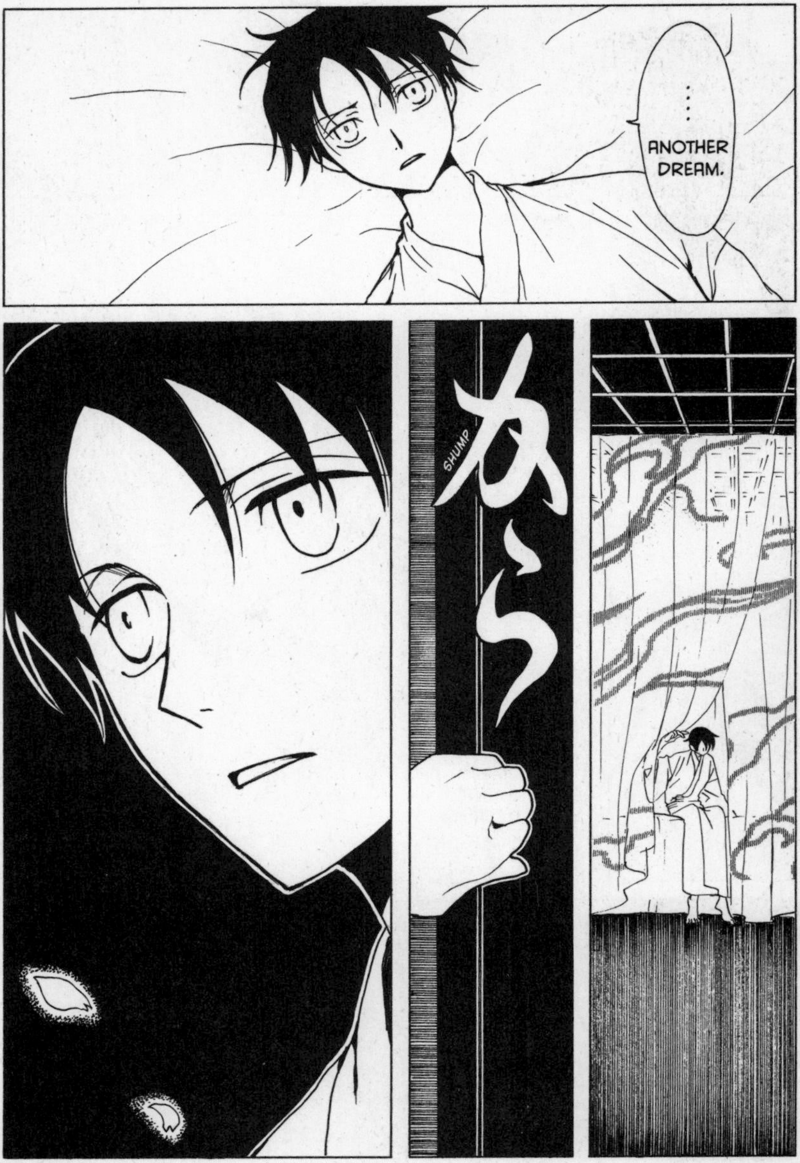
. . .
ANOTHER DREAM.
から
SHUMP

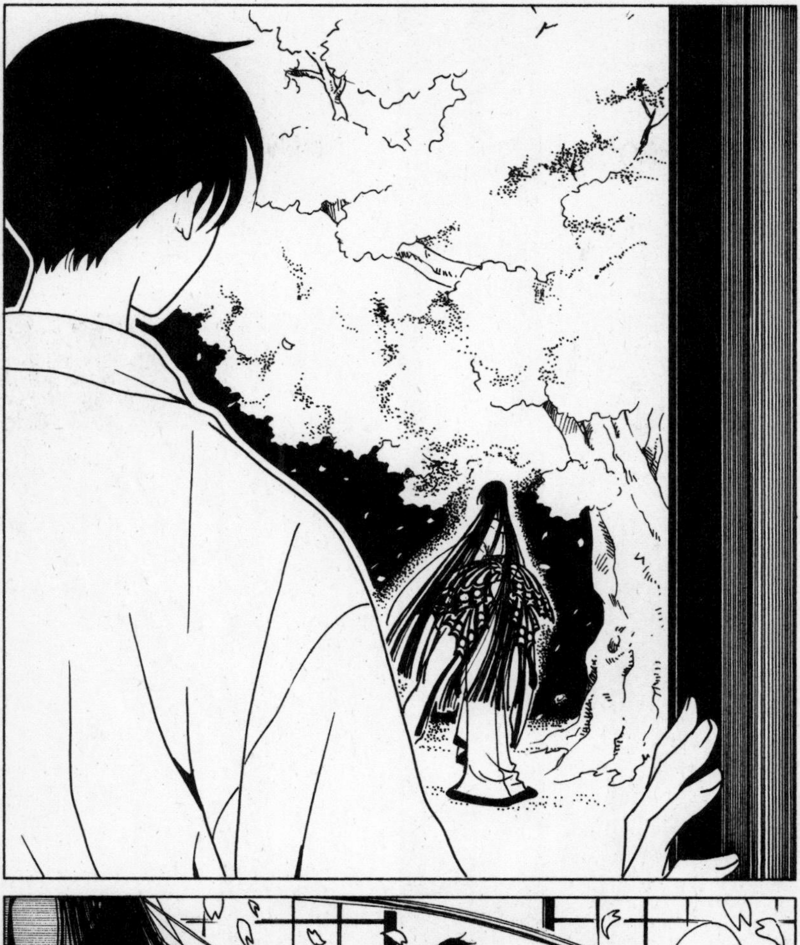

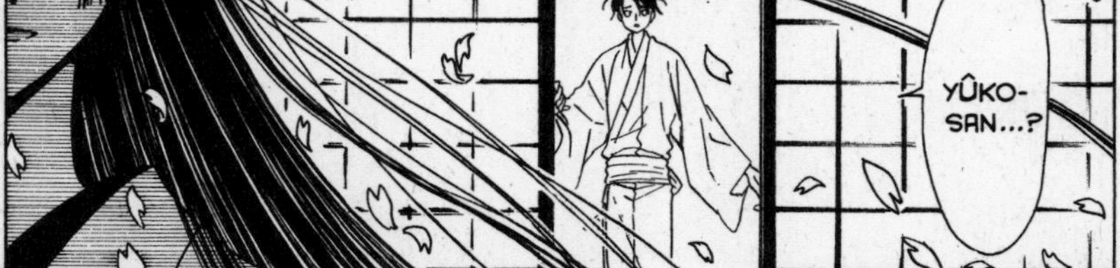
YÛKO-SAN...?

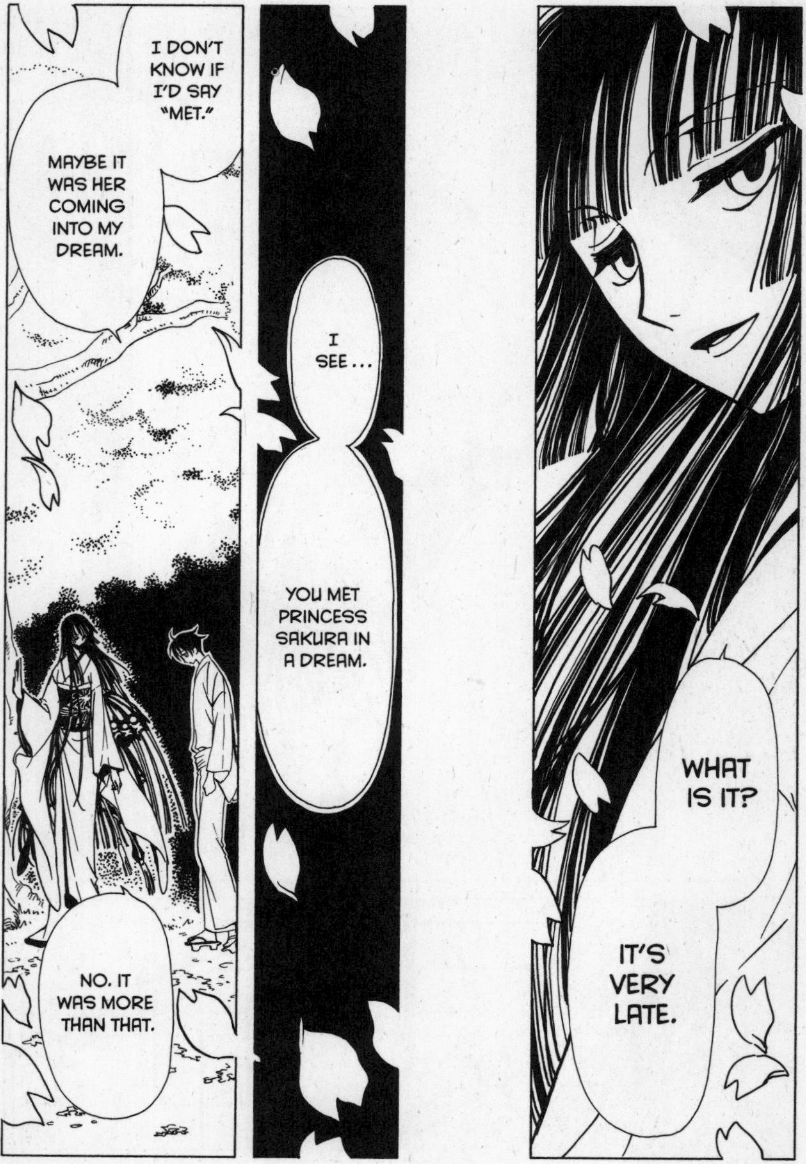
WHAT IS IT?
IT'S VERY LATE.
I SEE...
YOU MET PRINCESS SAKURA IN A DREAM.
I DON'T KNOW IF I'D SAY "MET."
MAYBE IT WAS HER COMING INTO MY DREAM.
NO. IT WAS MORE THAN THAT.

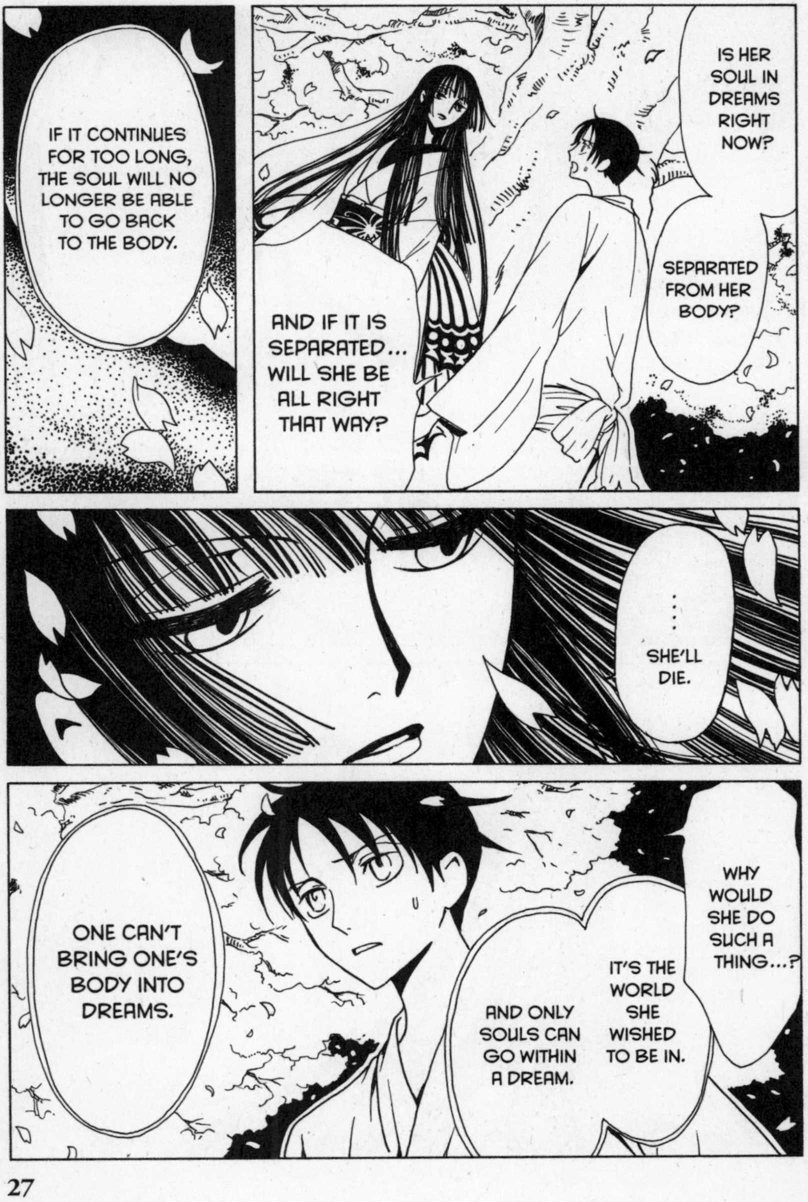
IS HER SOUL IN DREAMS RIGHT NOW?
SEPARATED FROM HER BODY?
AND IF IT IS SEPARATED... WILL SHE BE ALL RIGHT THAT WAY?
IF IT CONTINUES FOR TOO LONG, THE SOUL WILL NO LONGER BE ABLE TO GO BACK TO THE BODY.
......
SHE'LL DIE.
WHY WOULD SHE DO SUCH A THING...?
IT'S THE WORLD SHE WISHED TO BE IN.
AND ONLY SOULS CAN GO WITHIN A DREAM.
ONE CAN'T BRING ONE'S BODY INTO DREAMS.

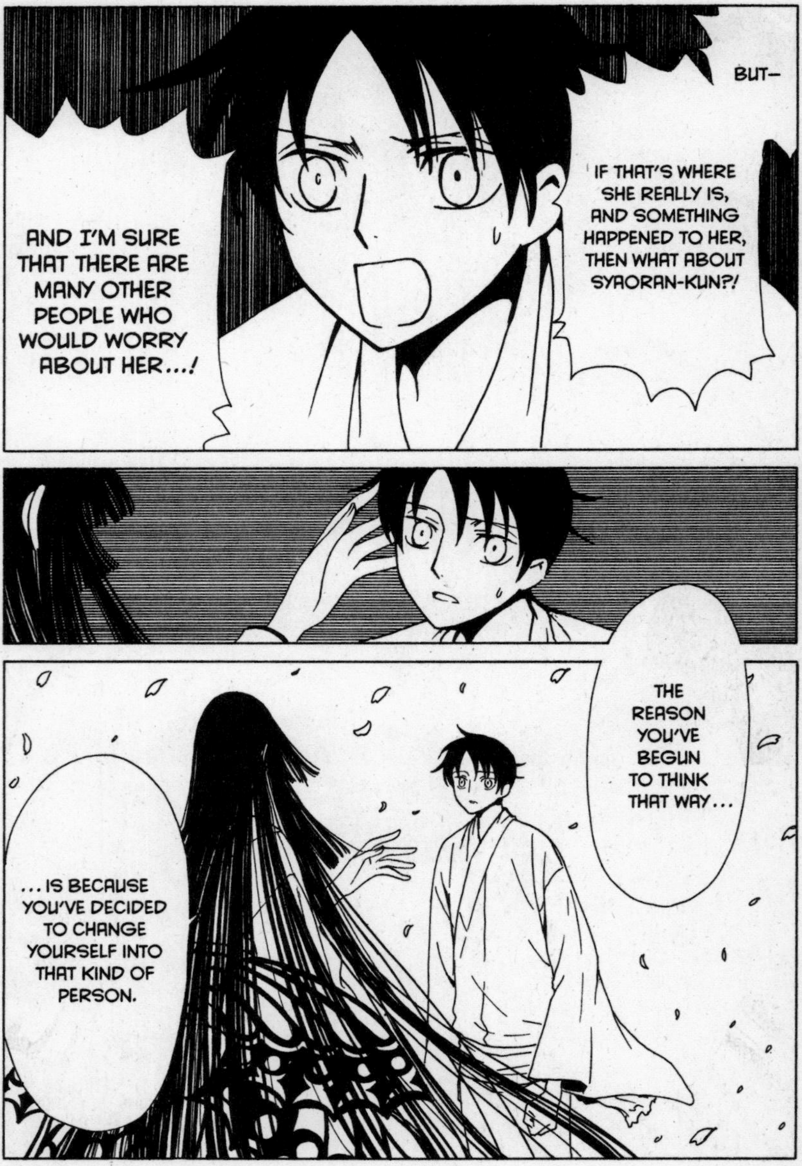
BUT—
IF THAT'S WHERE SHE REALLY IS, AND SOMETHING HAPPENED TO HER, THEN WHAT ABOUT SYAORAN-KUN?!
AND I'M SURE THAT THERE ARE MANY OTHER PEOPLE WHO WOULD WORRY ABOUT HER...!
THE REASON YOU'VE BEGUN TO THINK THAT WAY...
...IS BECAUSE YOU'VE DECIDED TO CHANGE YOURSELF INTO THAT KIND OF PERSON.

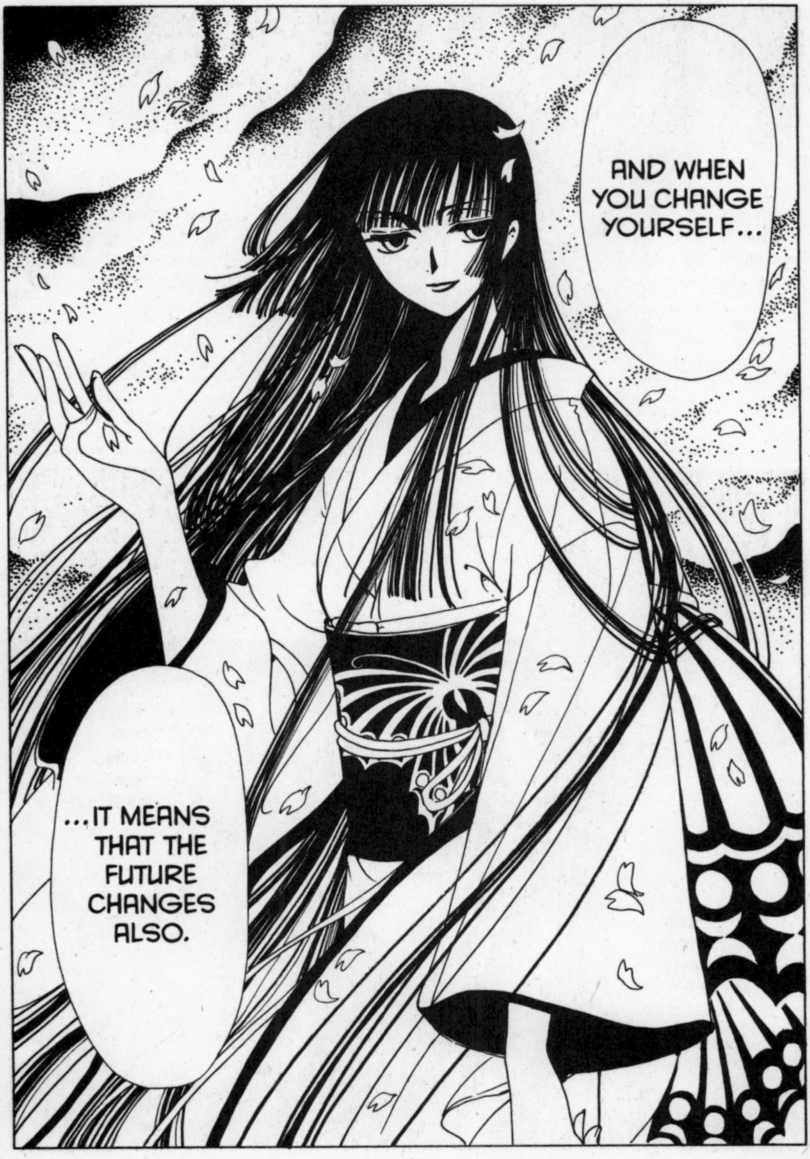
AND WHEN YOU CHANGE YOURSELF...
...IT MEANS THAT THE FUTURE CHANGES ALSO.

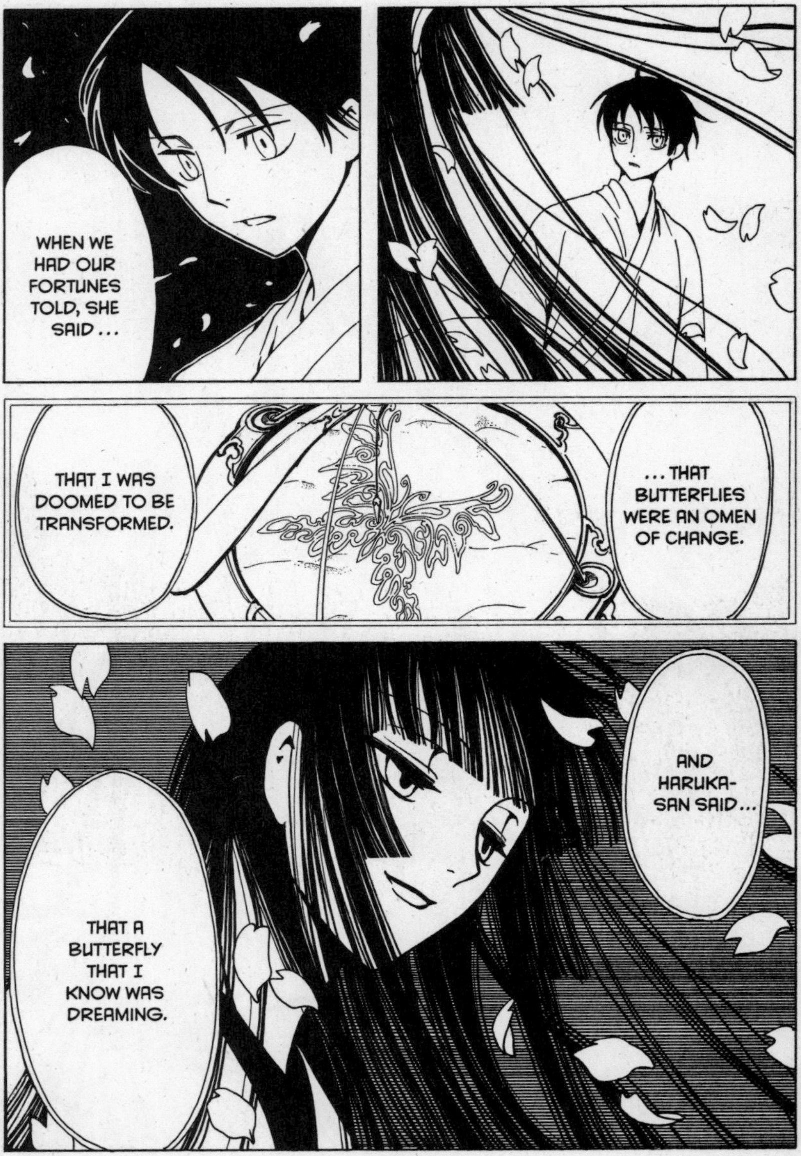
WHEN WE HAD OUR FORTUNES TOLD, SHE SAID...
...THAT BUTTERFLIES WERE AN OMEN OF CHANGE.
THAT I WAS DOOMED TO BE TRANSFORMED.
AND HARUKA-SAN SAID...
THAT A BUTTERFLY THAT I KNOW WAS DREAMING.

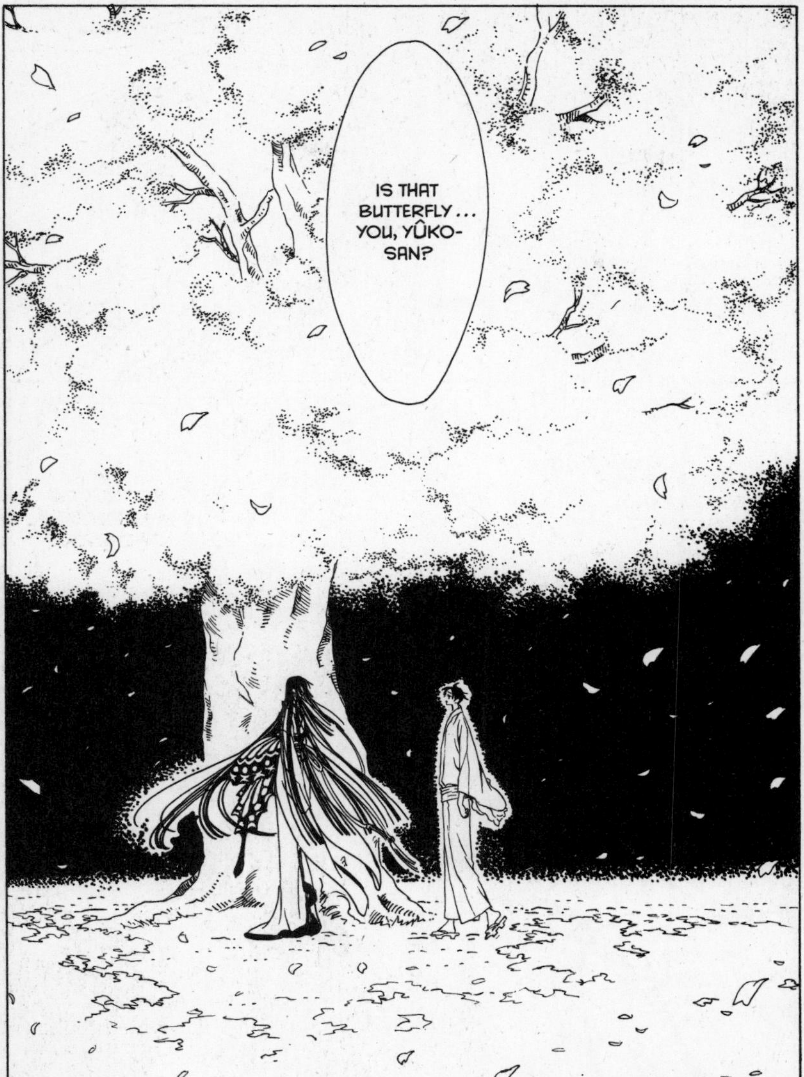
IS THAT BUTTERFLY . . . YOU, YÛKO-SAN?

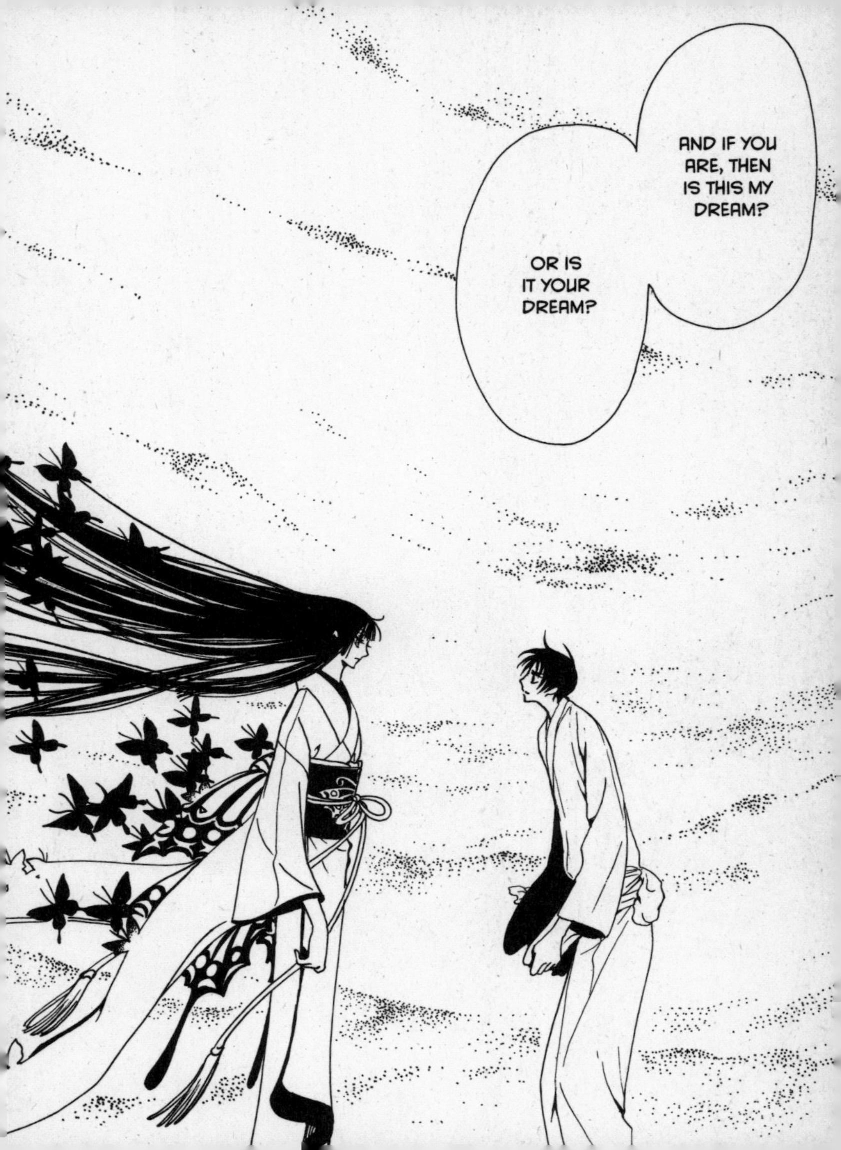
AND IF YOU ARE, THEN IS THIS MY DREAM?
OR IS IT YOUR DREAM?

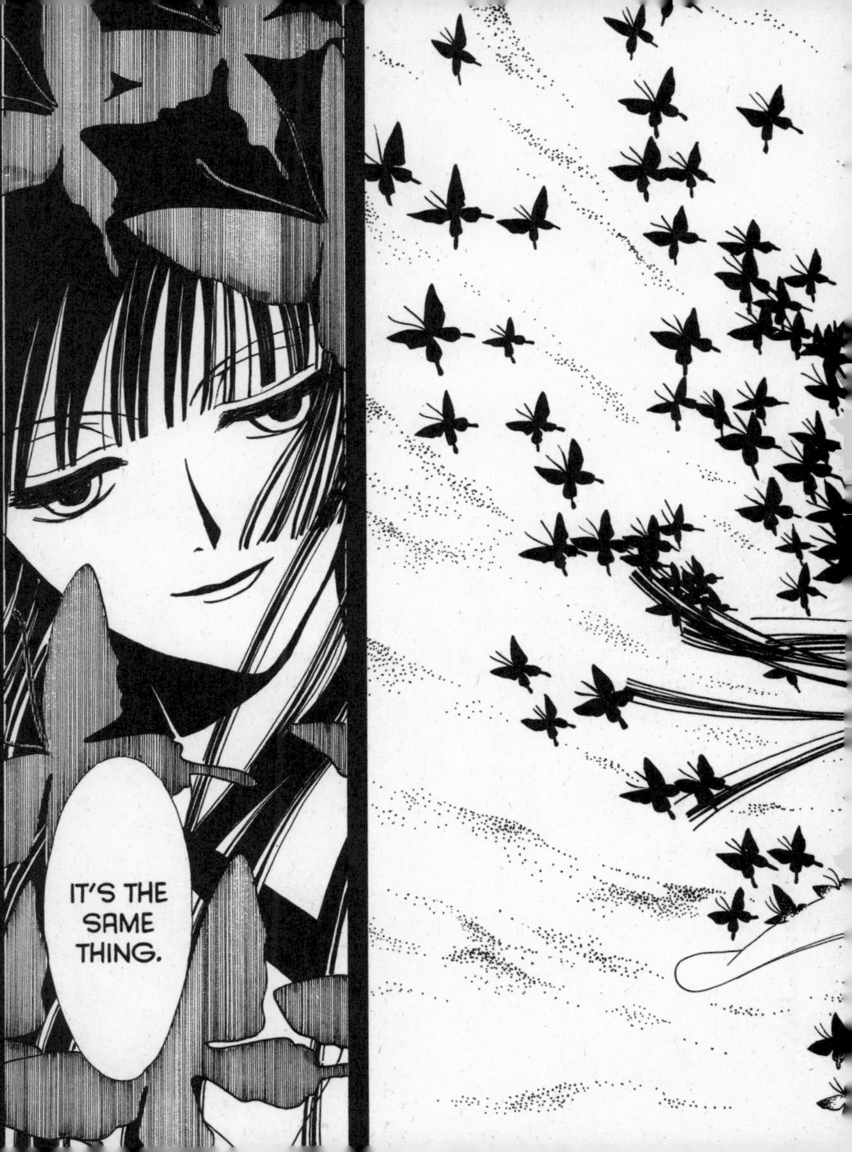
IT'S THE SAME THING.

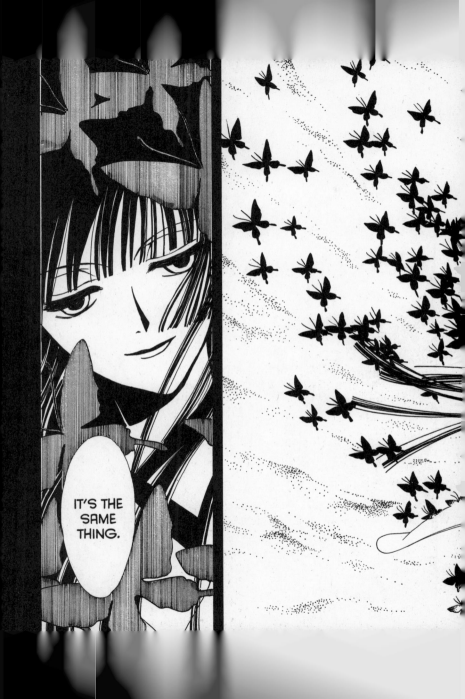

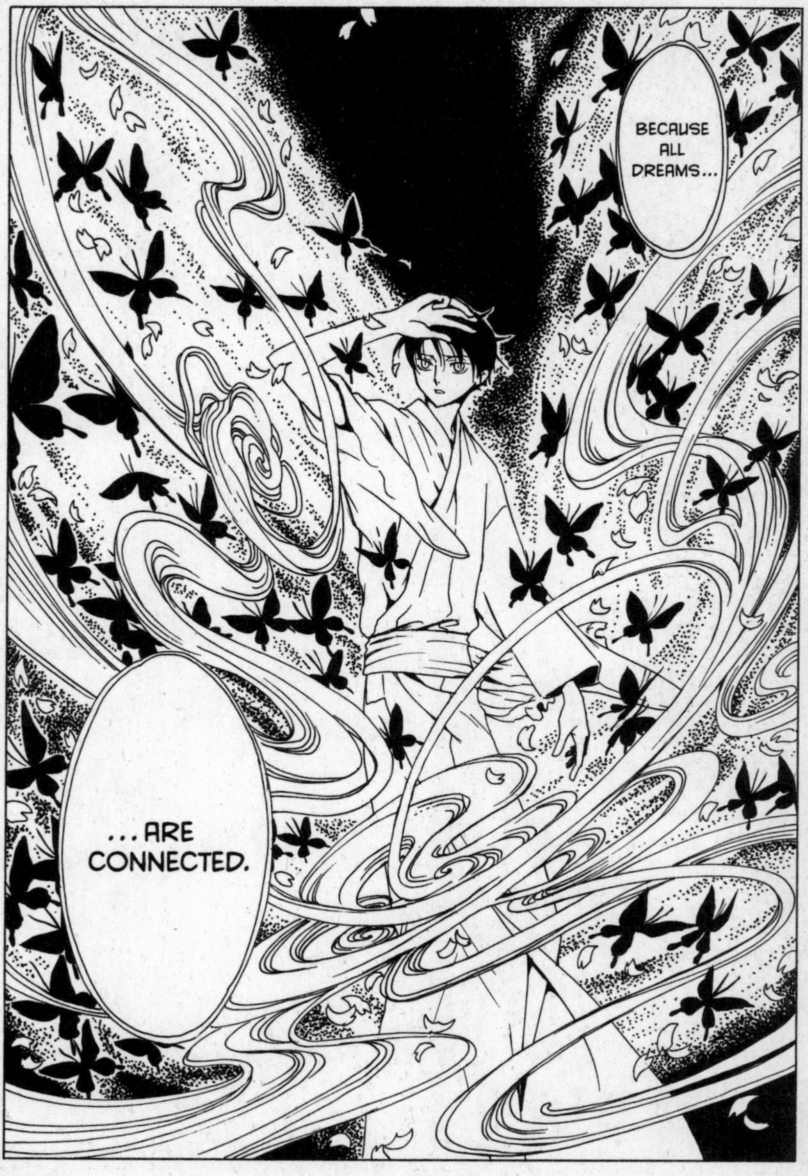
BECAUSE ALL DREAMS...
...ARE CONNECTED.

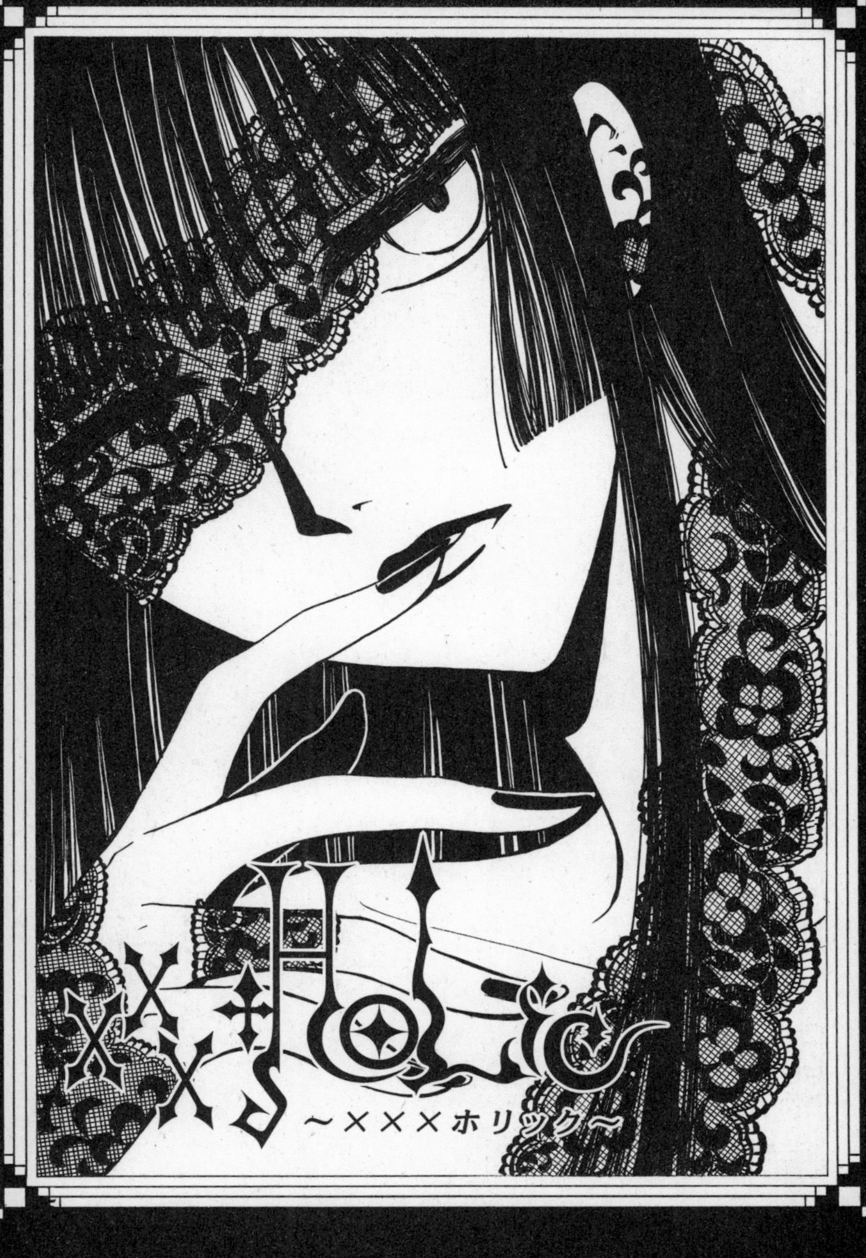
xxxHOLiC
~×××ホリック~

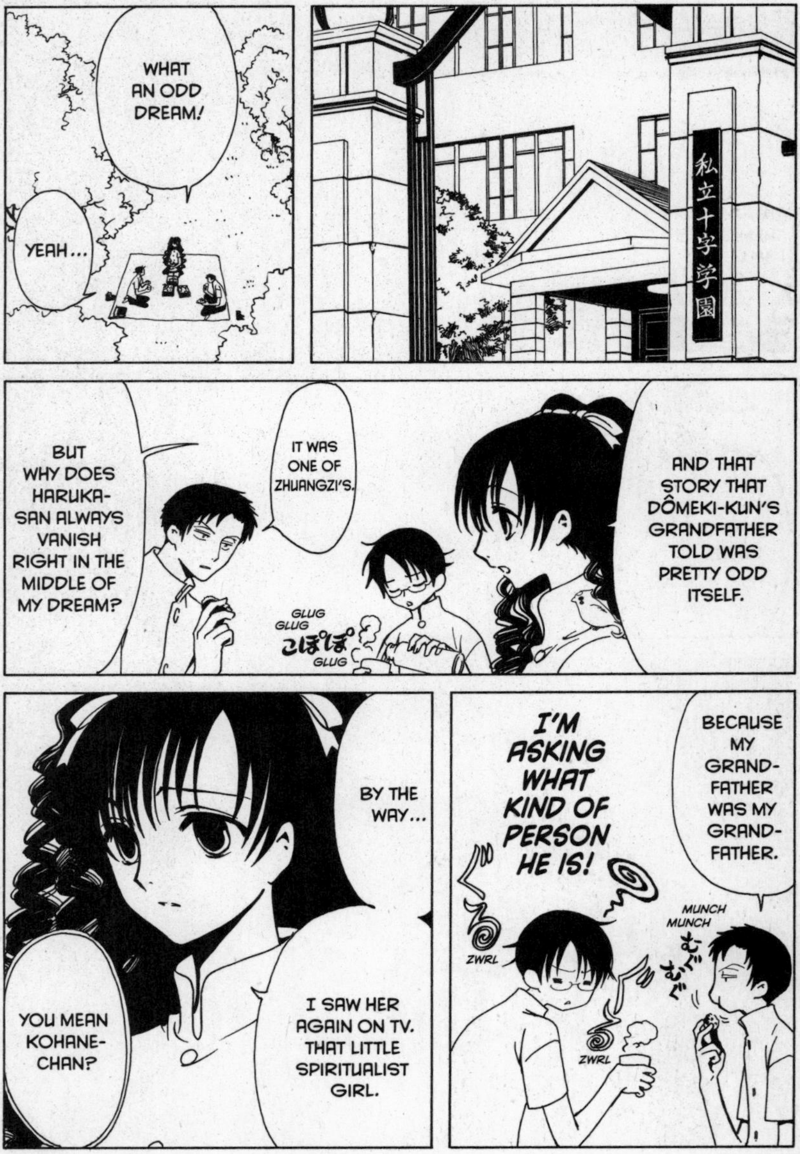
私立十字学園
WHAT AN ODD DREAM!
YEAH...
AND THAT STORY THAT DÔMEKI-KUN'S GRANDFATHER TOLD WAS PRETTY ODD ITSELF.
IT WAS ONE OF ZHUANGZI'S.
BUT WHY DOES HARUKA-SAN ALWAYS VANISH RIGHT IN THE MIDDLE OF MY DREAM?
GLUG GLUG こぽぽ GLUG
BECAUSE MY GRAND-FATHER WAS MY GRAND-FATHER.
I'M ASKING WHAT KIND OF PERSON HE IS!
MUNCH MUNCH むぐむぐ
ぐる ZWRL
ZWRL
BY THE WAY...
I SAW HER AGAIN ON TV. THAT LITTLE SPIRITUALIST GIRL.
YOU MEAN KOHANE-CHAN?

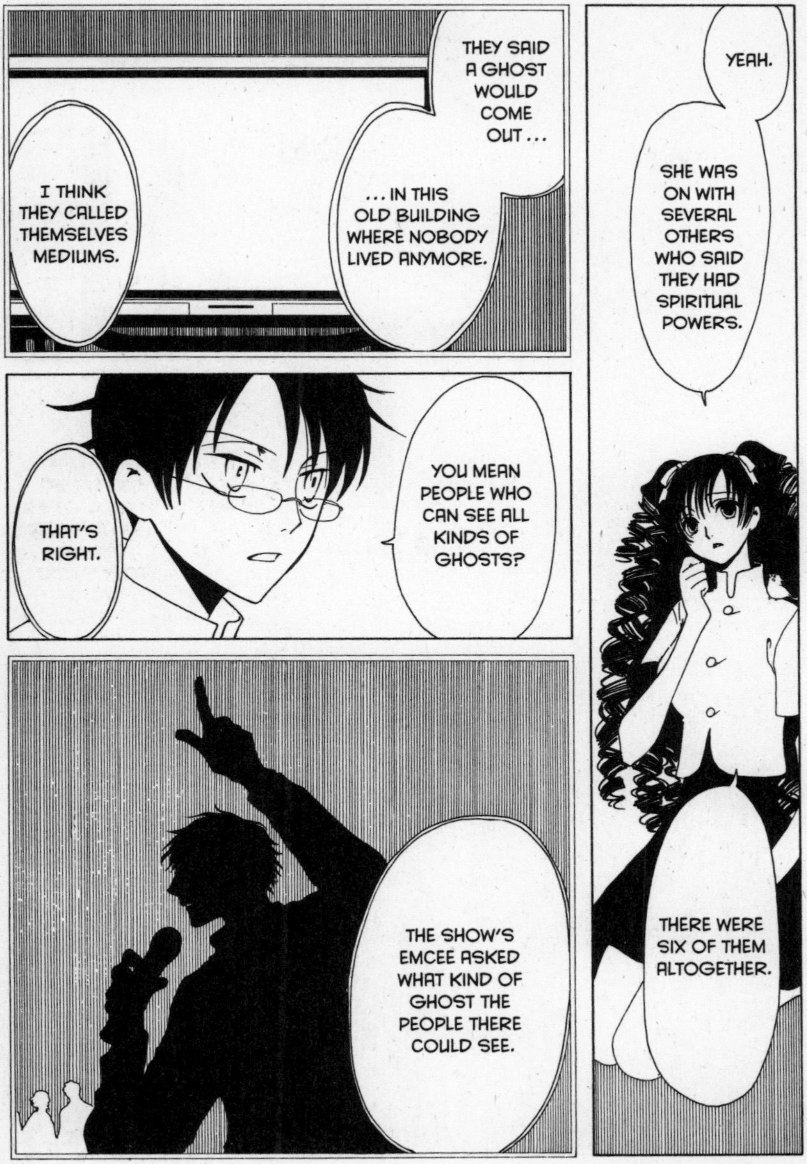
YEAH.
SHE WAS ON WITH SEVERAL OTHERS WHO SAID THEY HAD SPIRITUAL POWERS.
THERE WERE SIX OF THEM ALTOGETHER.
THEY SAID A GHOST WOULD COME OUT ...
... IN THIS OLD BUILDING WHERE NOBODY LIVED ANYMORE.
I THINK THEY CALLED THEMSELVES MEDIUMS.
YOU MEAN PEOPLE WHO CAN SEE ALL KINDS OF GHOSTS?
THAT'S RIGHT.
THE SHOW'S EMCEE ASKED WHAT KIND OF GHOST THE PEOPLE THERE COULD SEE.

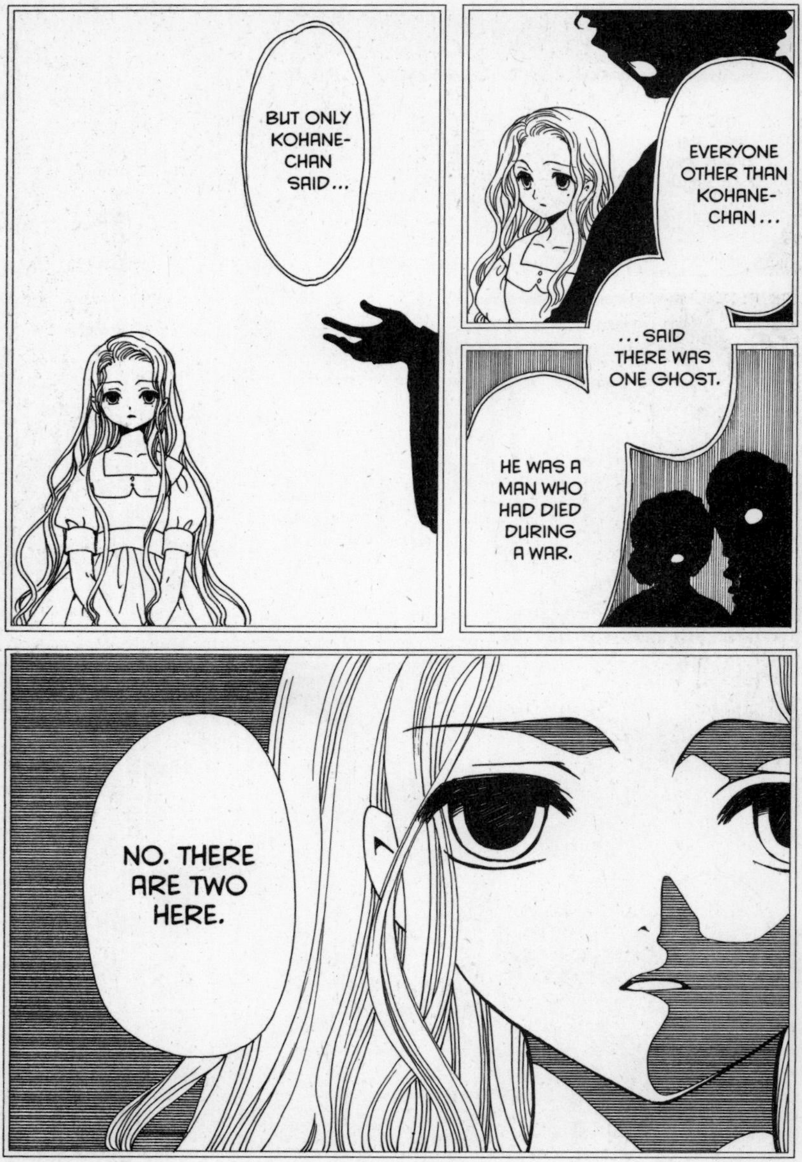
EVERYONE OTHER THAN KOHANE-CHAN...
...SAID THERE WAS ONE GHOST.
HE WAS A MAN WHO HAD DIED DURING A WAR.
BUT ONLY KOHANE-CHAN SAID...
NO. THERE ARE TWO HERE.

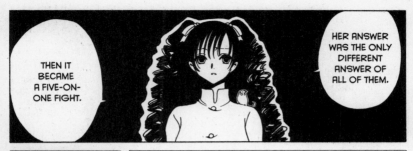

HER ANSWER WAS THE ONLY DIFFERENT ANSWER OF ALL OF THEM.
THEN IT BECAME A FIVE-ON-ONE FIGHT.
THE OTHER SPIRITU-ALISTS...
...ALL ATTACKED HER AS IF KOHANE-CHAN WAS LYING TO THEM..
BUT EVEN UNDER ALL THAT, KOHANE-CHAN REFUSED TO CHANGE HER STORY.
THE TV SHOW ENDED LIKE THAT.

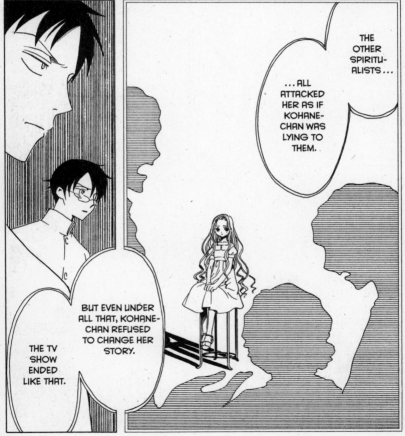

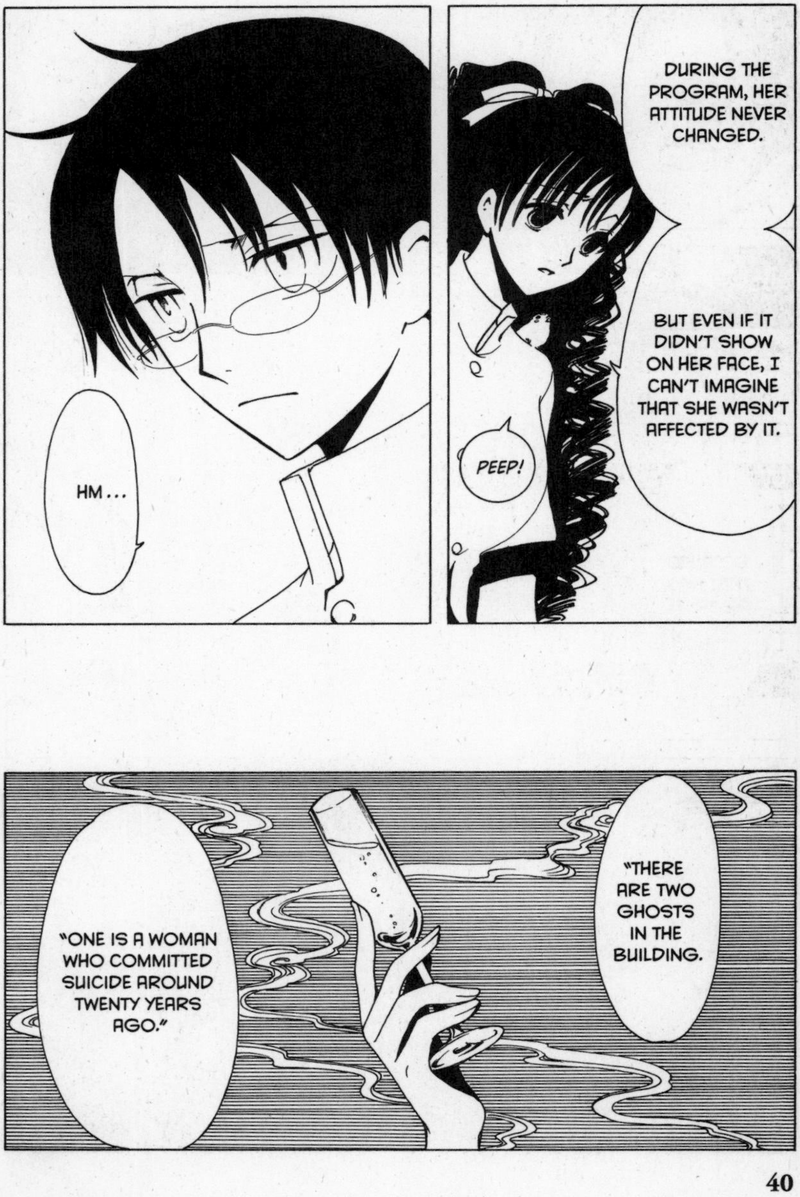
DURING THE PROGRAM, HER ATTITUDE NEVER CHANGED.
BUT EVEN IF IT DIDN'T SHOW ON HER FACE, I CAN'T IMAGINE THAT SHE WASN'T AFFECTED BY IT.
PEEP!
HM . . .
"THERE ARE TWO GHOSTS IN THE BUILDING.
"ONE IS A WOMAN WHO COMMITTED SUICIDE AROUND TWENTY YEARS AGO."

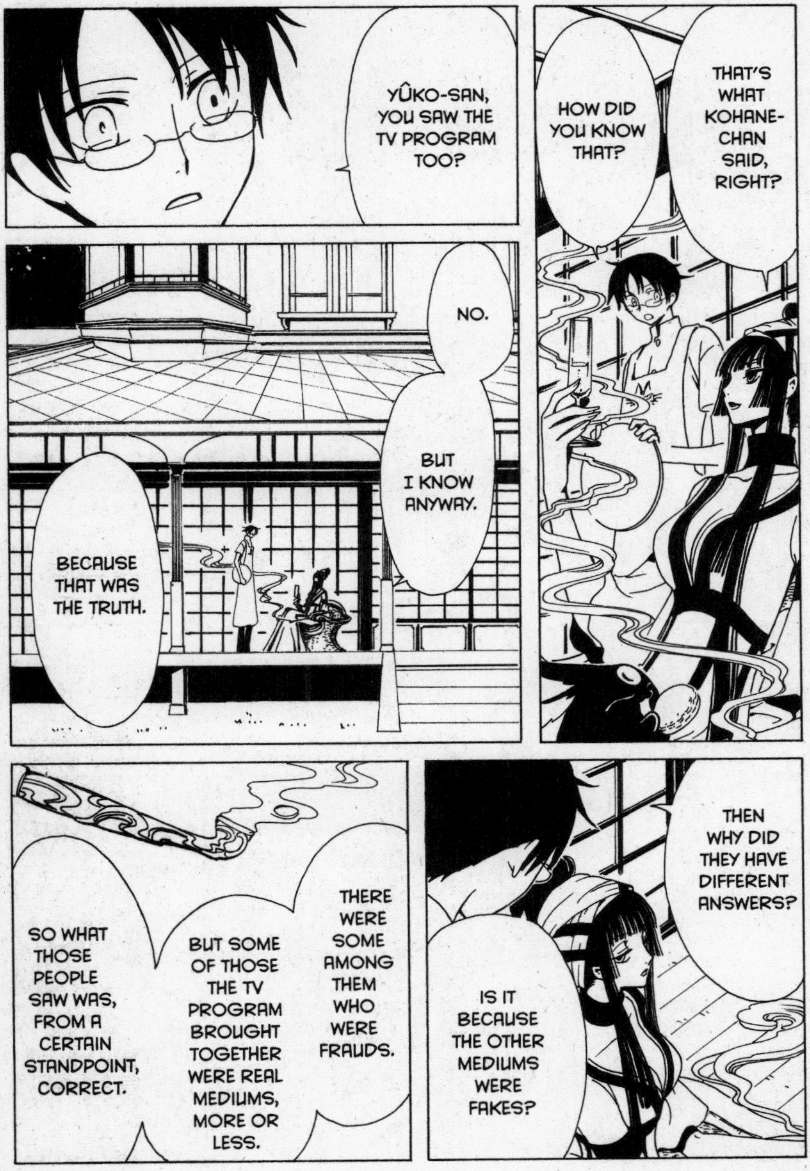
THAT'S WHAT KOHANE-CHAN SAID, RIGHT?
HOW DID YOU KNOW THAT?
YÛKO-SAN, YOU SAW THE TV PROGRAM TOO?
NO.
BUT I KNOW ANYWAY.
BECAUSE THAT WAS THE TRUTH.
THEN WHY DID THEY HAVE DIFFERENT ANSWERS?
IS IT BECAUSE THE OTHER MEDIUMS WERE FAKES?
THERE WERE SOME AMONG THEM WHO WERE FRAUDS.
BUT SOME OF THOSE THE TV PROGRAM BROUGHT TOGETHER WERE REAL MEDIUMS, MORE OR LESS.
SO WHAT THOSE PEOPLE SAW WAS, FROM A CERTAIN STANDPOINT, CORRECT.

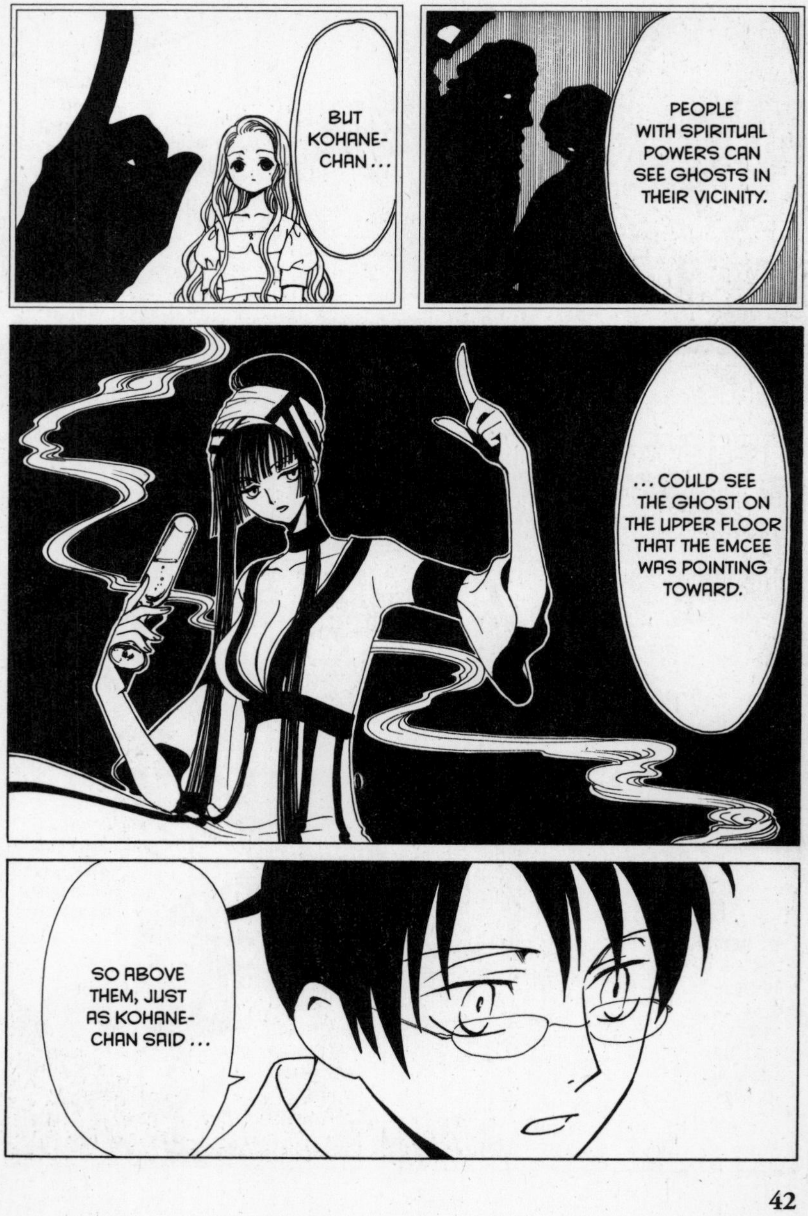
PEOPLE WITH SPIRITUAL POWERS CAN SEE GHOSTS IN THEIR VICINITY.
BUT KOHANE-CHAN...
...COULD SEE THE GHOST ON THE UPPER FLOOR THAT THE EMCEE WAS POINTING TOWARD.
SO ABOVE THEM, JUST AS KOHANE-CHAN SAID...

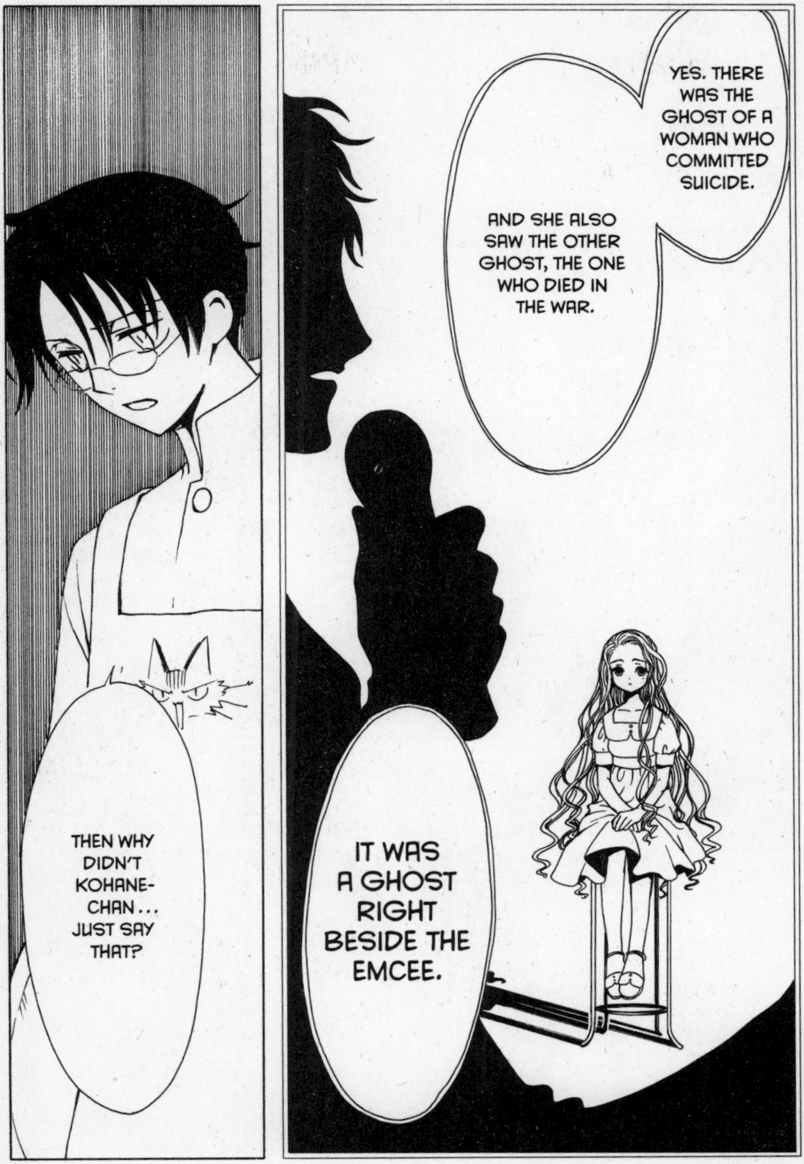
YES. THERE WAS THE GHOST OF A WOMAN WHO COMMITTED SUICIDE.
AND SHE ALSO SAW THE OTHER GHOST, THE ONE WHO DIED IN THE WAR.
IT WAS A GHOST RIGHT BESIDE THE EMCEE.
THEN WHY DIDN'T KOHANE-CHAN... JUST SAY THAT?

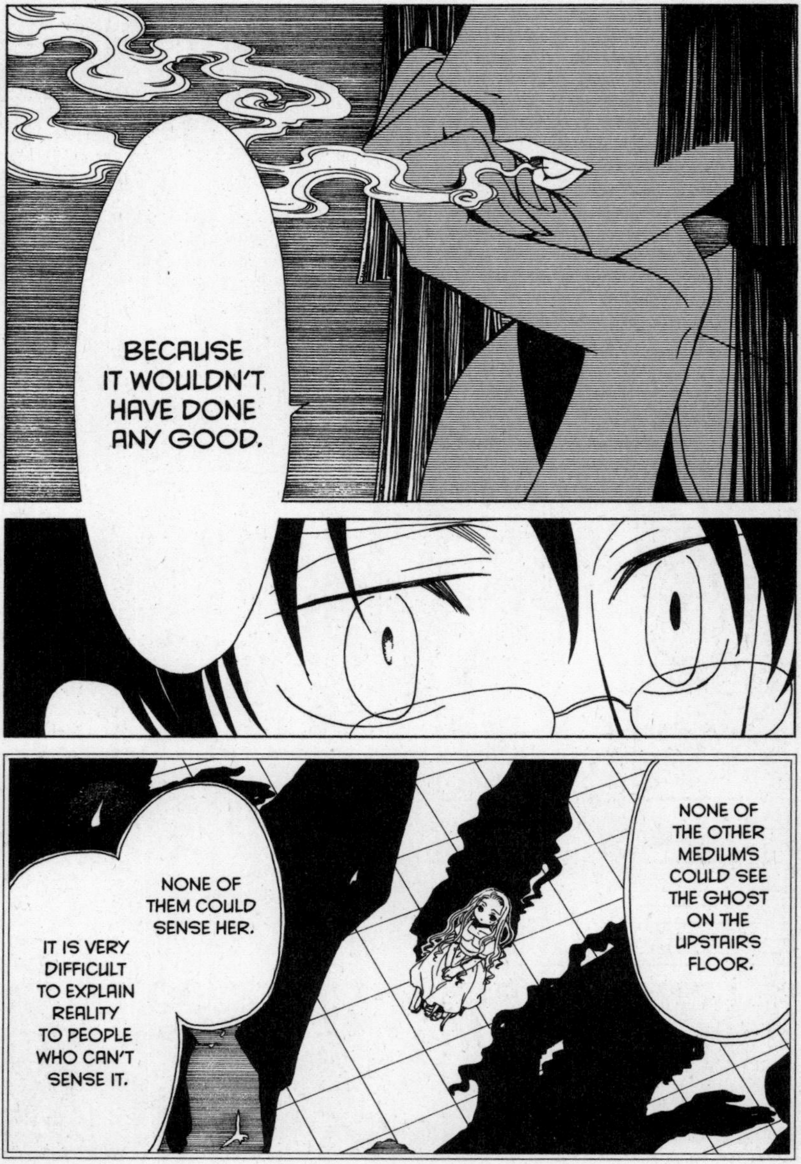
BECAUSE IT WOULDN'T HAVE DONE ANY GOOD.
NONE OF THE OTHER MEDIUMS COULD SEE THE GHOST ON THE UPSTAIRS FLOOR.
NONE OF THEM COULD SENSE HER.
IT IS VERY DIFFICULT TO EXPLAIN REALITY TO PEOPLE WHO CAN'T SENSE IT.

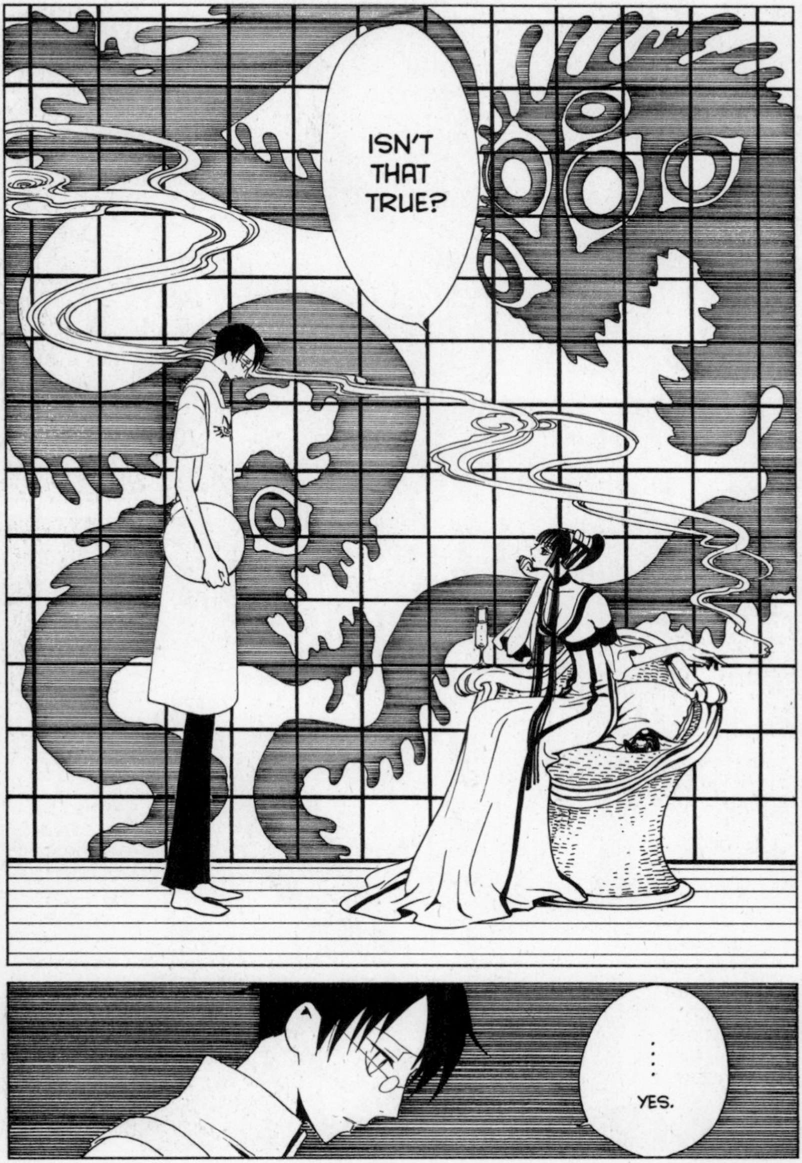
ISN'T THAT TRUE?
. . . .
YES.

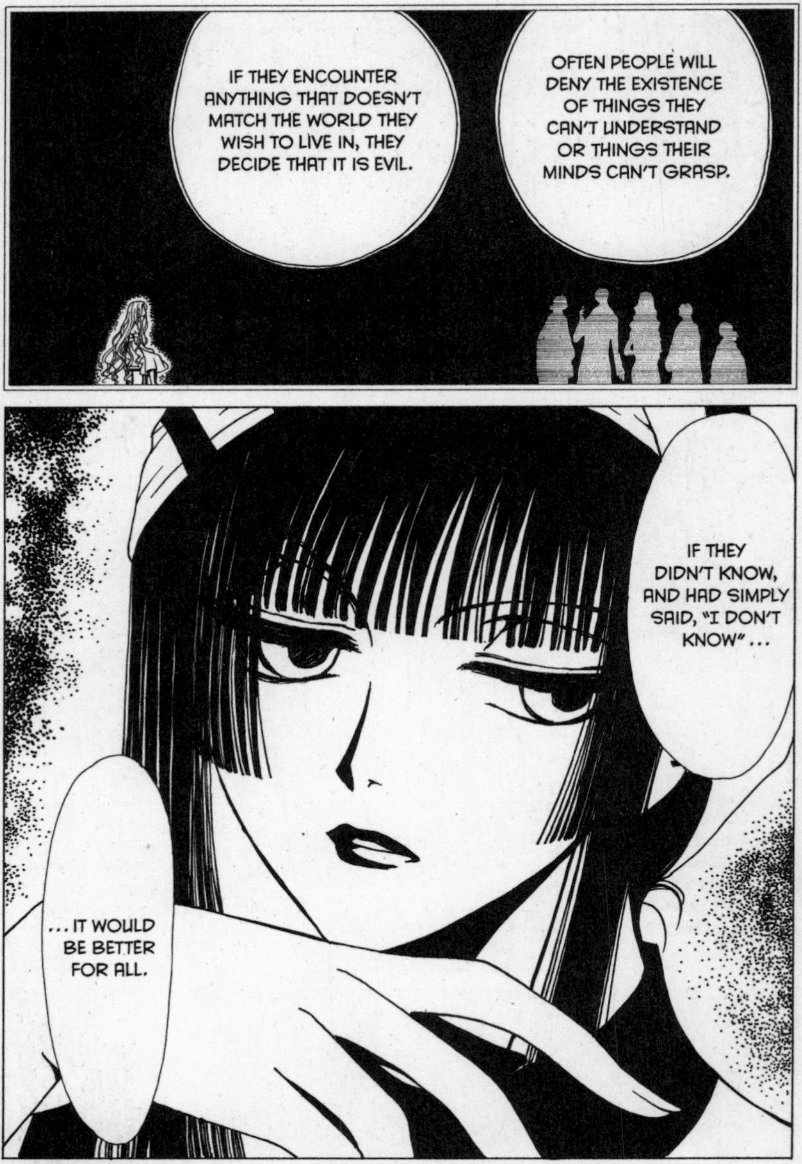
OFTEN PEOPLE WILL DENY THE EXISTENCE OF THINGS THEY CAN'T UNDERSTAND OR THINGS THEIR MINDS CAN'T GRASP.
IF THEY ENCOUNTER ANYTHING THAT DOESN'T MATCH THE WORLD THEY WISH TO LIVE IN, THEY DECIDE THAT IT IS EVIL.
IF THEY DIDN'T KNOW, AND HAD SIMPLY SAID, "I DON'T KNOW"...
...IT WOULD BE BETTER FOR ALL.

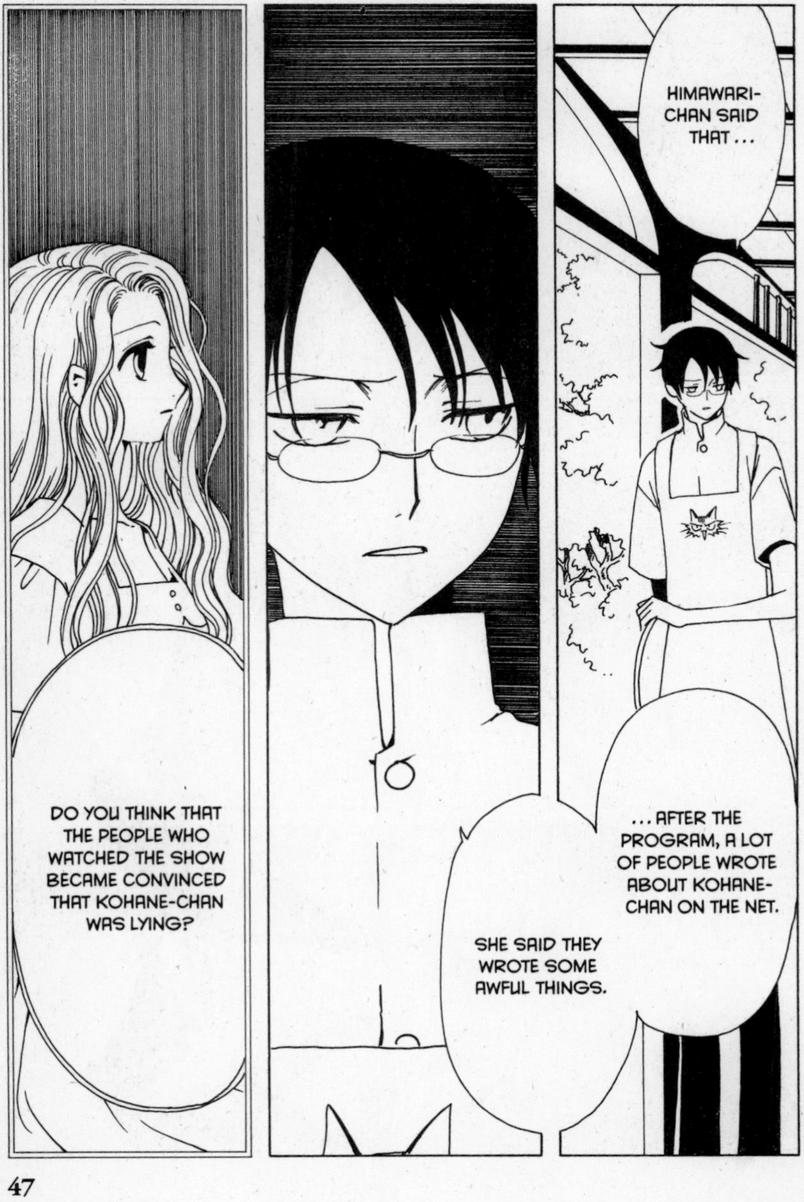
HIMAWARI-CHAN SAID THAT...
...AFTER THE PROGRAM, A LOT OF PEOPLE WROTE ABOUT KOHANE-CHAN ON THE NET.
SHE SAID THEY WROTE SOME AWFUL THINGS.
DO YOU THINK THAT THE PEOPLE WHO WATCHED THE SHOW BECAME CONVINCED THAT KOHANE-CHAN WAS LYING?

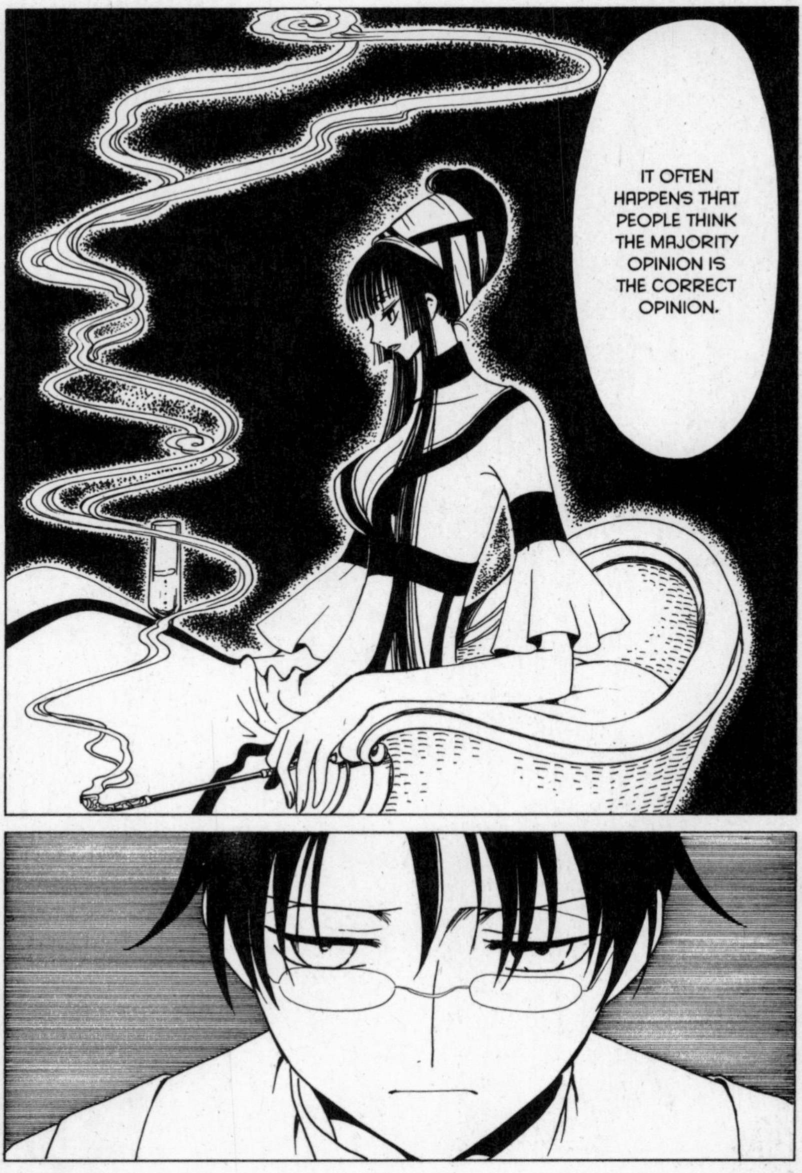
IT OFTEN HAPPENS THAT PEOPLE THINK THE MAJORITY OPINION IS THE CORRECT OPINION.

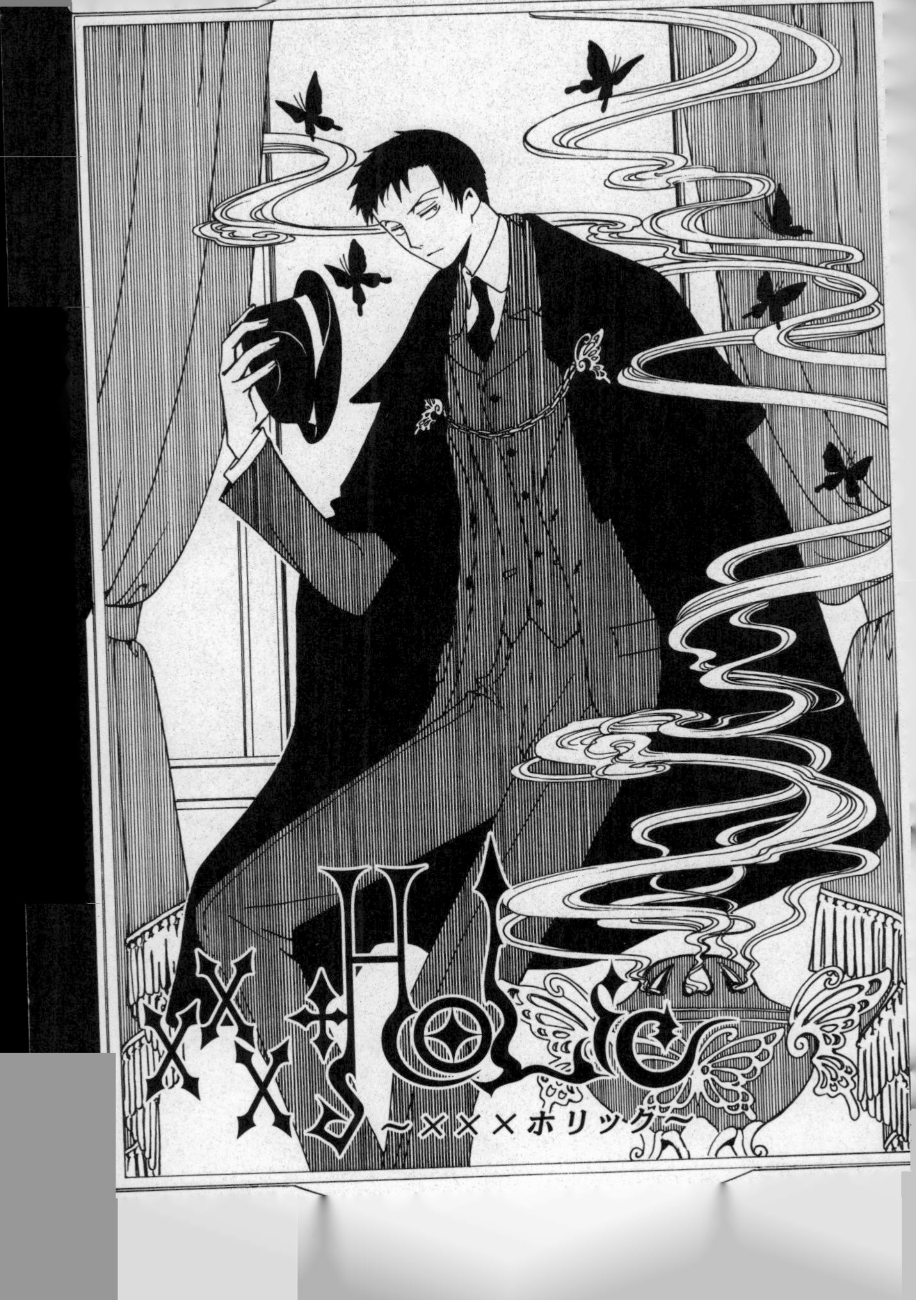
xxxHOLiC
〜×××ホリック〜

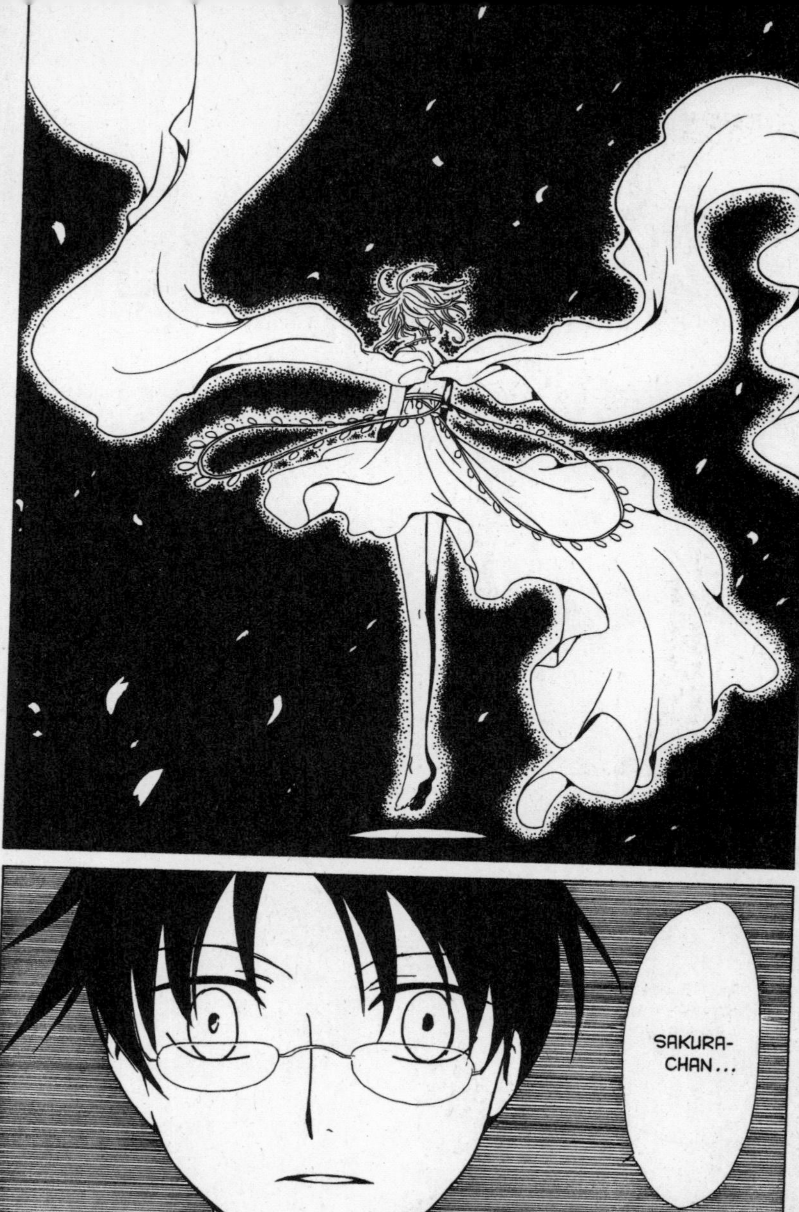
SAKURA-
CHAN...

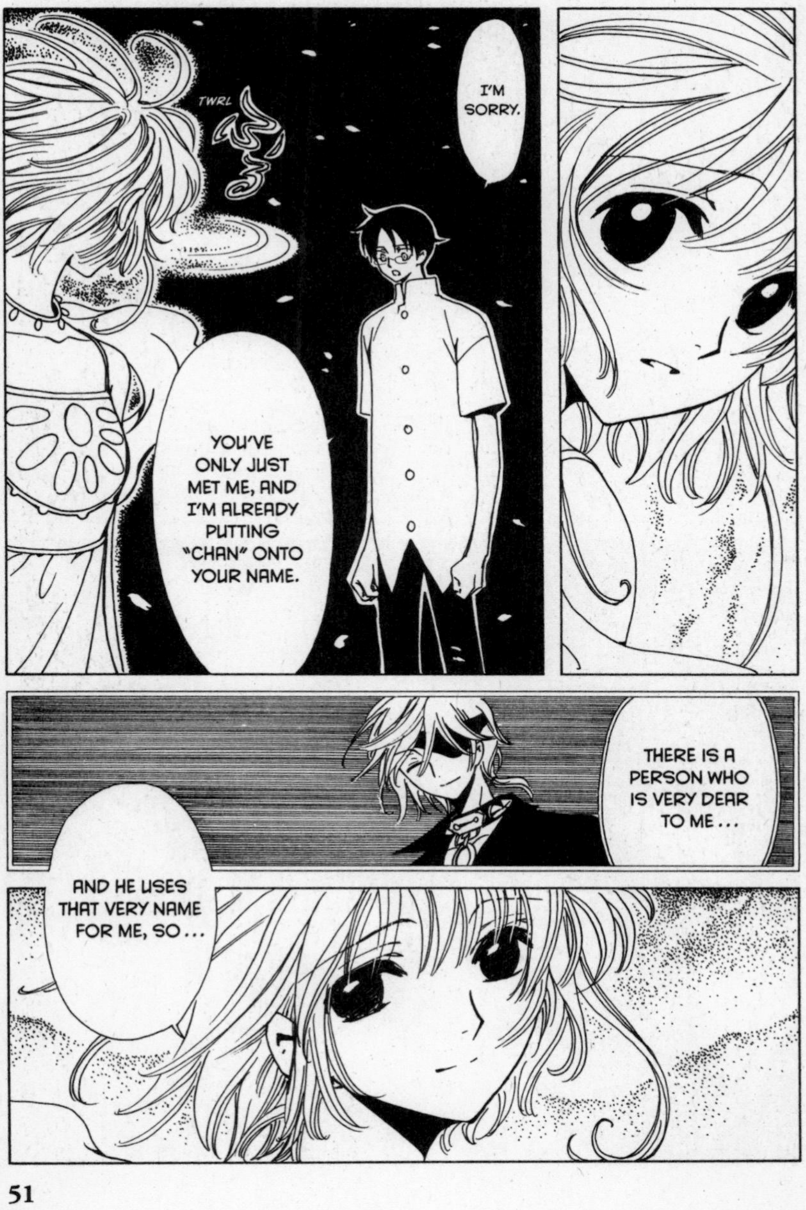
I'M SORRY.
TWRL
YOU'VE ONLY JUST MET ME, AND I'M ALREADY PUTTING "CHAN" ONTO YOUR NAME.
THERE IS A PERSON WHO IS VERY DEAR TO ME...
AND HE USES THAT VERY NAME FOR ME, SO...

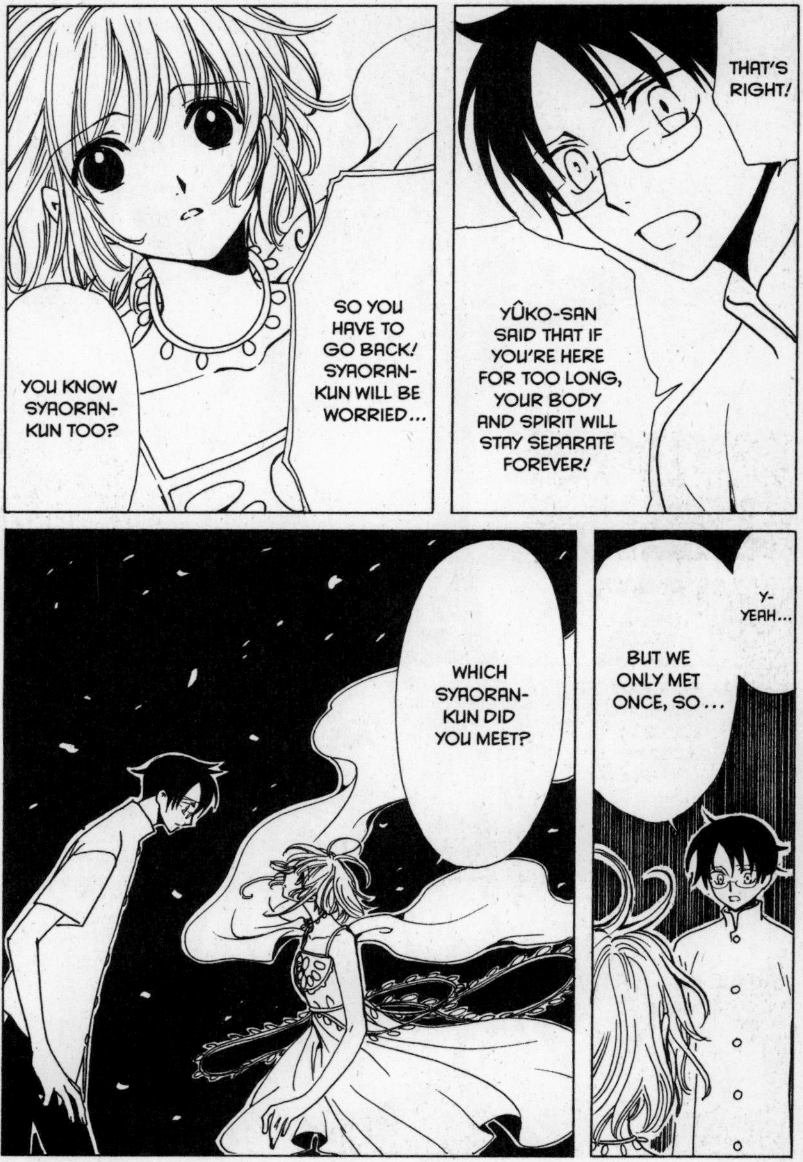
THAT'S RIGHT!
YÛKO-SAN SAID THAT IF YOU'RE HERE FOR TOO LONG, YOUR BODY AND SPIRIT WILL STAY SEPARATE FOREVER!
SO YOU HAVE TO GO BACK! SYAORAN-KUN WILL BE WORRIED...
YOU KNOW SYAORAN-KUN TOO?
Y-YEAH...
BUT WE ONLY MET ONCE, SO...
WHICH SYAORAN-KUN DID YOU MEET?

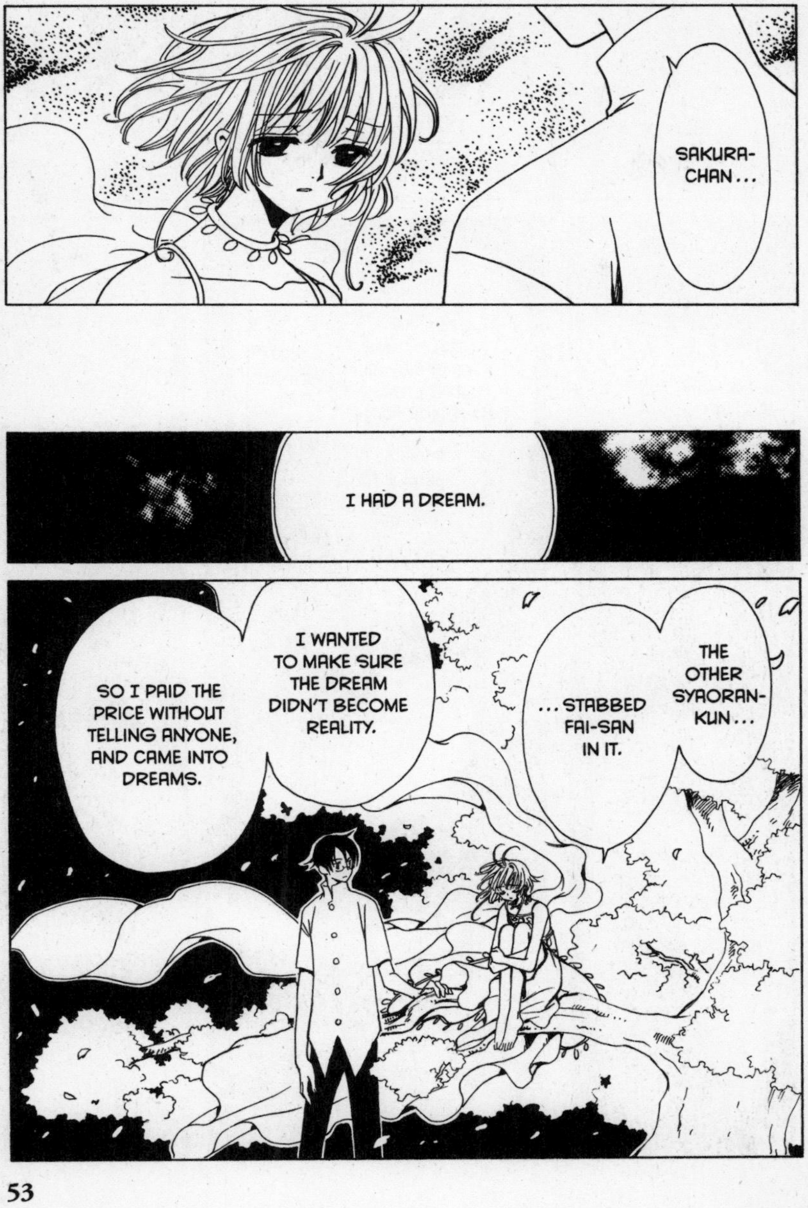
SAKURA-CHAN…
I HAD A DREAM.
THE OTHER SYAORAN-KUN…
…STABBED FAI-SAN IN IT.
I WANTED TO MAKE SURE THE DREAM DIDN'T BECOME REALITY.
SO I PAID THE PRICE WITHOUT TELLING ANYONE, AND CAME INTO DREAMS.

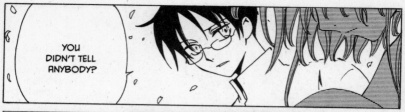

YOU DIDN'T TELL ANYBODY?
IT IS VERY DIFFICULT TO CHANGE THE FUTURE.
IF I HAD TOLD ANY-ONE, THEN THE NUMBER OF CHANGES IN PEOPLE'S CHOICES WOULD INCREASE.
I DIDN'T HAVE TIME.
ASSUMING I TOLD THEM, A DIFFERENT FUTURE WOULD BE BORN FROM THAT, AND I DIDN'T KNOW IF I'D BE ABLE TO SEE THAT FUTURE IN A DREAM.
BE-SIDES...
...EVEN IF I SAW THAT FUTURE IN A DREAM, I COULDN'T... TELL ANYONE OF WHAT FAI-SAN HAS KEPT HIDDEN ALL THIS TIME.

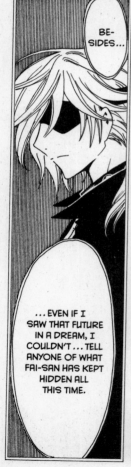

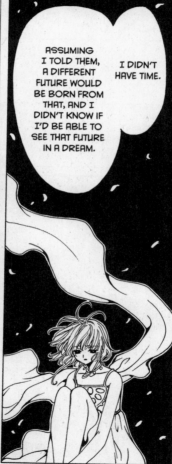

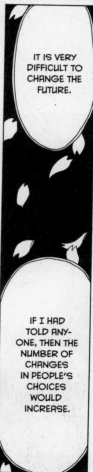

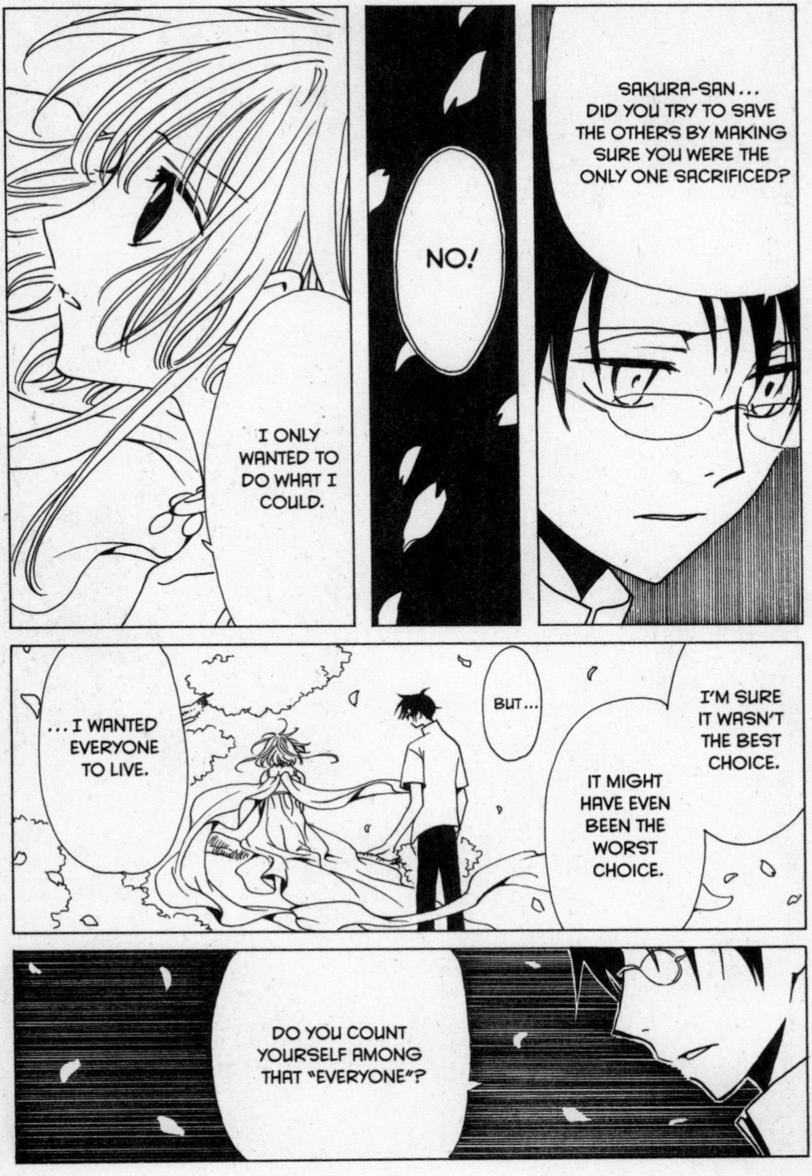
SAKURA-SAN... DID YOU TRY TO SAVE THE OTHERS BY MAKING SURE YOU WERE THE ONLY ONE SACRIFICED?
NO!
I ONLY WANTED TO DO WHAT I COULD.
I'M SURE IT WASN'T THE BEST CHOICE.
IT MIGHT HAVE EVEN BEEN THE WORST CHOICE.
BUT...
...I WANTED EVERYONE TO LIVE.
DO YOU COUNT YOURSELF AMONG THAT "EVERYONE"?

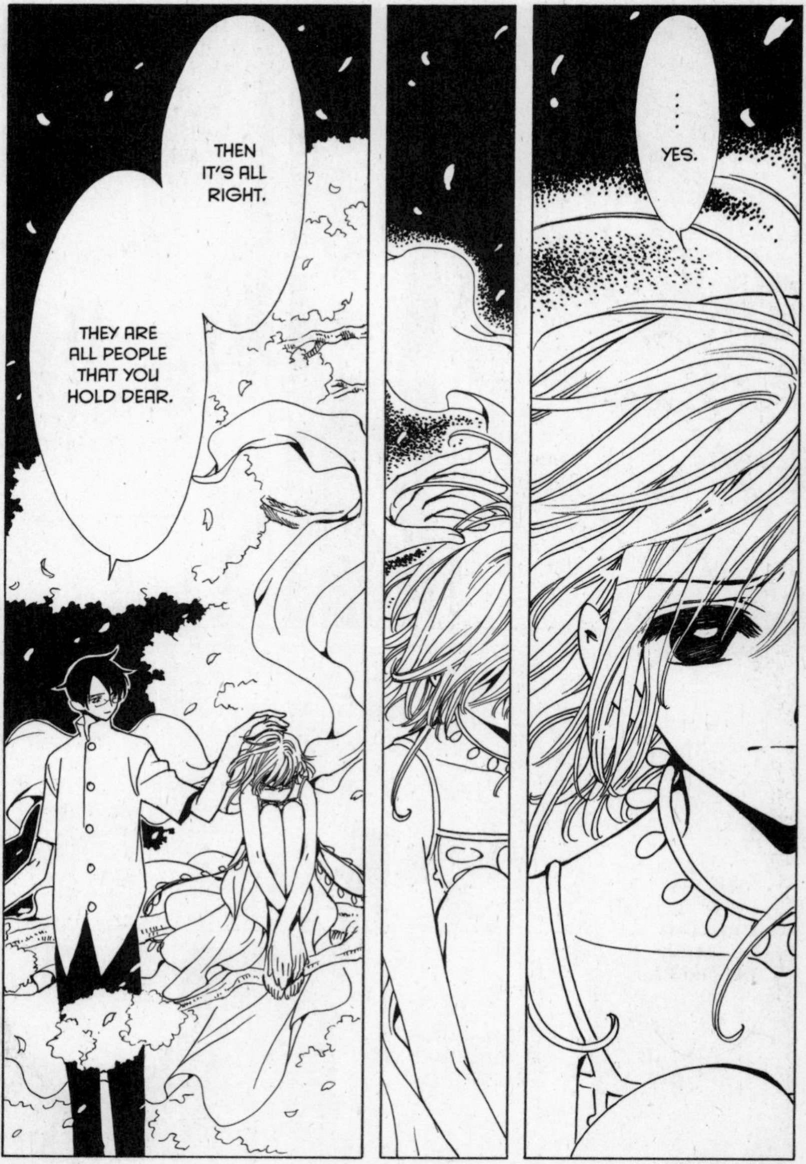
......YES.
THEN IT'S ALL RIGHT.
THEY ARE ALL PEOPLE THAT YOU HOLD DEAR.

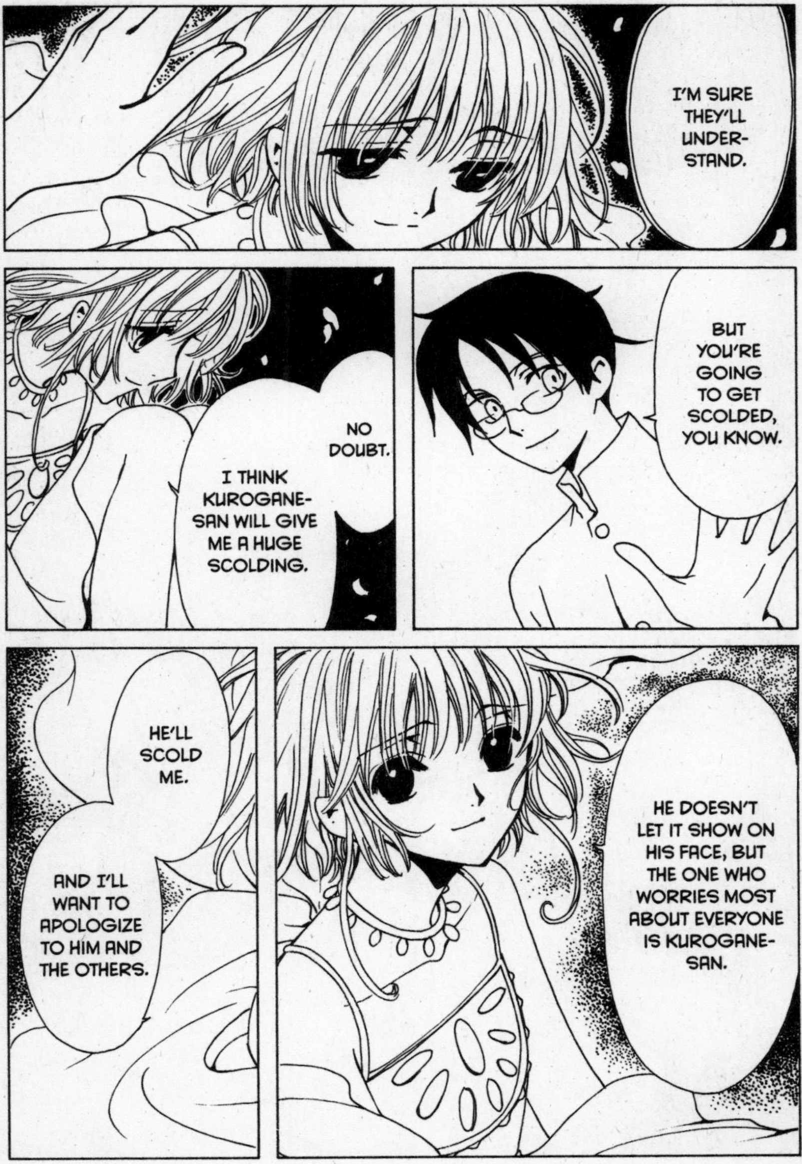
I'M SURE THEY'LL UNDER-STAND.
BUT YOU'RE GOING TO GET SCOLDED, YOU KNOW.
NO DOUBT.
I THINK KUROGANE-SAN WILL GIVE ME A HUGE SCOLDING.
HE DOESN'T LET IT SHOW ON HIS FACE, BUT THE ONE WHO WORRIES MOST ABOUT EVERYONE IS KUROGANE-SAN.
HE'LL SCOLD ME.
AND I'LL WANT TO APOLOGIZE TO HIM AND THE OTHERS.

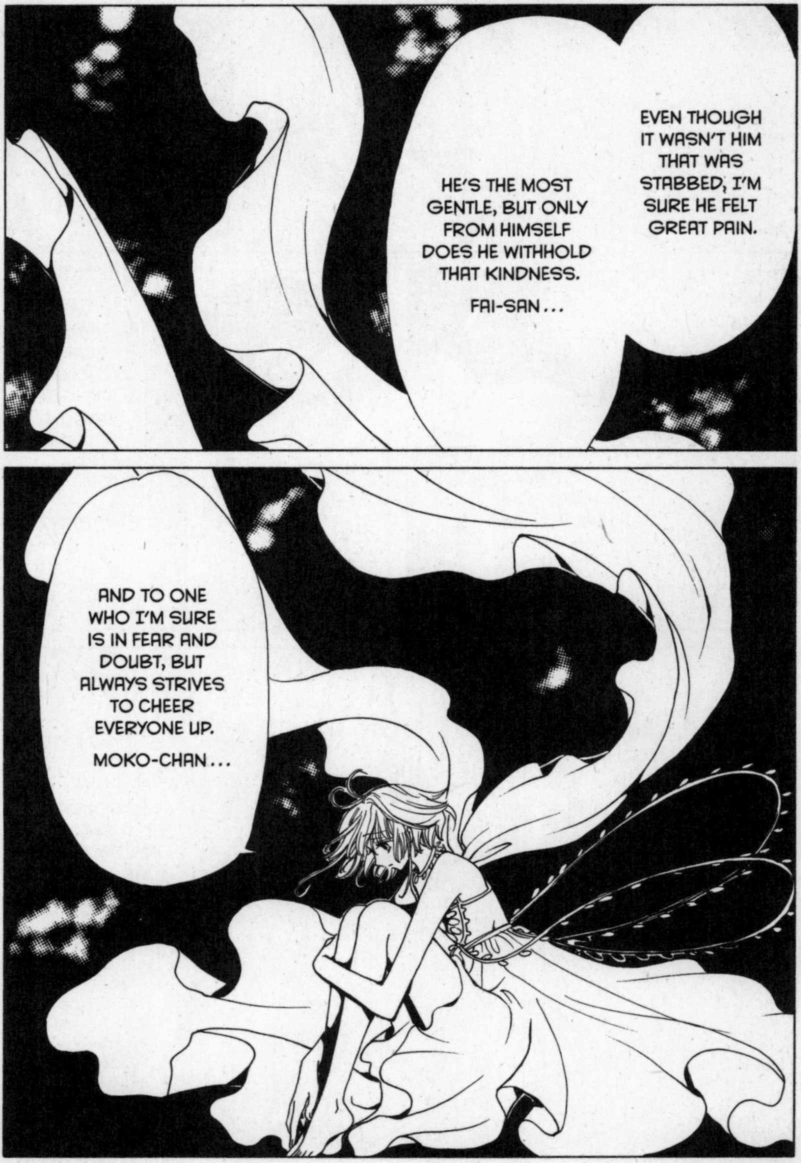
EVEN THOUGH IT WASN'T HIM THAT WAS STABBED, I'M SURE HE FELT GREAT PAIN.
HE'S THE MOST GENTLE, BUT ONLY FROM HIMSELF DOES HE WITHHOLD THAT KINDNESS.
FAI-SAN...
AND TO ONE WHO I'M SURE IS IN FEAR AND DOUBT, BUT ALWAYS STRIVES TO CHEER EVERYONE UP.
MOKO-CHAN...

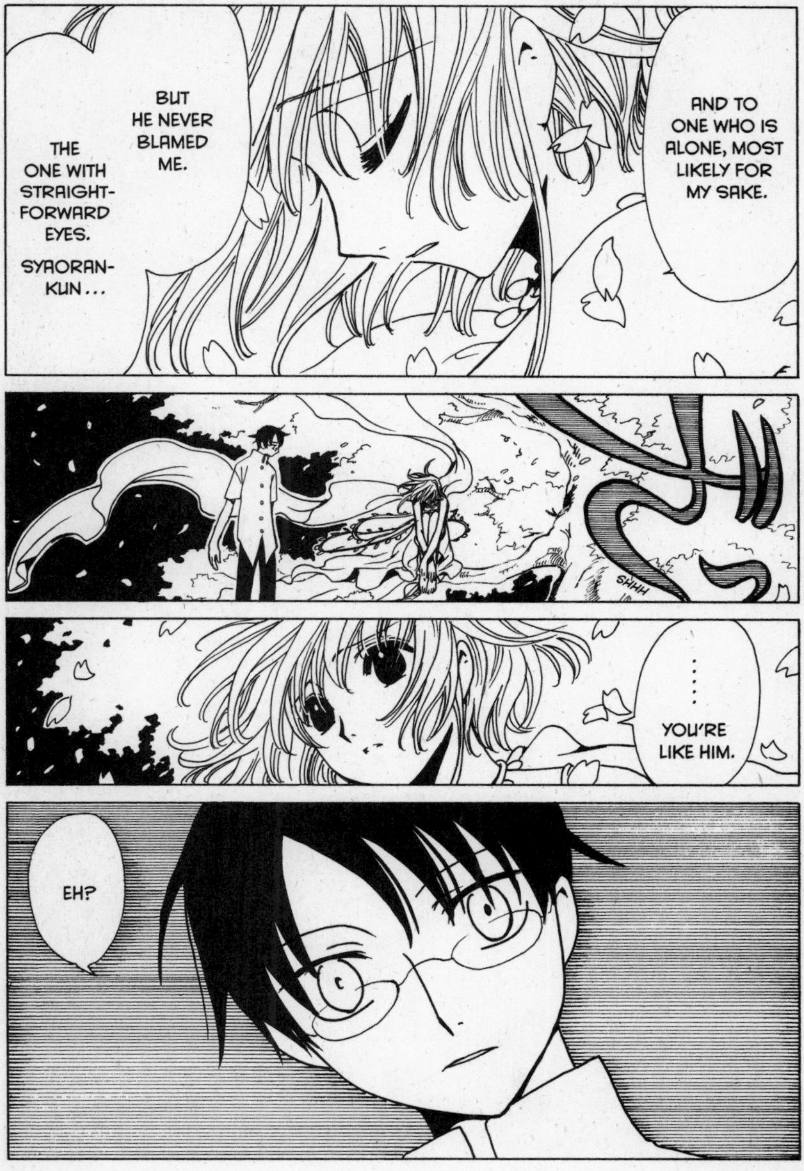
AND TO ONE WHO IS ALONE, MOST LIKELY FOR MY SAKE.
BUT HE NEVER BLAMED ME.
THE ONE WITH STRAIGHT-FORWARD EYES.
SYAORAN-KUN...
SHHH
...... YOU'RE LIKE HIM.
EH?

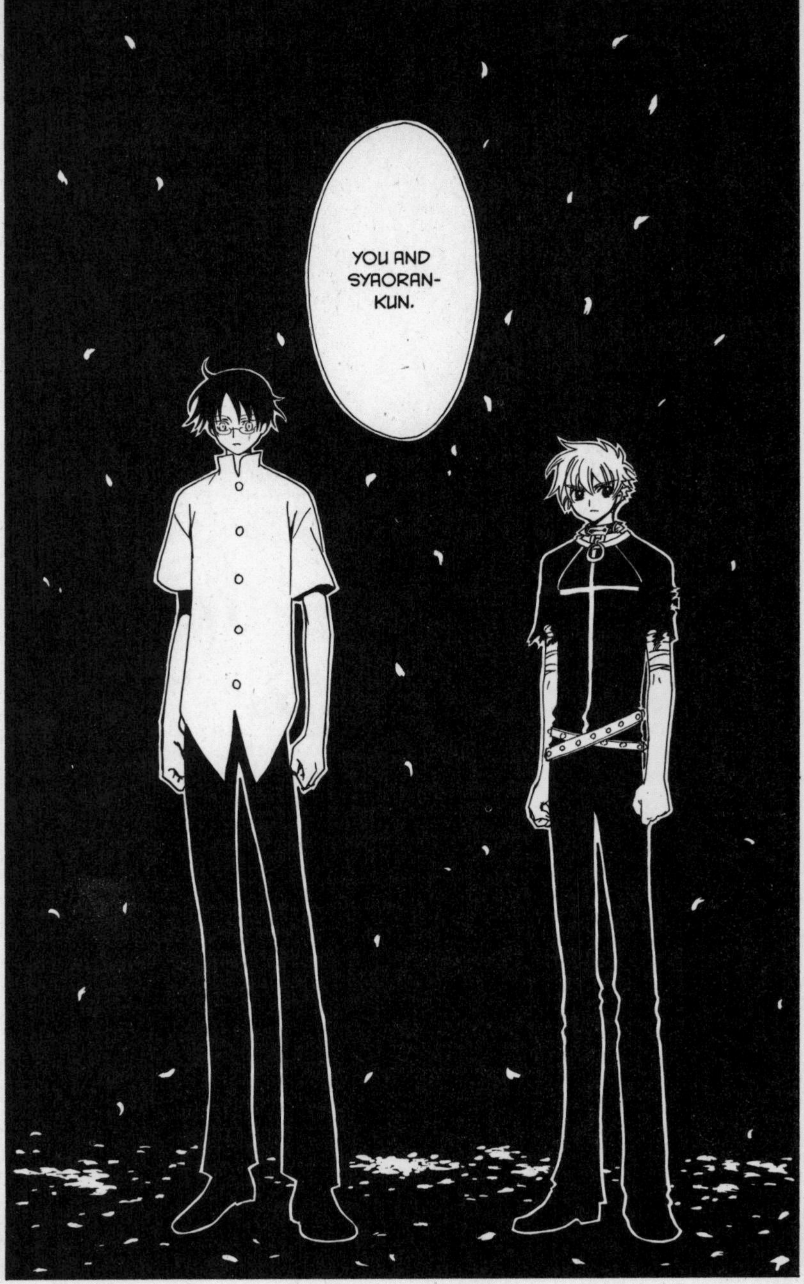
YOU AND SYAORAN-KUN.

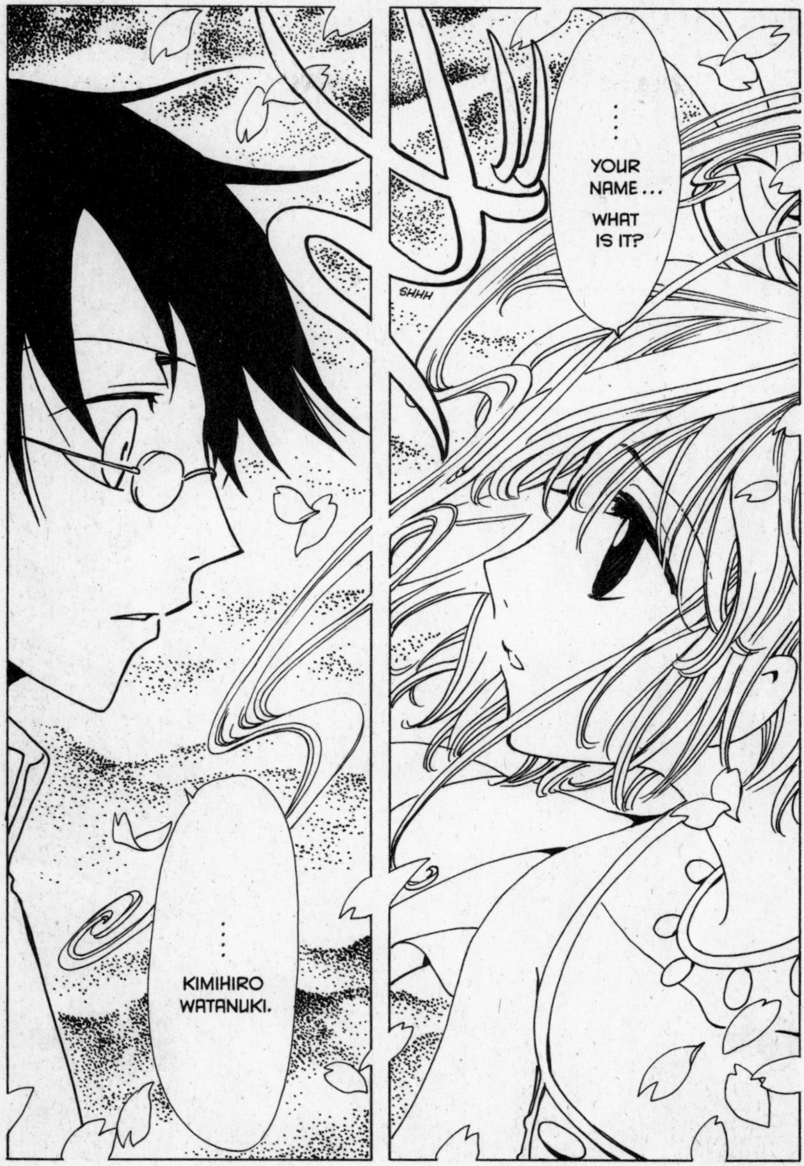
. . .
YOUR NAME . . .
WHAT IS IT?
SHHH
. . .
KIMIHIRO WATANUKI.

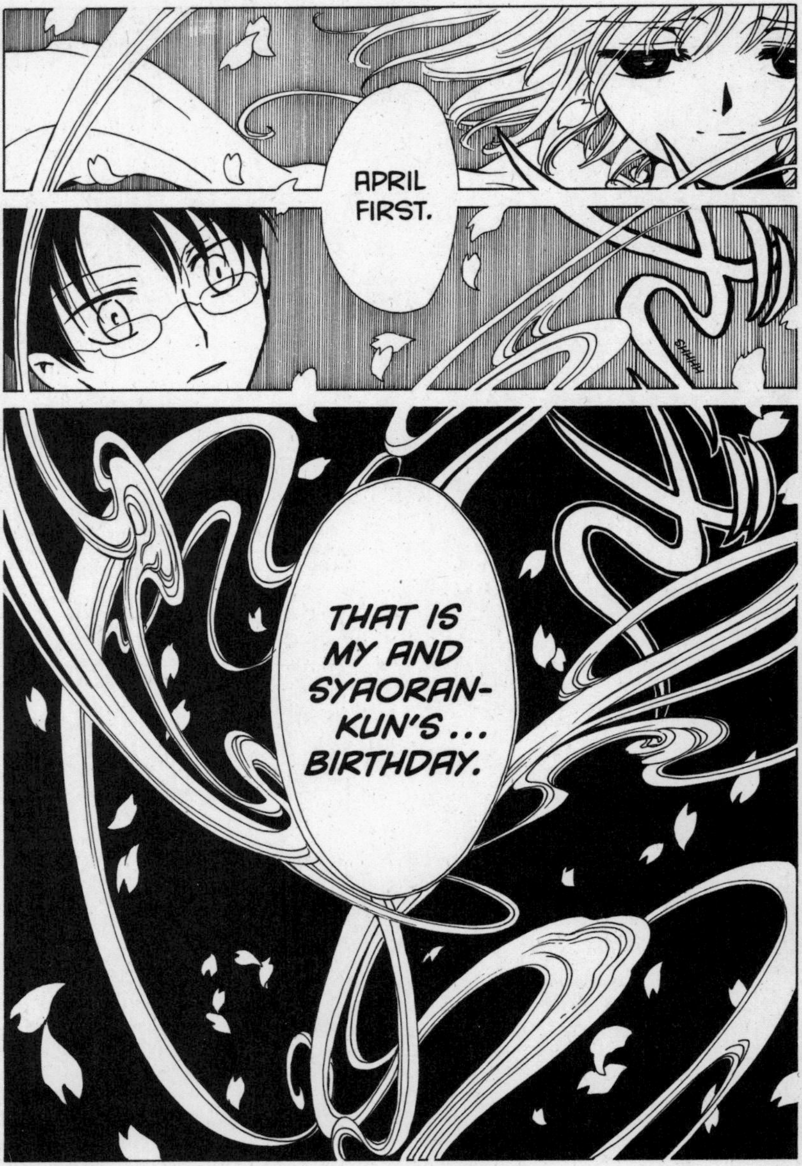
APRIL FIRST.
SHHHH
THAT IS MY AND SYAORAN-KUN'S ... BIRTHDAY.

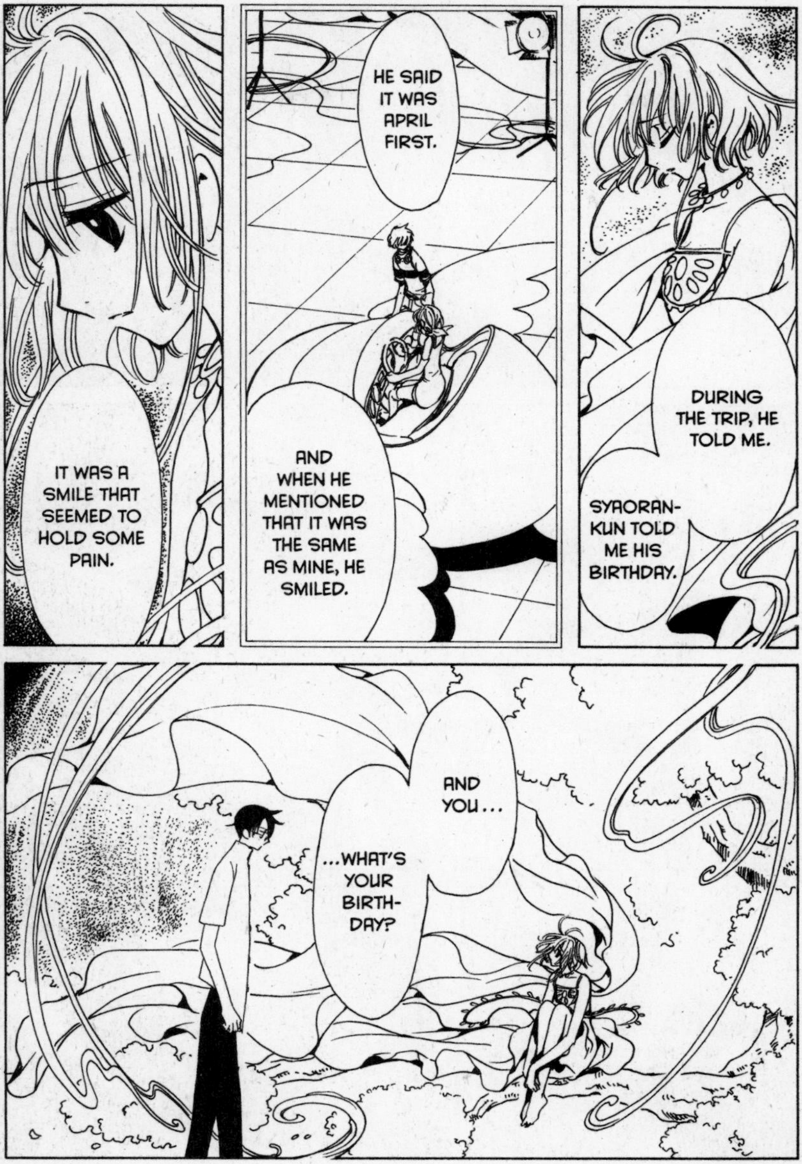
DURING THE TRIP, HE TOLD ME.
SYAORAN-KUN TOLD ME HIS BIRTHDAY.
HE SAID IT WAS APRIL FIRST.
AND WHEN HE MENTIONED THAT IT WAS THE SAME AS MINE, HE SMILED.
IT WAS A SMILE THAT SEEMED TO HOLD SOME PAIN.
AND YOU...
...WHAT'S YOUR BIRTH-DAY?

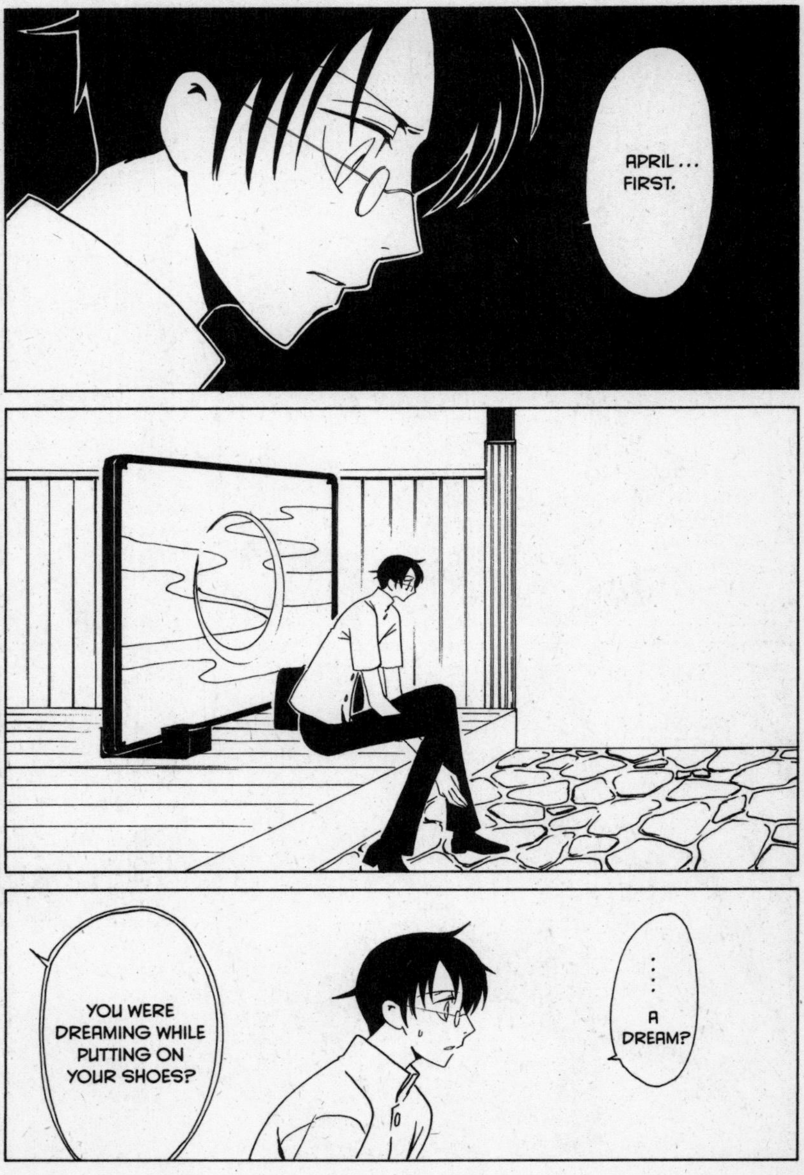
APRIL... FIRST.
... A DREAM?
YOU WERE DREAMING WHILE PUTTING ON YOUR SHOES?

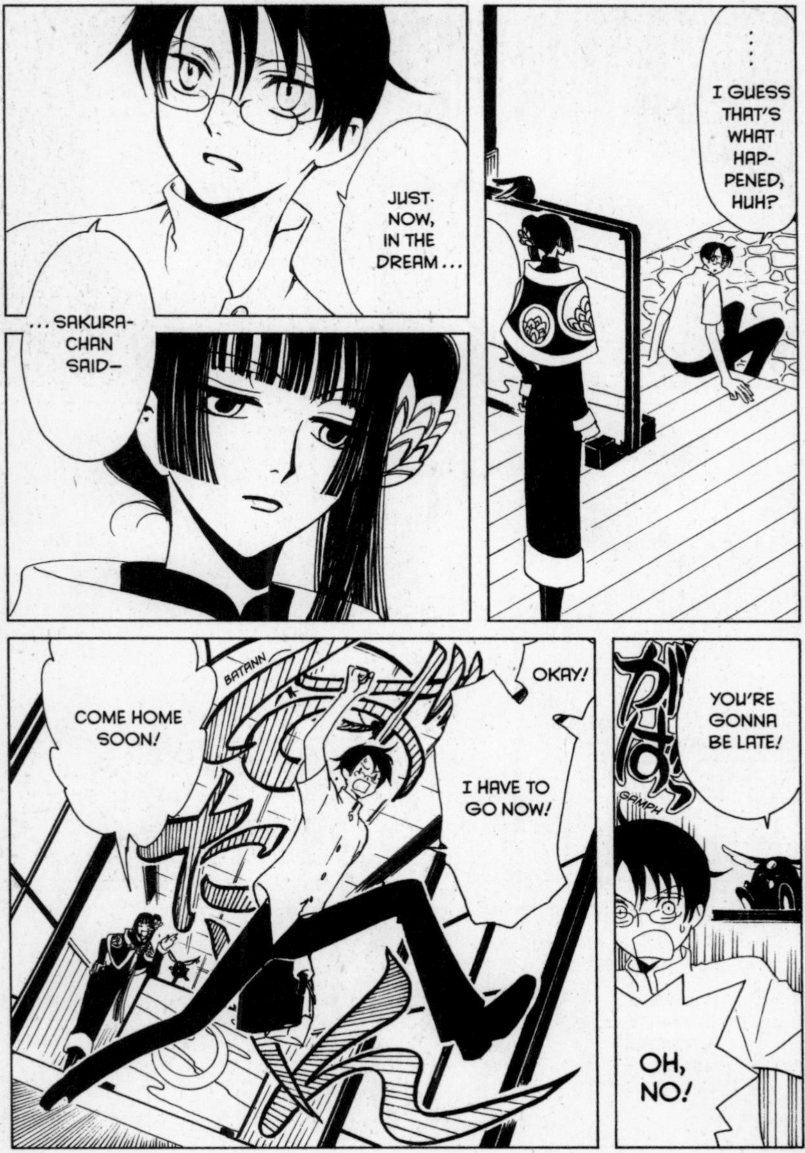
. . . .
I GUESS THAT'S WHAT HAP-PENED, HUH?
JUST. NOW, IN THE DREAM . . .
. . . SAKURA-CHAN SAID–
かはっ
GAMPH
YOU'RE GONNA BE LATE!
OH, NO!
OKAY!
I HAVE TO GO NOW!
BATANN
COME HOME SOON!

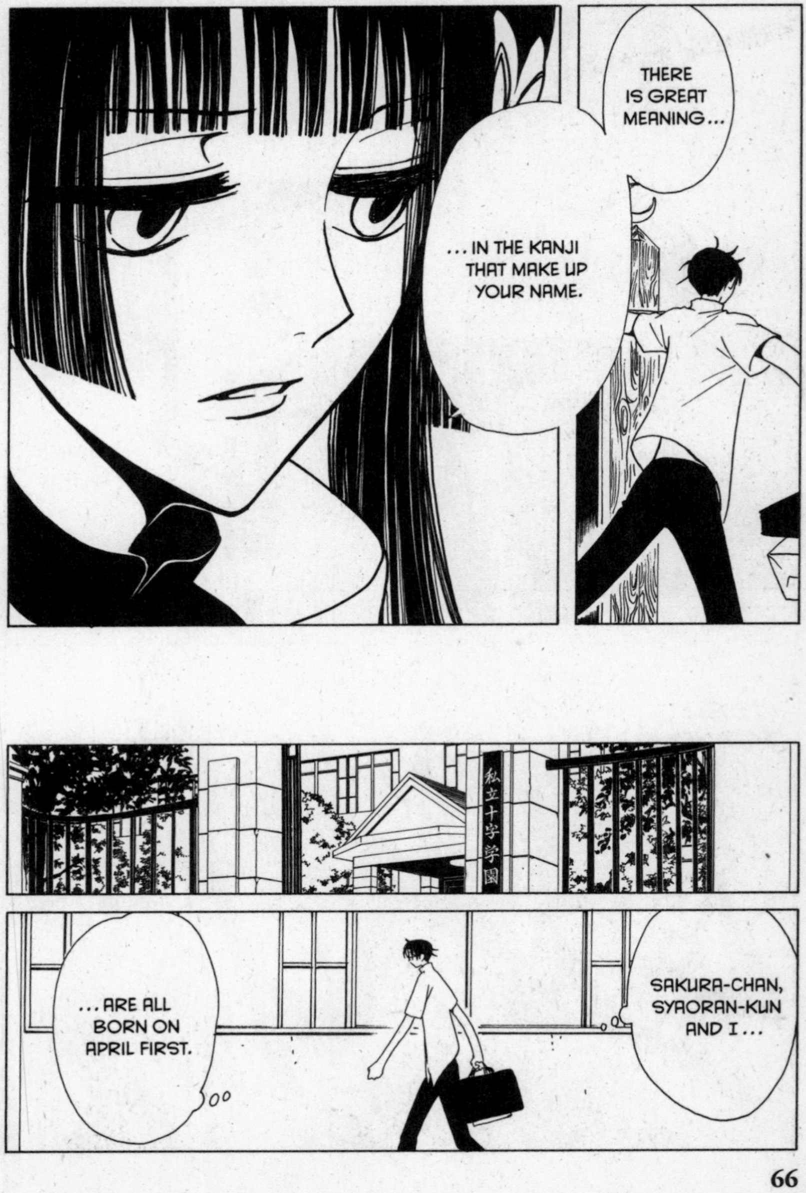
THERE IS GREAT MEANING...
...IN THE KANJI THAT MAKE UP YOUR NAME.
SAKURA-CHAN, SYAORAN-KUN AND I...
...ARE ALL BORN ON APRIL FIRST.

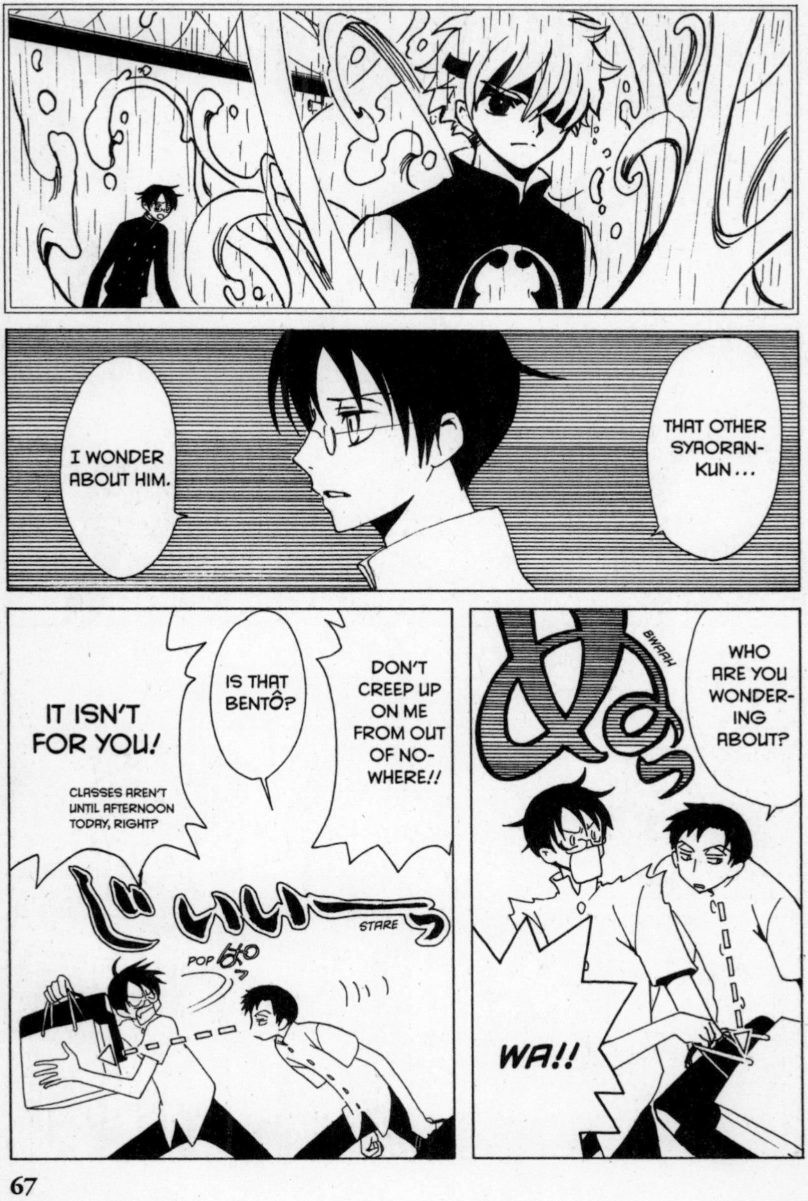

THAT OTHER SYAORAN-KUN...
I WONDER ABOUT HIM.
WHO ARE YOU WONDERING ABOUT?
BWAAH
WA!!
DON'T CREEP UP ON ME FROM OUT OF NOWHERE!!
IS THAT BENTÔ?
IT ISN'T FOR YOU!
CLASSES AREN'T UNTIL AFTERNOON TODAY, RIGHT?
STARE
POP

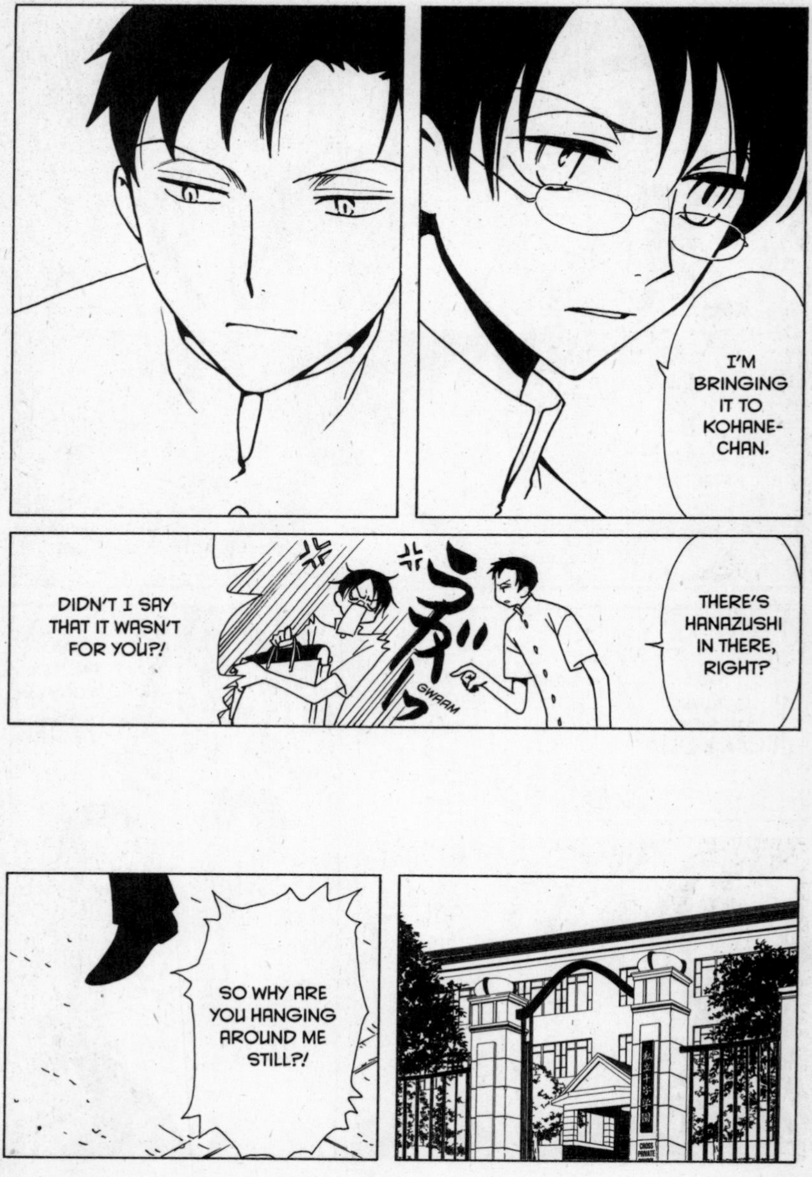
I'M BRINGING IT TO KOHANE-CHAN.
THERE'S HANAZUSHI IN THERE, RIGHT?
GWAAM
DIDN'T I SAY THAT IT WASN'T FOR YOU?!
SO WHY ARE YOU HANGING AROUND ME STILL?!

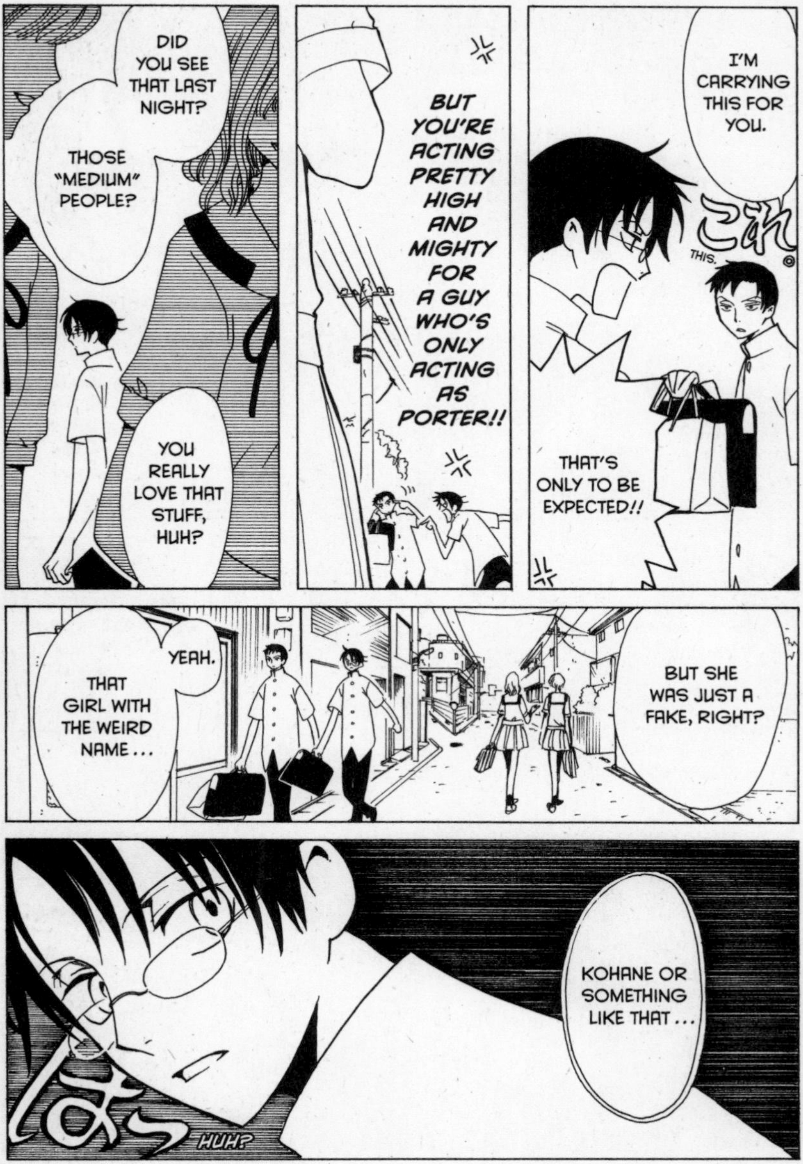

I'M CARRYING THIS FOR YOU.
これ
THIS.
THAT'S ONLY TO BE EXPECTED!!
BUT YOU'RE ACTING PRETTY HIGH AND MIGHTY FOR A GUY WHO'S ONLY ACTING AS PORTER!!
DID YOU SEE THAT LAST NIGHT?
THOSE "MEDIUM" PEOPLE?
YOU REALLY LOVE THAT STUFF, HUH?
BUT SHE WAS JUST A FAKE, RIGHT?
YEAH.
THAT GIRL WITH THE WEIRD NAME...
KOHANE OR SOMETHING LIKE THAT...
はっ
HUH?

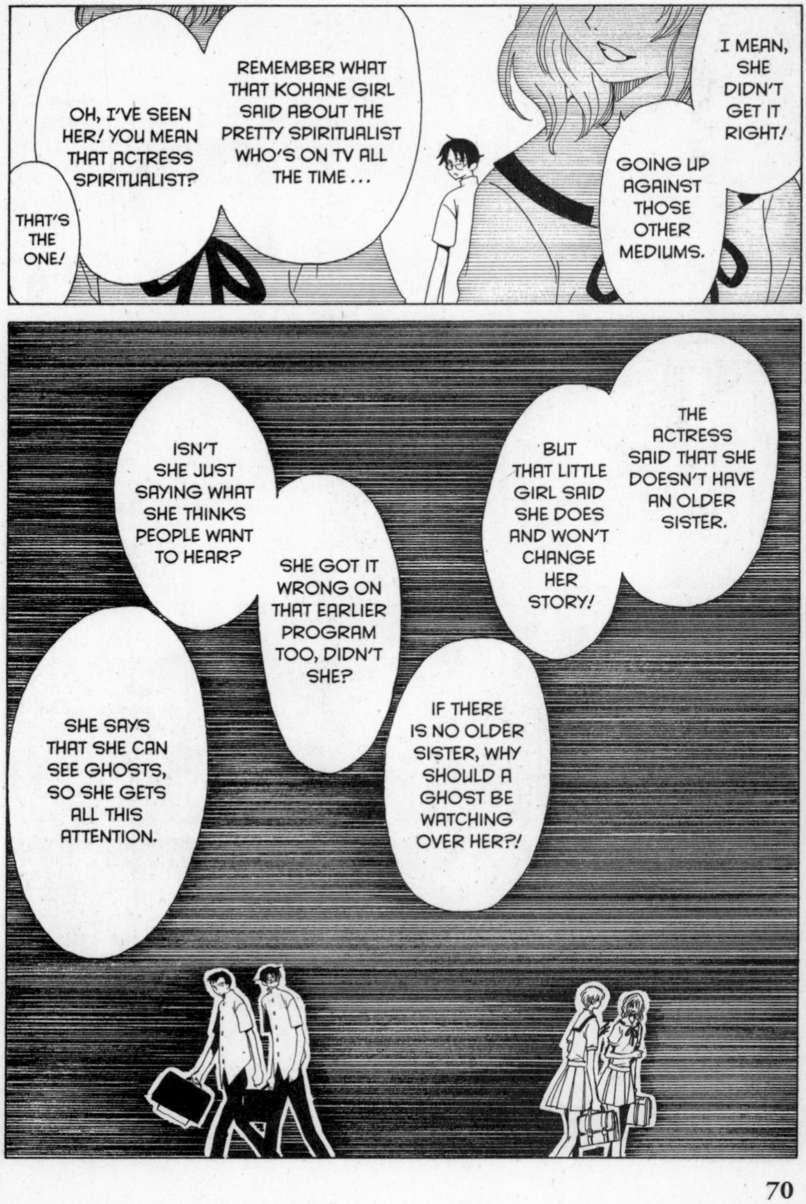
I MEAN, SHE DIDN'T GET IT RIGHT!
GOING UP AGAINST THOSE OTHER MEDIUMS.
REMEMBER WHAT THAT KOHANE GIRL SAID ABOUT THE PRETTY SPIRITUALIST WHO'S ON TV ALL THE TIME . . .
OH, I'VE SEEN HER! YOU MEAN THAT ACTRESS SPIRITUALIST?
THAT'S THE ONE!
THE ACTRESS SAID THAT SHE DOESN'T HAVE AN OLDER SISTER.
BUT THAT LITTLE GIRL SAID SHE DOES AND WON'T CHANGE HER STORY!
ISN'T SHE JUST SAYING WHAT SHE THINKS PEOPLE WANT TO HEAR?
SHE GOT IT WRONG ON THAT EARLIER PROGRAM TOO, DIDN'T SHE?
IF THERE IS NO OLDER SISTER, WHY SHOULD A GHOST BE WATCHING OVER HER?!
SHE SAYS THAT SHE CAN SEE GHOSTS, SO SHE GETS ALL THIS ATTENTION.

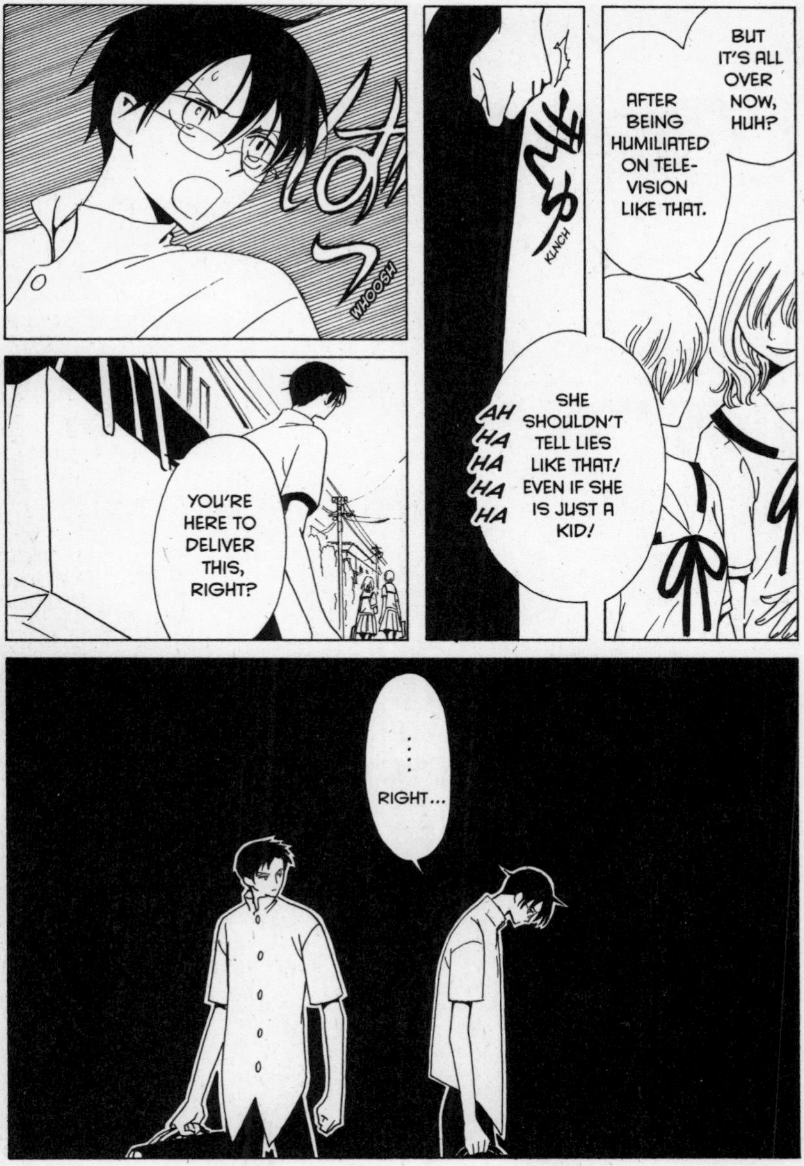
BUT IT'S ALL OVER NOW, HUH?
AFTER BEING HUMILIATED ON TELE- VISION LIKE THAT.
SHE SHOULDN'T TELL LIES LIKE THAT! EVEN IF SHE IS JUST A KID!
AH HA HA HA HA HA
KLNCH
WHOOSH
YOU'RE HERE TO DELIVER THIS, RIGHT?
....
RIGHT...

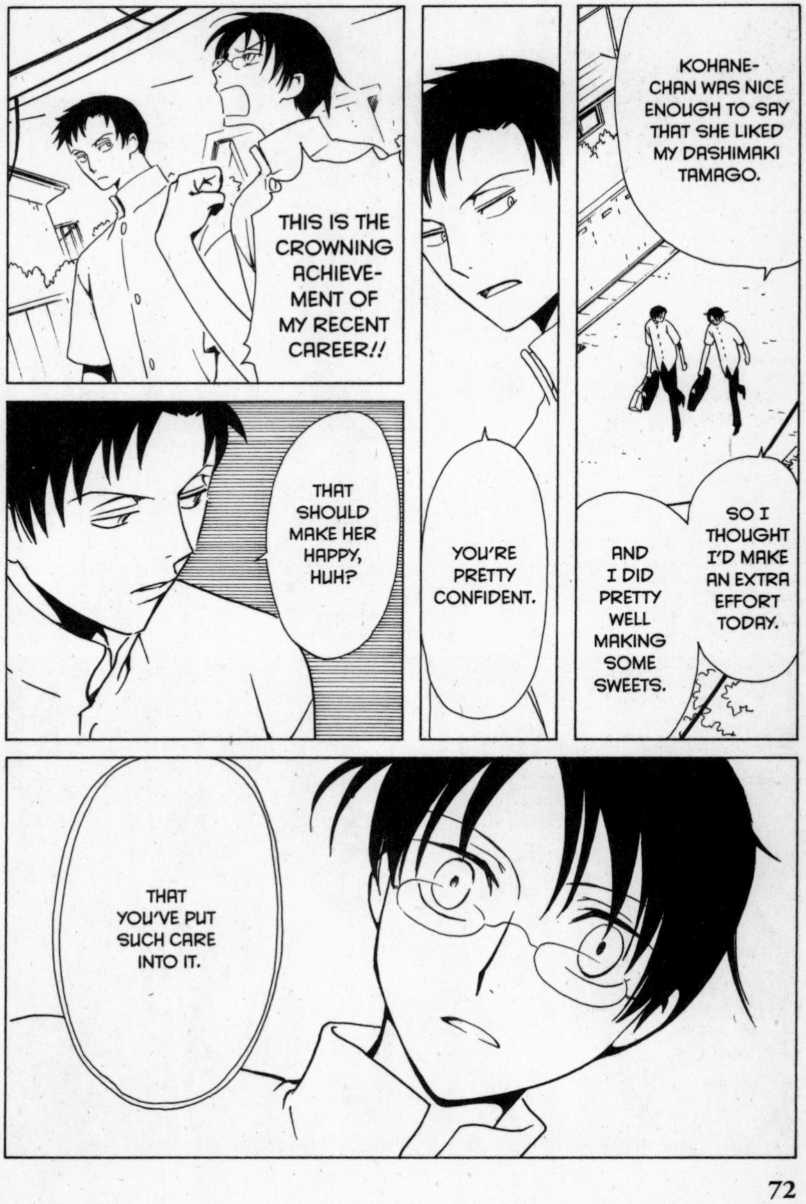
KOHANE-CHAN WAS NICE ENOUGH TO SAY THAT SHE LIKED MY DASHIMAKI TAMAGO.
SO I THOUGHT I'D MAKE AN EXTRA EFFORT TODAY.
AND I DID PRETTY WELL MAKING SOME SWEETS.
YOU'RE PRETTY CONFIDENT.
THIS IS THE CROWNING ACHIEVE-MENT OF MY RECENT CAREER!!
THAT SHOULD MAKE HER HAPPY, HUH?
THAT YOU'VE PUT SUCH CARE INTO IT.

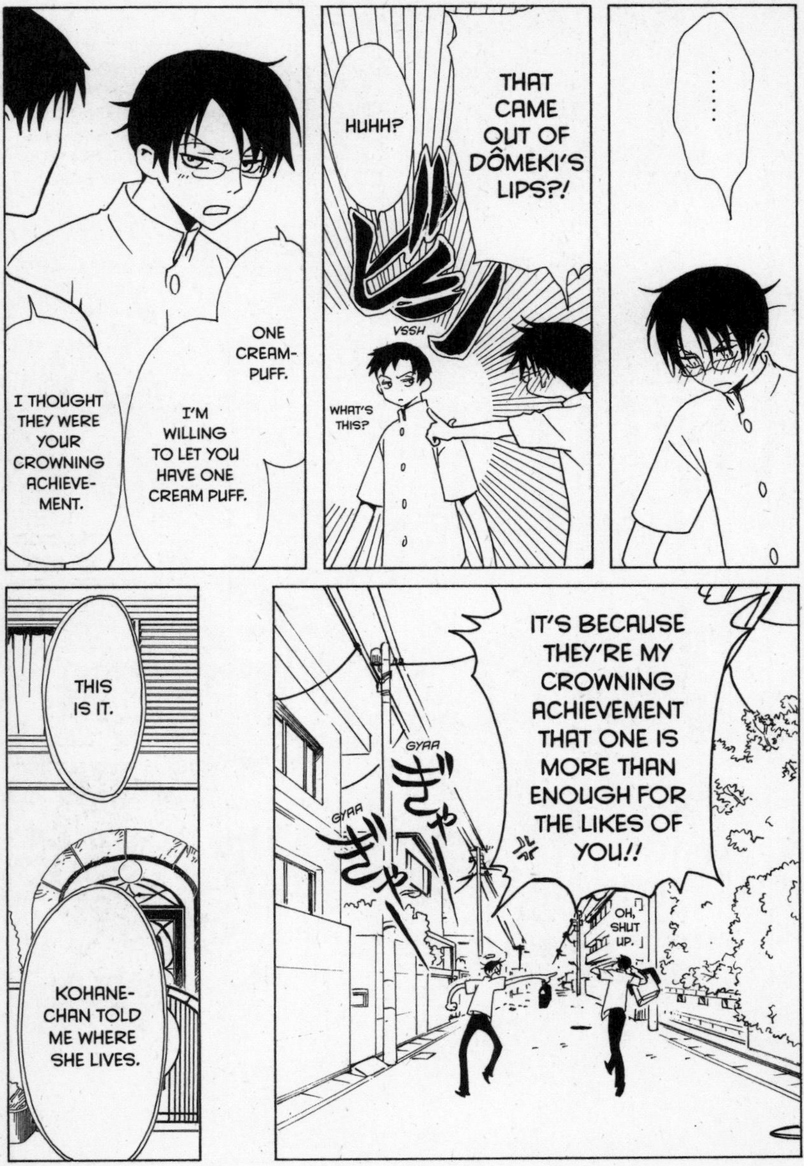
......
THAT CAME OUT OF DÔMEKI'S LIPS?!
HUHH?
VSSH
WHAT'S THIS?
ONE CREAM-PUFF.
I'M WILLING TO LET YOU HAVE ONE CREAM PUFF.
I THOUGHT THEY WERE YOUR CROWNING ACHIEVEMENT.
IT'S BECAUSE THEY'RE MY CROWNING ACHIEVEMENT THAT ONE IS MORE THAN ENOUGH FOR THE LIKES OF YOU!!
OH, SHUT UP.
GYAA
GYAA
THIS IS IT.
KOHANE-CHAN TOLD ME WHERE SHE LIVES.

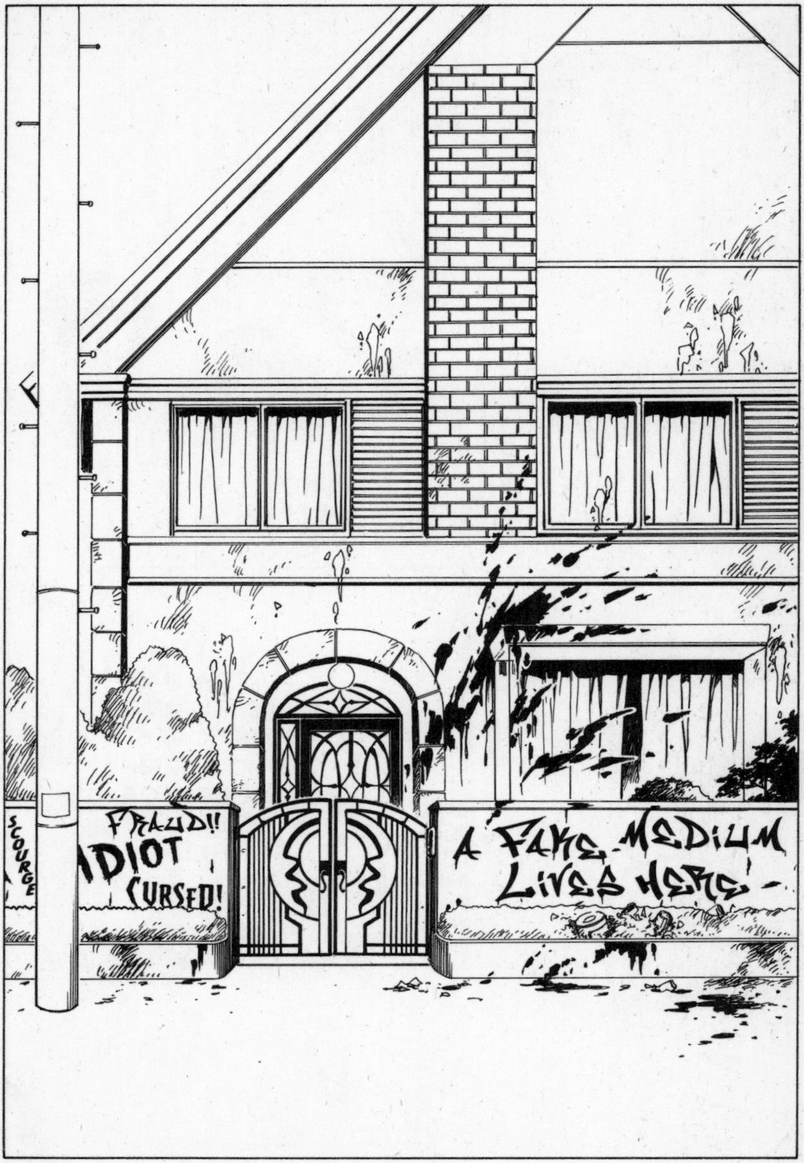
A FAKE MEDIUM
LIVES HERE
FRAUD!!
SCOURGE
IDIOT
CURSED!

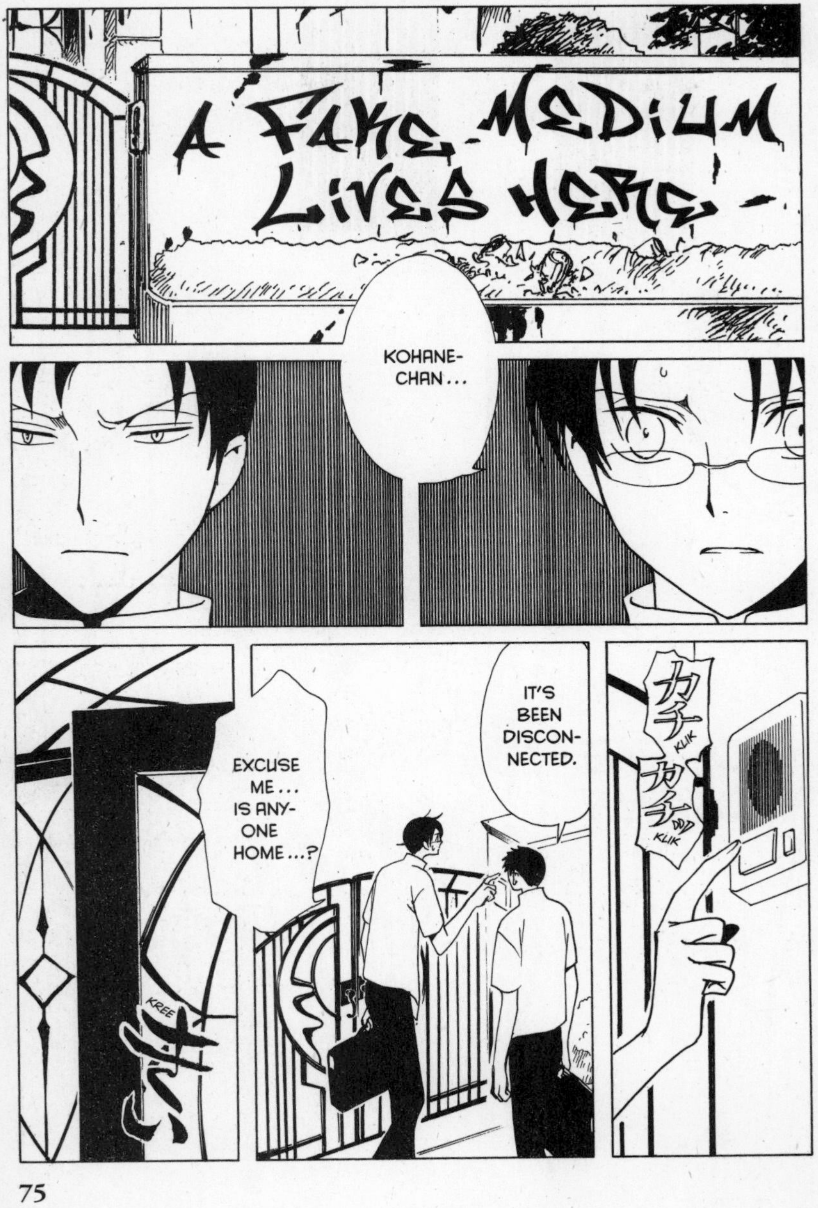
A FAKE MEDIUM LIVES HERE
KOHANE-CHAN...
カチ
KLIK
カチ
KLIK
IT'S BEEN DISCONNECTED.
EXCUSE ME... IS ANYONE HOME...?
KREE

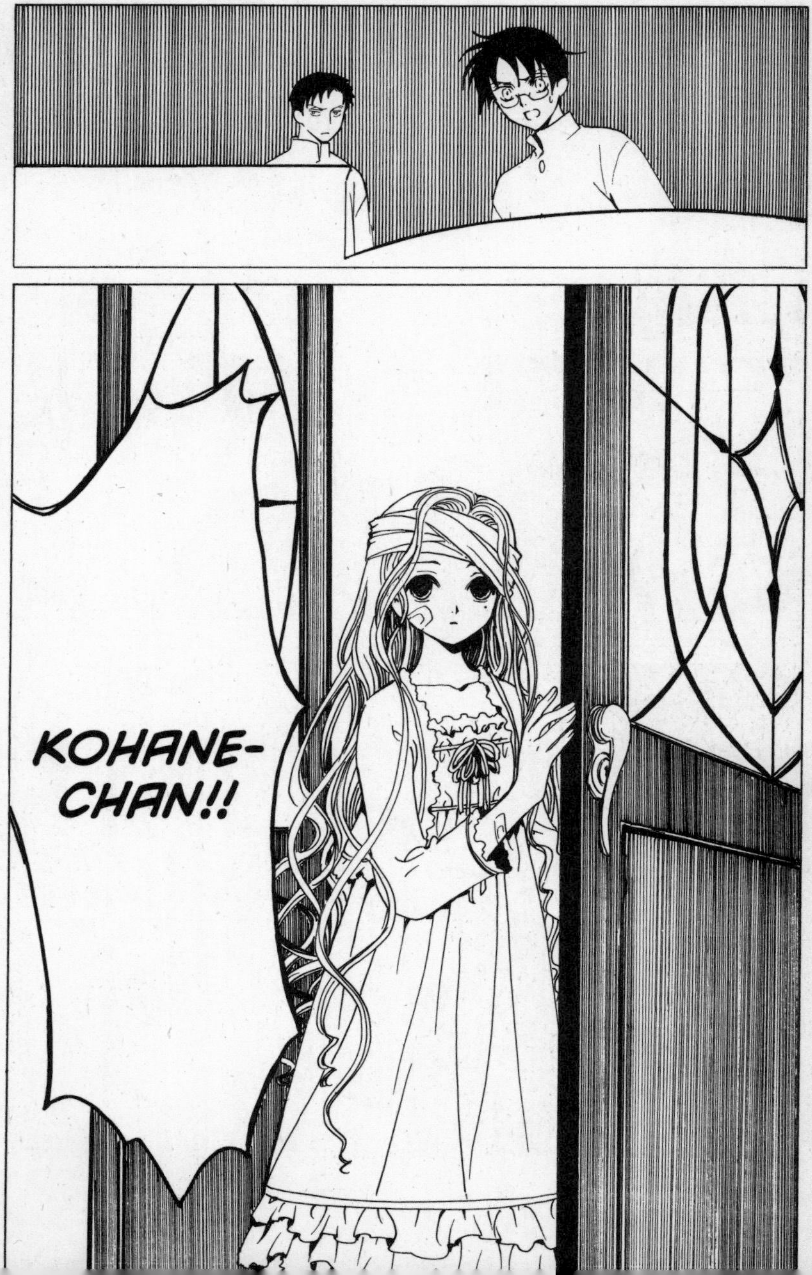
KOHANE-CHAN!!

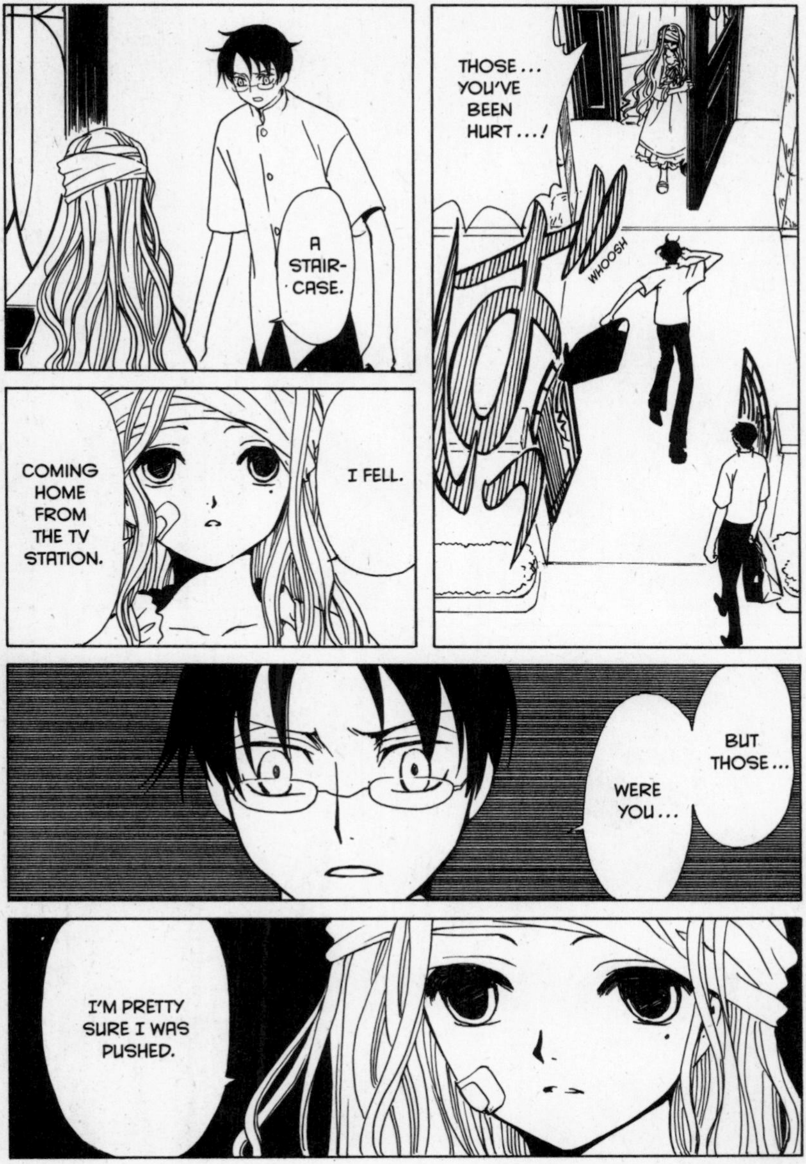
THOSE... YOU'VE BEEN HURT...!
WHOOSH
A STAIR-CASE.
I FELL.
COMING HOME FROM THE TV STATION.
BUT THOSE...
WERE YOU...
I'M PRETTY SURE I WAS PUSHED.

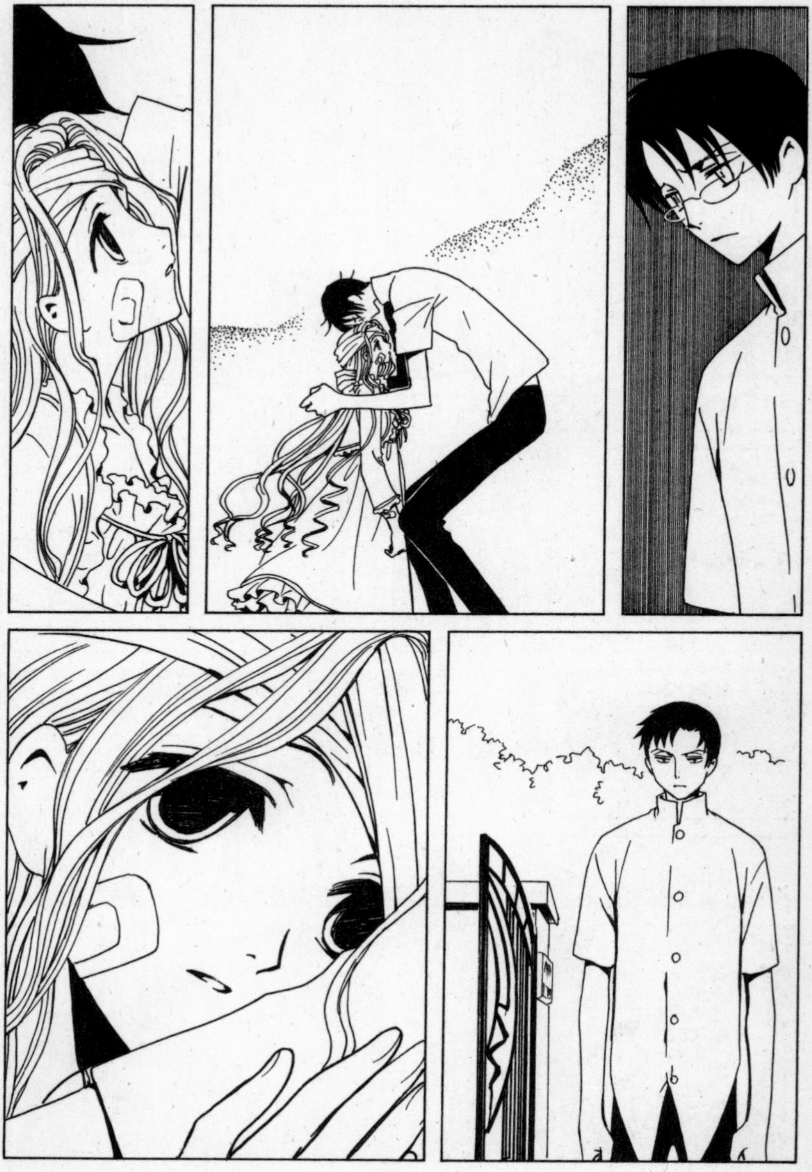

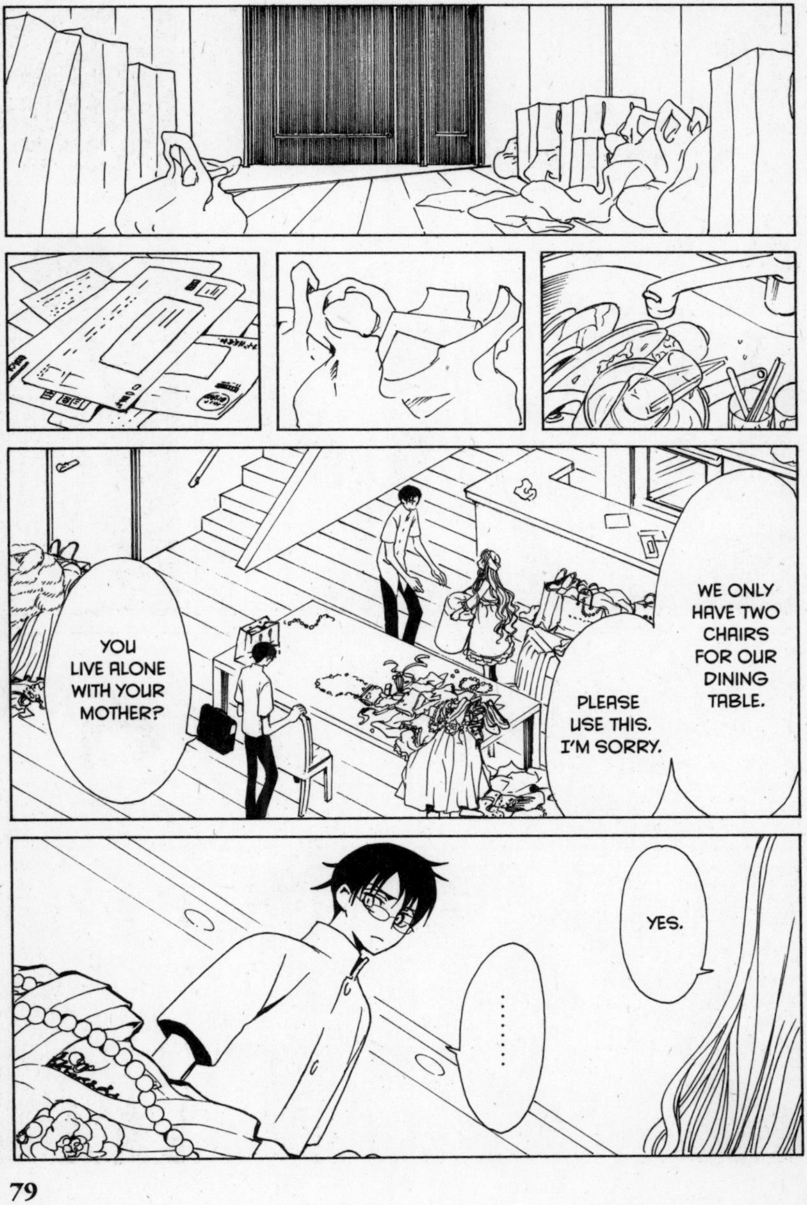
WE ONLY HAVE TWO CHAIRS FOR OUR DINING TABLE.
PLEASE USE THIS. I'M SORRY.
YOU LIVE ALONE WITH YOUR MOTHER?
YES.
......

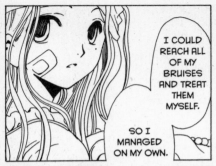

HAVE YOU BEEN TO A HOSPITAL FOR YOUR INJURIES?
NO, I HAVEN'T.
I COULD REACH ALL OF MY BRUISES AND TREAT THEM MYSELF.
SO I MANAGED ON MY OWN.
トゥルルルル
RRRRNG
トゥルルル
RRRRNG
カチ
CHK
ピー
PEEEP

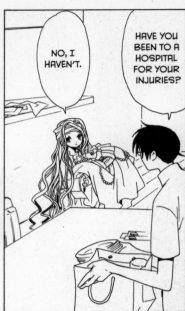

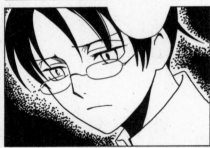

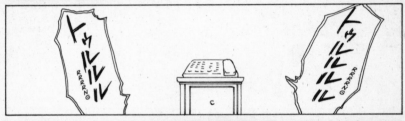

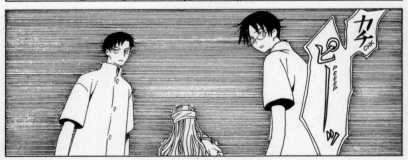

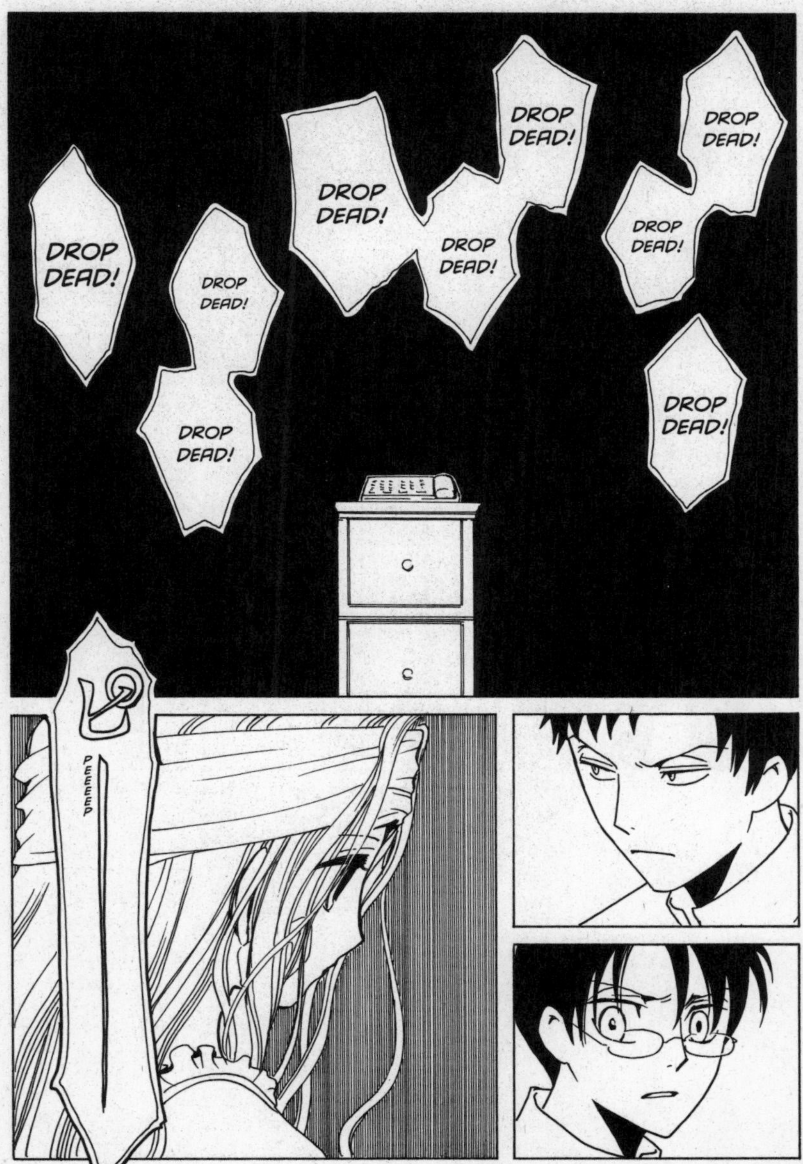
DROP DEAD!
DROP DEAD!
DROP DEAD!
DROP DEAD!
DROP DEAD!
DROP DEAD!
DROP DEAD!
DROP DEAD!
DROP DEAD!
PEEEEP

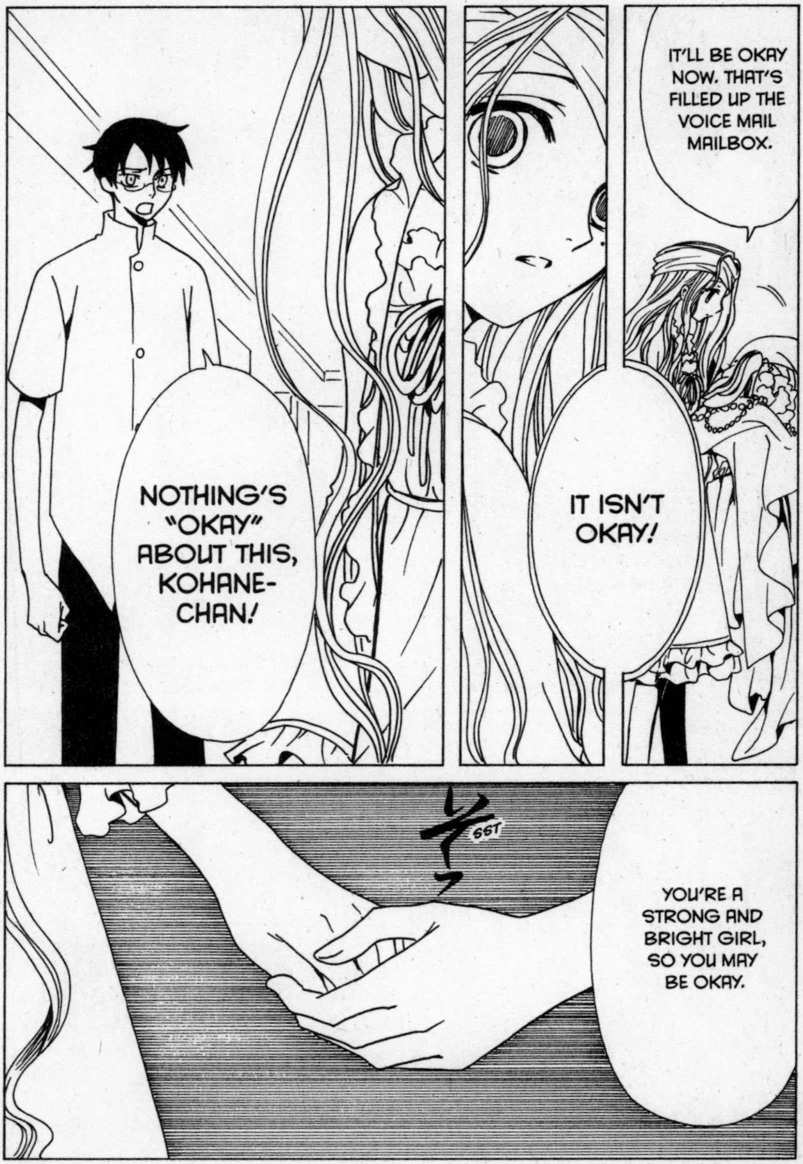
IT'LL BE OKAY NOW. THAT'S FILLED UP THE VOICE MAIL MAILBOX.
IT ISN'T OKAY!
NOTHING'S "OKAY" ABOUT THIS, KOHANE-CHAN!
YOU'RE A STRONG AND BRIGHT GIRL, SO YOU MAY BE OKAY.
SST

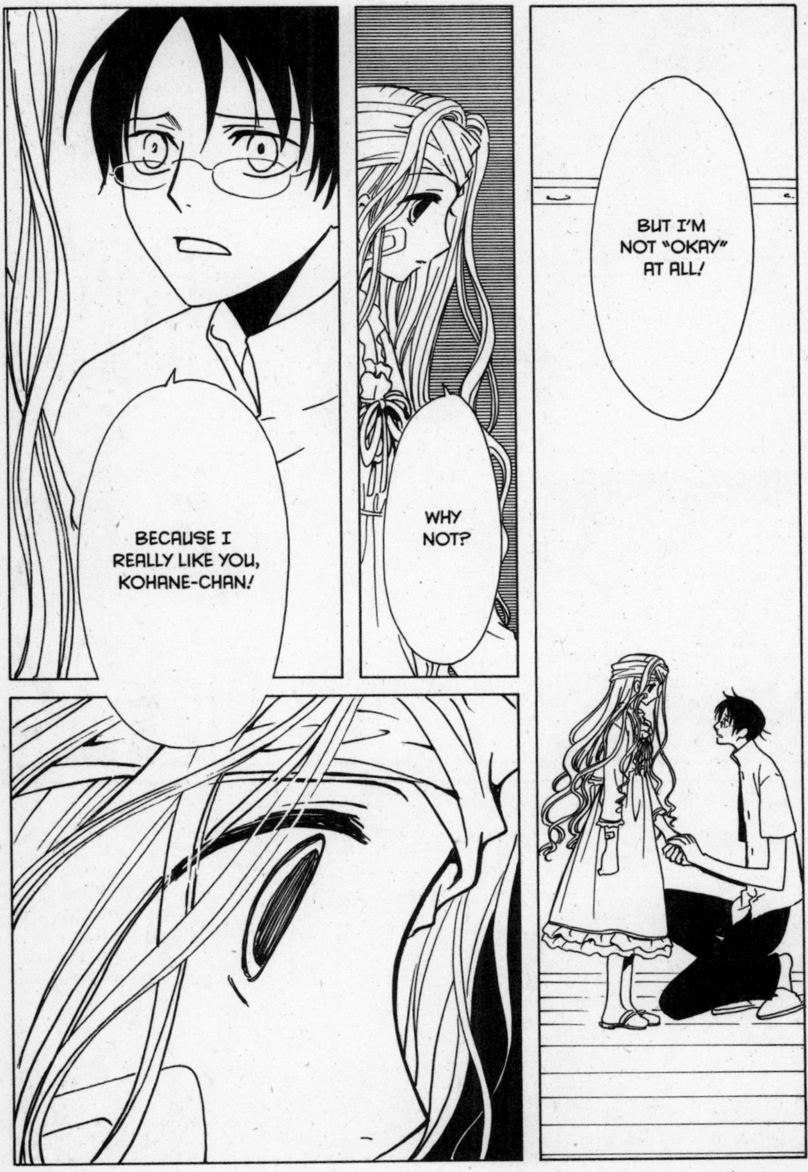
BUT I'M NOT "OKAY" AT ALL!
WHY NOT?
BECAUSE I REALLY LIKE YOU, KOHANE-CHAN!

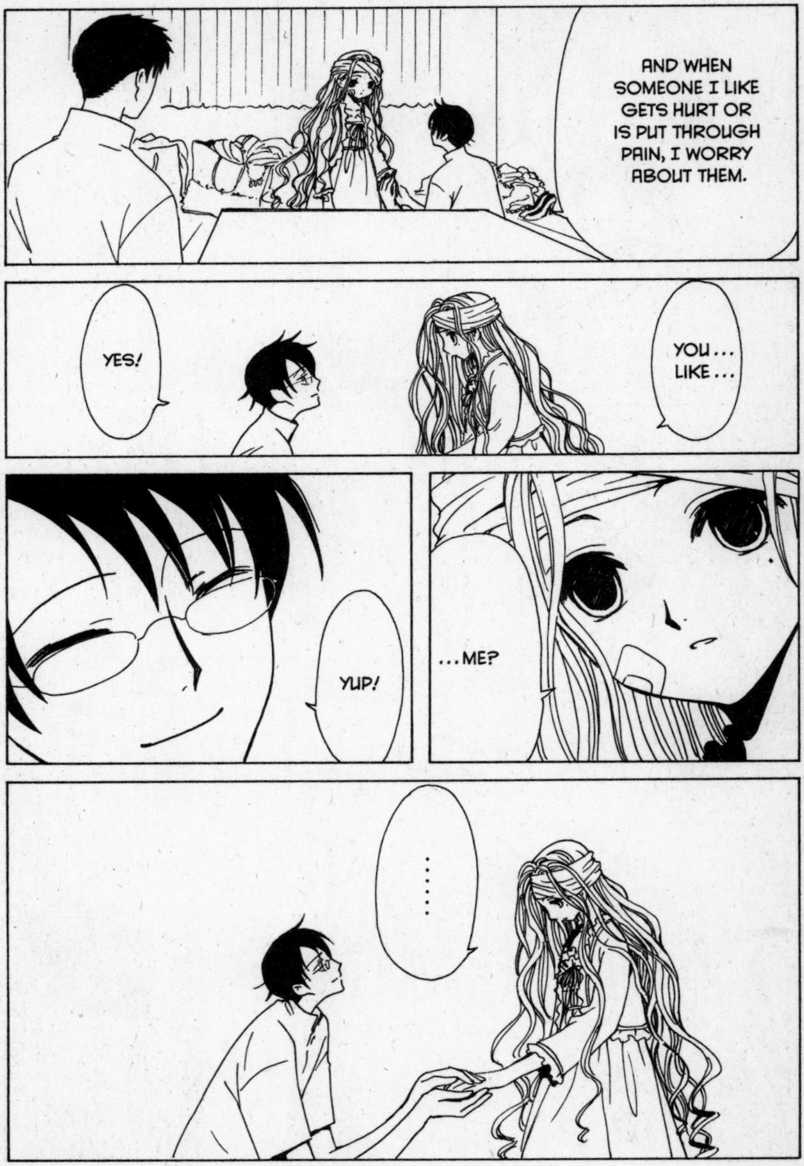
AND WHEN SOMEONE I LIKE GETS HURT OR IS PUT THROUGH PAIN, I WORRY ABOUT THEM.
YOU... LIKE...
YES!
...ME?
YUP!
......

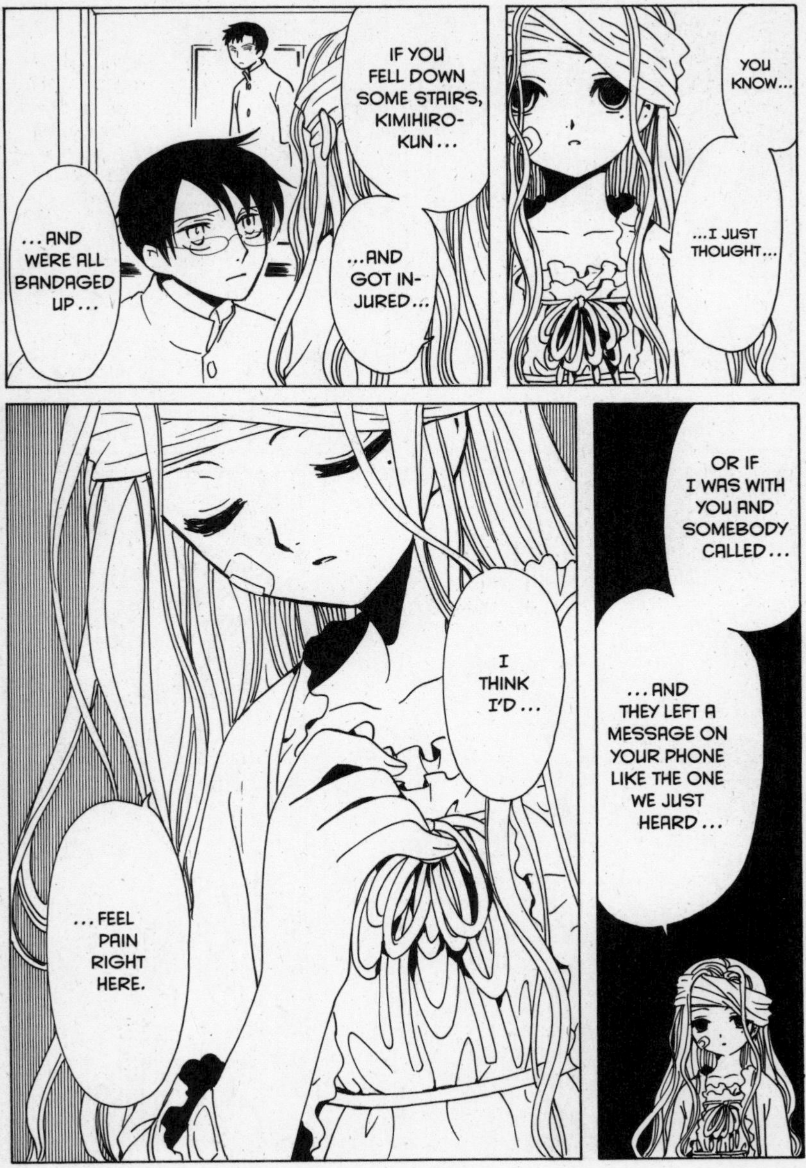
YOU KNOW...
...I JUST THOUGHT...
IF YOU FELL DOWN SOME STAIRS, KIMIHIRO-KUN...
...AND GOT IN-JURED...
...AND WERE ALL BANDAGED UP...
OR IF I WAS WITH YOU AND SOMEBODY CALLED...
...AND THEY LEFT A MESSAGE ON YOUR PHONE LIKE THE ONE WE JUST HEARD...
I THINK I'D...
...FEEL PAIN RIGHT HERE.

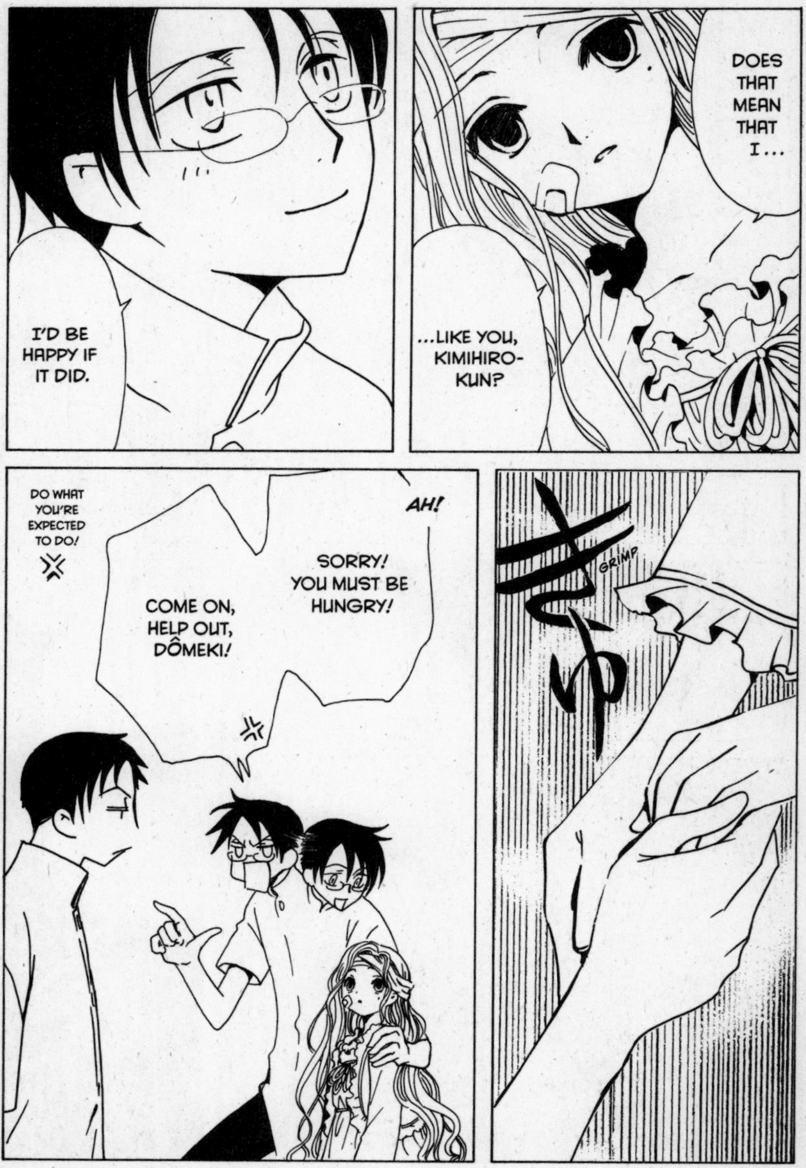

DOES THAT MEAN THAT I...
...LIKE YOU, KIMIHIRO-KUN?
I'D BE HAPPY IF IT DID.
きゅ
GRIMP
AH!
SORRY! YOU MUST BE HUNGRY!
COME ON, HELP OUT, DÔMEKI!
DO WHAT YOU'RE EXPECTED TO DO!

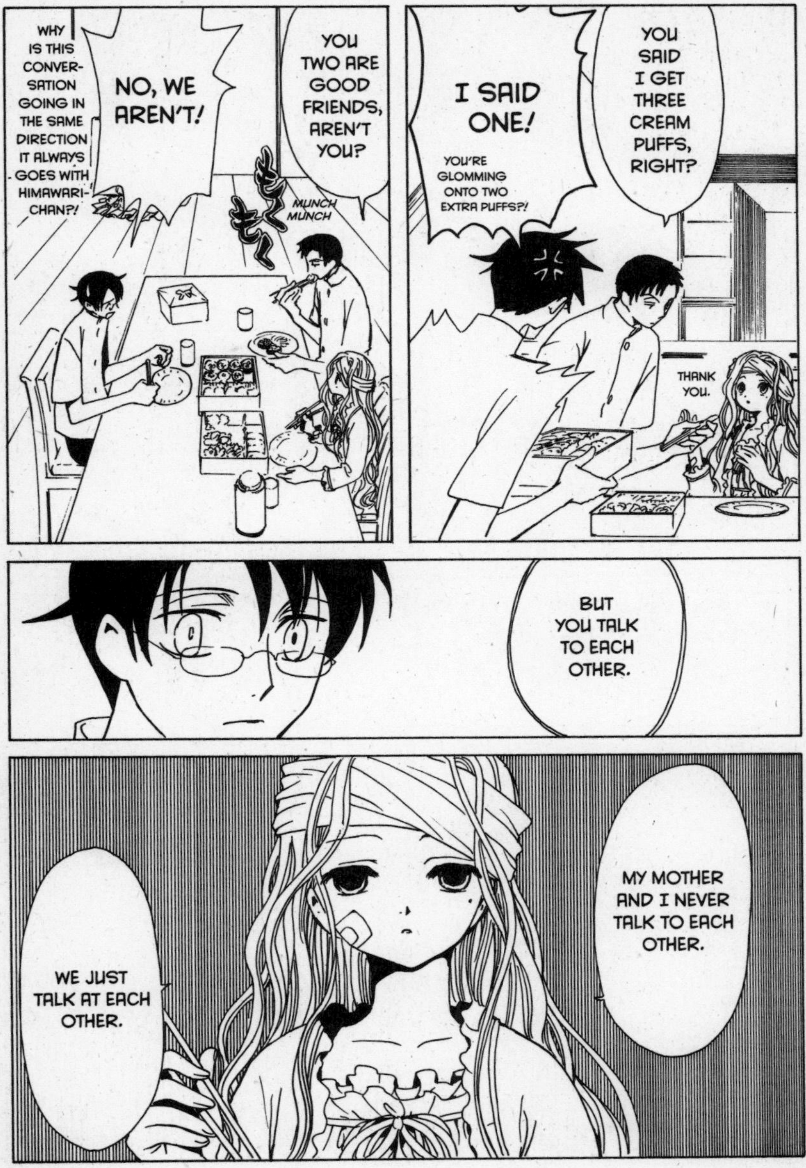
YOU SAID I GET THREE CREAM PUFFS, RIGHT?
I SAID ONE!
YOU'RE GLOMMING ONTO TWO EXTRA PUFFS?!
THANK YOU.
YOU TWO ARE GOOD FRIENDS, AREN'T YOU?
NO, WE AREN'T!
WHY IS THIS CONVER-SATION GOING IN THE SAME DIRECTION IT ALWAYS GOES WITH HIMAWARI-CHAN?!
MUNCH MUNCH
BUT YOU TALK TO EACH OTHER.
MY MOTHER AND I NEVER TALK TO EACH OTHER.
WE JUST TALK AT EACH OTHER.

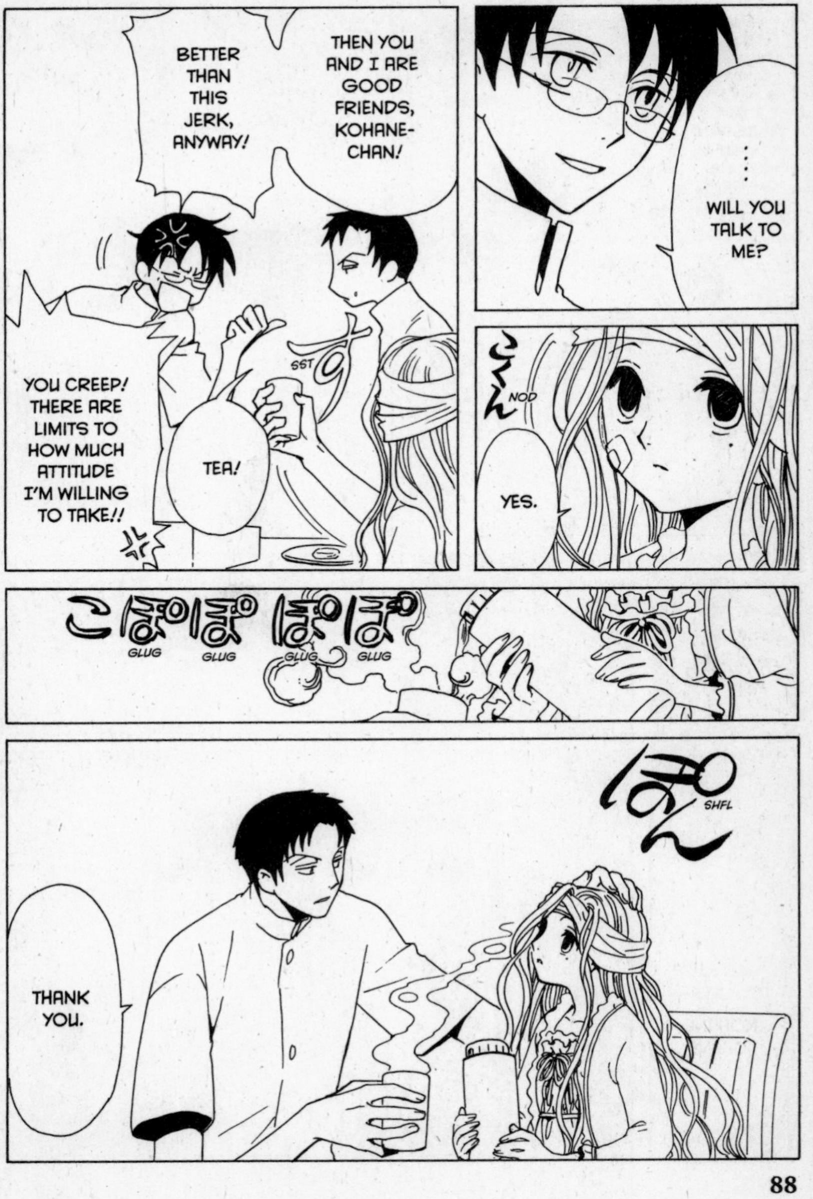
. . . . .
WILL YOU TALK TO ME?
こくん
NOD
YES.
THEN YOU AND I ARE GOOD FRIENDS, KOHANE-CHAN!
BETTER THAN THIS JERK, ANYWAY!
SST
TEA!
YOU CREEP! THERE ARE LIMITS TO HOW MUCH ATTITUDE I'M WILLING TO TAKE!!
こぽぽ ぽぽ
GLUG GLUG GLUG GLUG
ぽん
SHFL
THANK YOU.

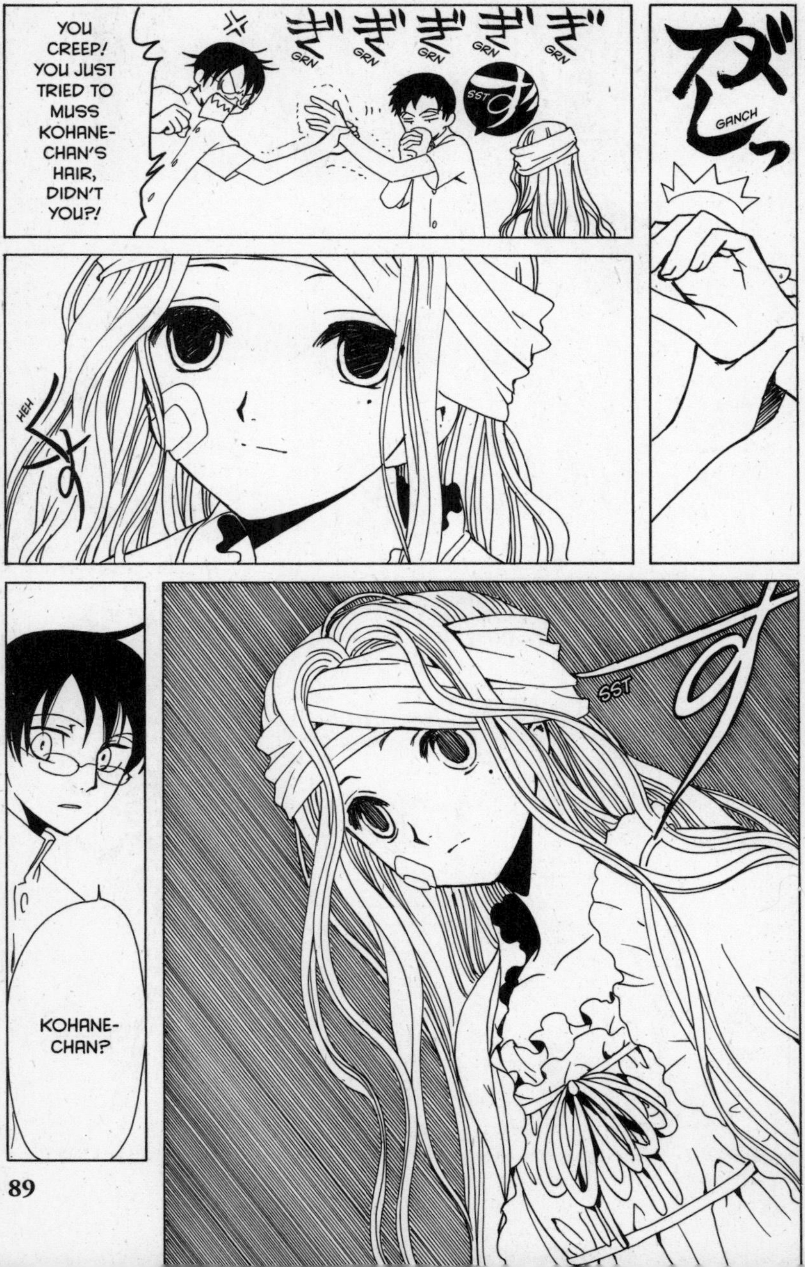
GANCH
GRN GRN GRN GRN GRN
SST
YOU CREEP! YOU JUST TRIED TO MUSS KOHANE-CHAN'S HAIR, DIDN'T YOU?!
HEH
SST
KOHANE-CHAN?

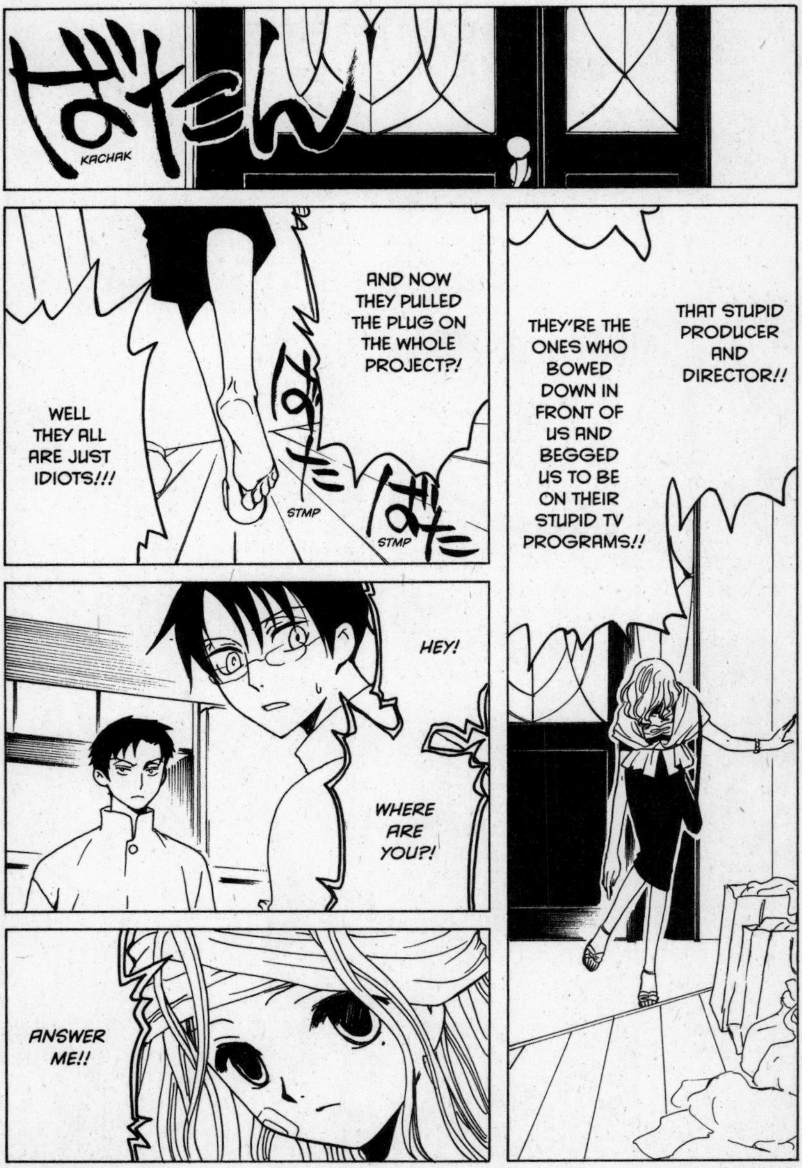
ばたん
KACHAK
THAT STUPID PRODUCER AND DIRECTOR!!
THEY'RE THE ONES WHO BOWED DOWN IN FRONT OF US AND BEGGED US TO BE ON THEIR STUPID TV PROGRAMS!!
AND NOW THEY PULLED THE PLUG ON THE WHOLE PROJECT?!
STMP
STMP
WELL THEY ALL ARE JUST IDIOTS!!!
HEY!
WHERE ARE YOU?!
ANSWER ME!!

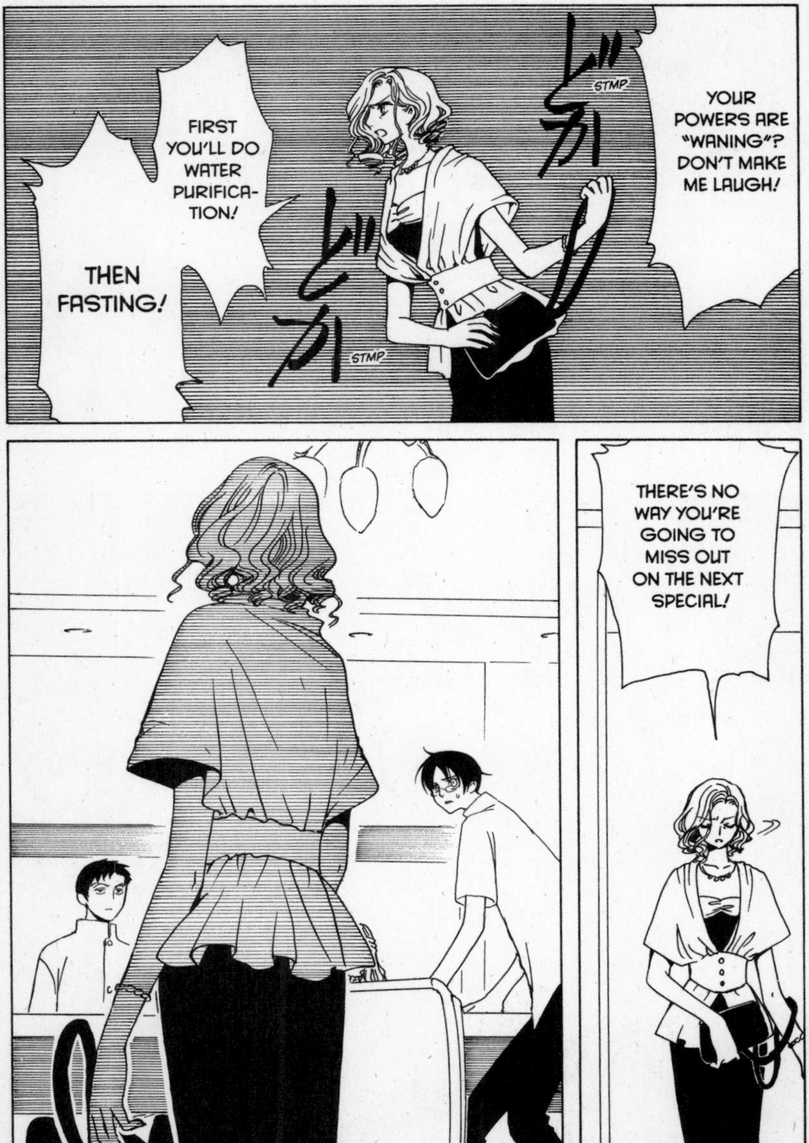
YOUR POWERS ARE "WANING"? DON'T MAKE ME LAUGH!
STMP
STMP
FIRST YOU'LL DO WATER PURIFICA-TION!
THEN FASTING!
THERE'S NO WAY YOU'RE GOING TO MISS OUT ON THE NEXT SPECIAL!

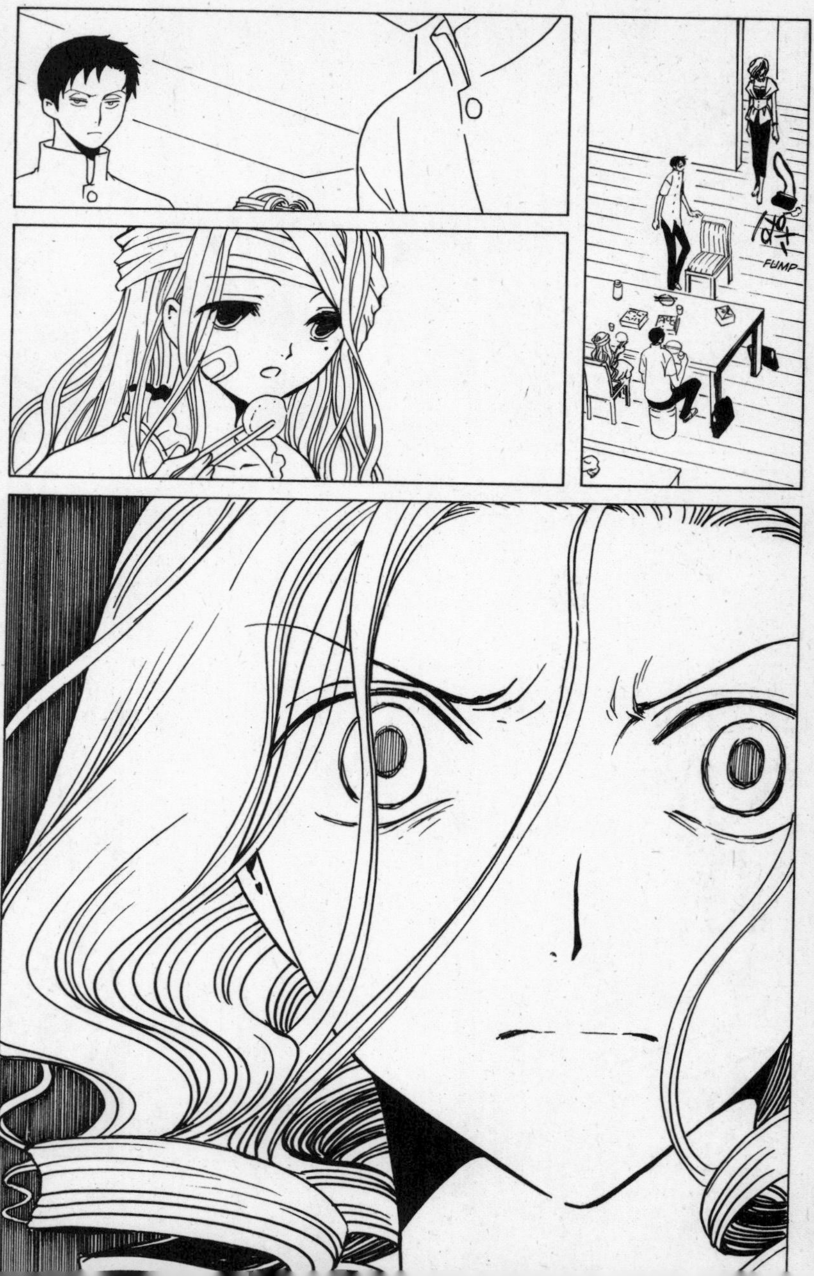
FUMP

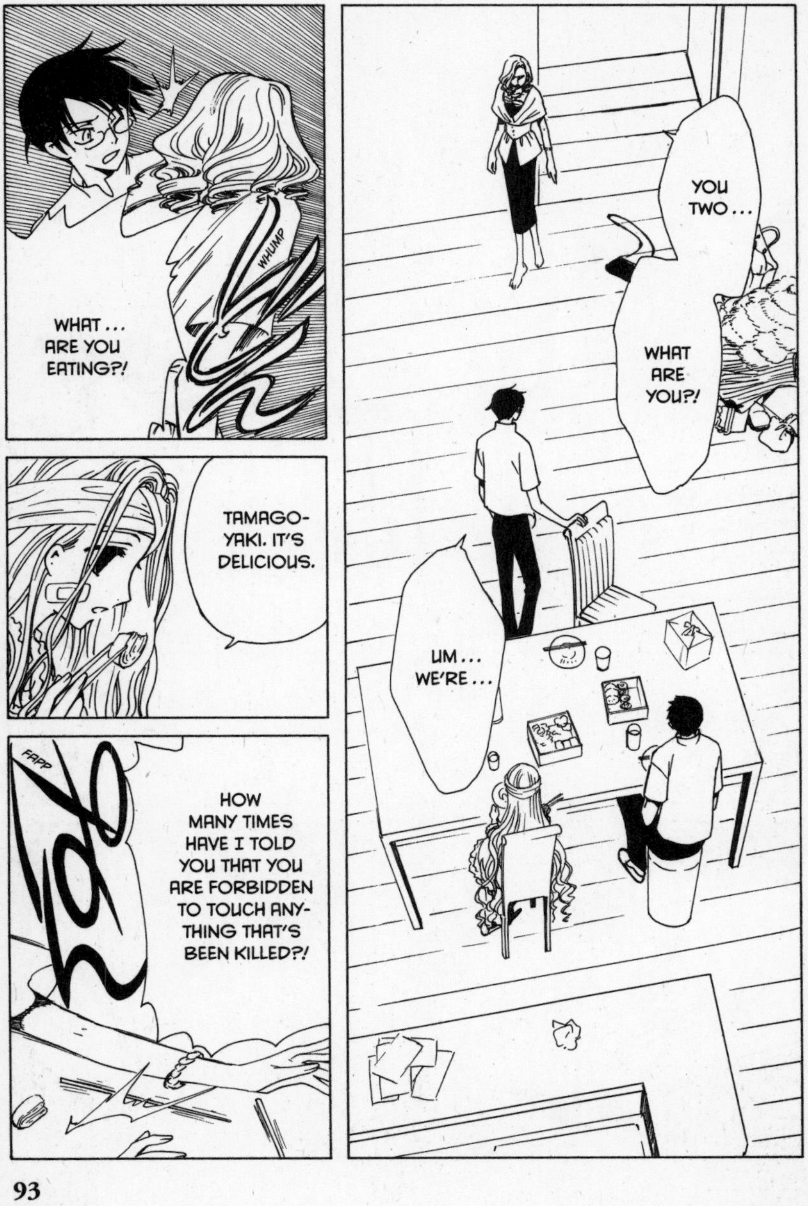
YOU TWO...
WHAT ARE YOU?!
UM... WE'RE...
WHUMP
WHAT... ARE YOU EATING?!
TAMAGO-YAKI. IT'S DELICIOUS.
FAPP
HOW MANY TIMES HAVE I TOLD YOU THAT YOU ARE FORBIDDEN TO TOUCH ANYTHING THAT'S BEEN KILLED?!

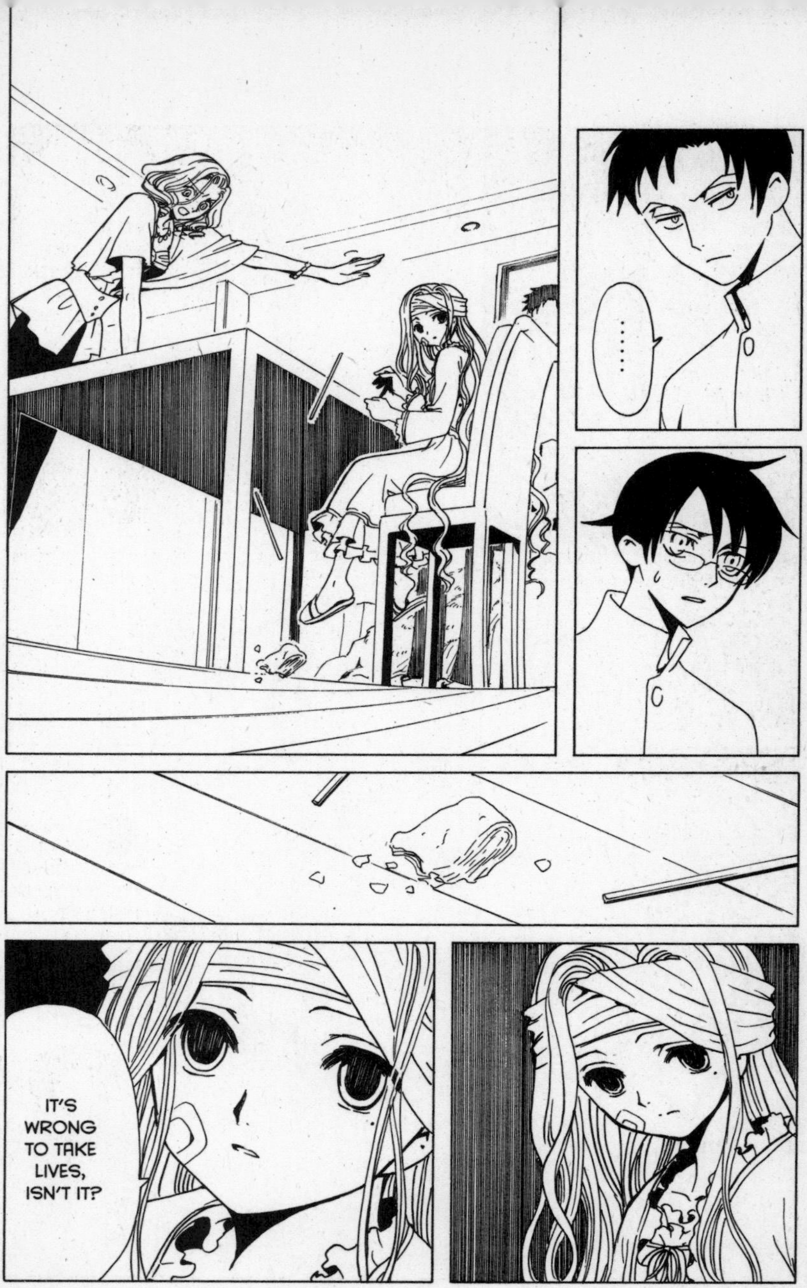
......
IT'S WRONG TO TAKE LIVES, ISN'T IT?

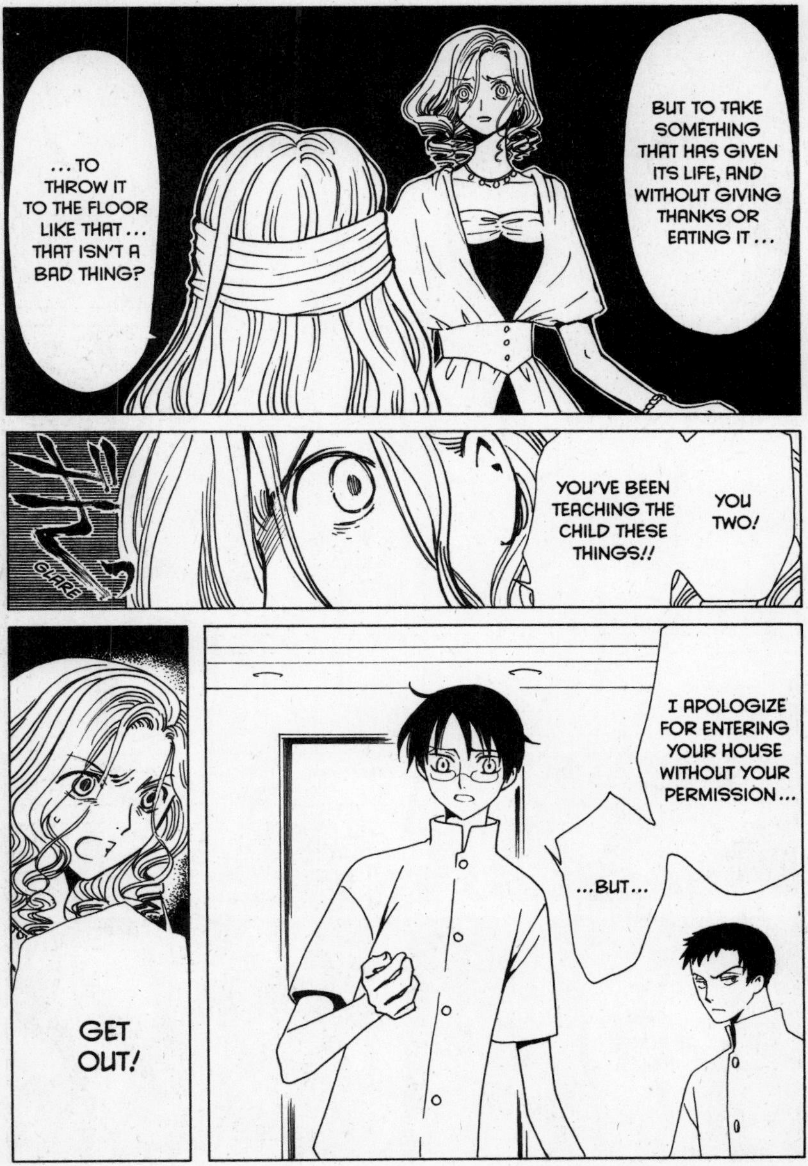
BUT TO TAKE SOMETHING THAT HAS GIVEN ITS LIFE, AND WITHOUT GIVING THANKS OR EATING IT...
...TO THROW IT TO THE FLOOR LIKE THAT... THAT ISN'T A BAD THING?
YOU TWO!
YOU'VE BEEN TEACHING THE CHILD THESE THINGS!!
GLARE
I APOLOGIZE FOR ENTERING YOUR HOUSE WITHOUT YOUR PERMISSION...
...BUT...
GET OUT!

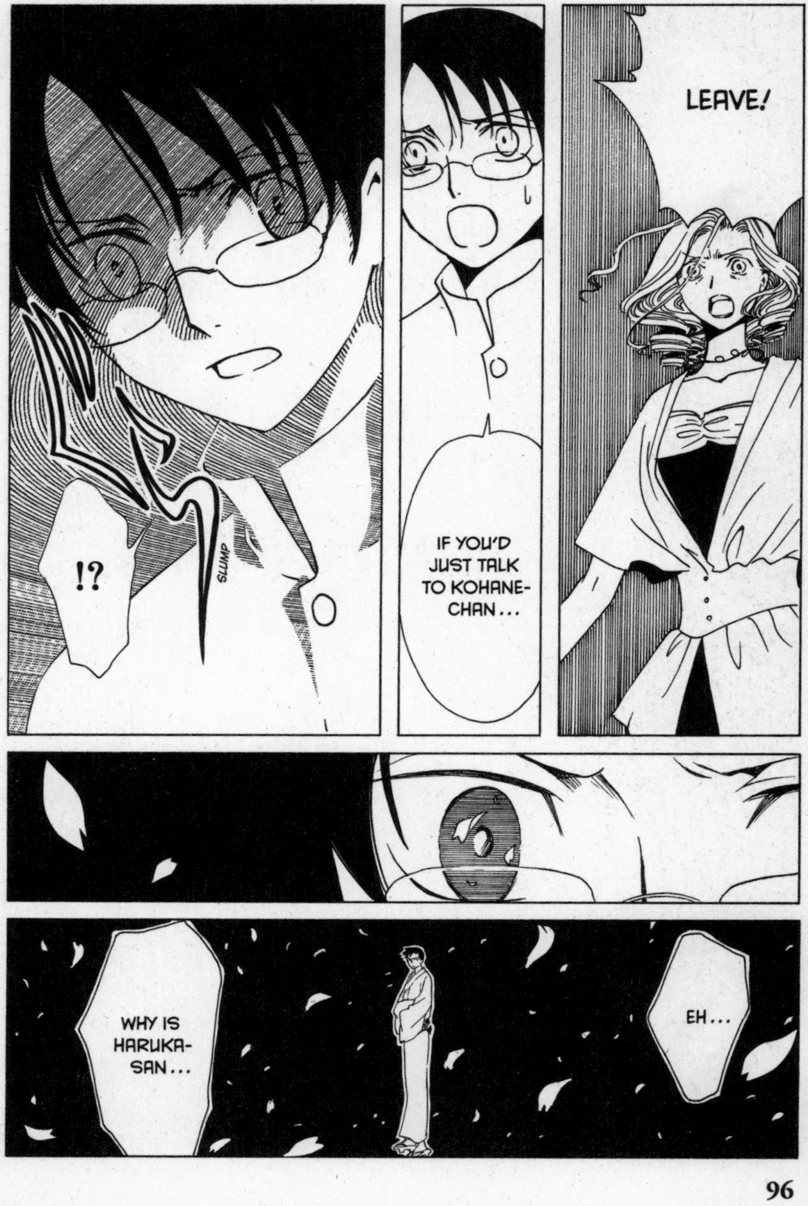
LEAVE!
IF YOU'D JUST TALK TO KOHANE-CHAN...
!?
SLUMP
EH...
WHY IS HARUKA-SAN...

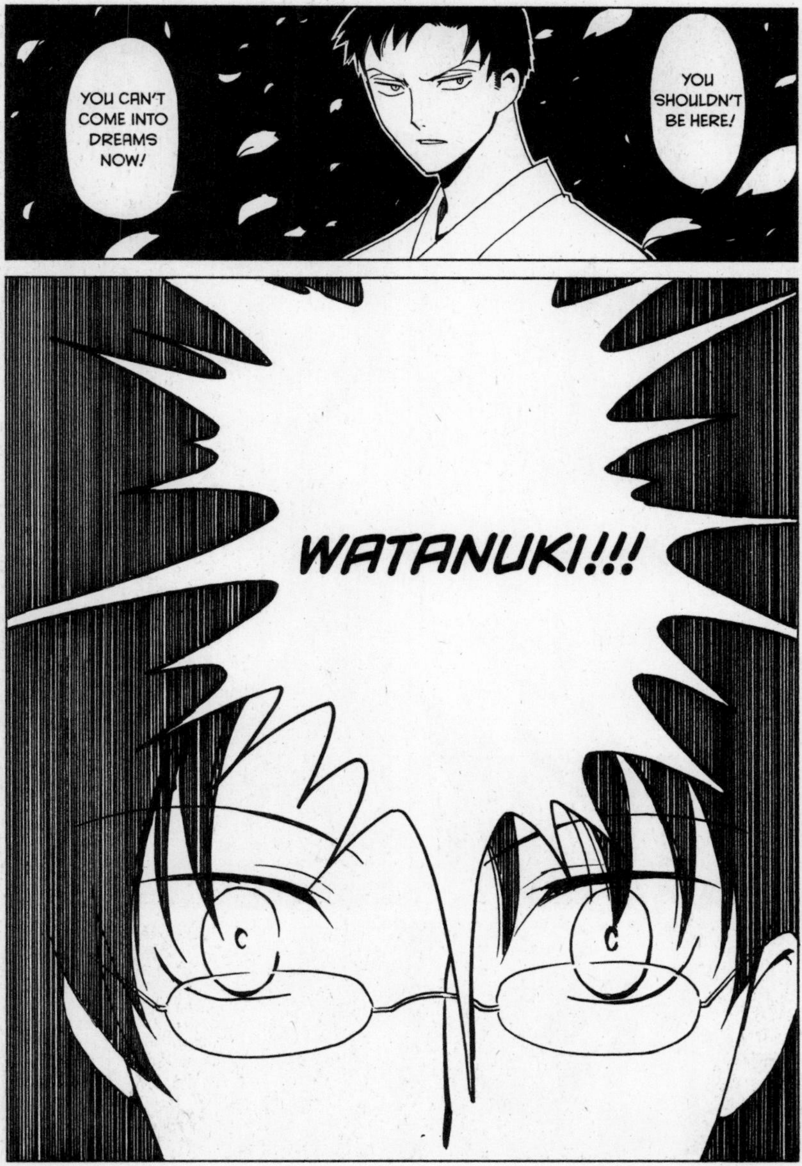
YOU SHOULDN'T BE HERE!
YOU CAN'T COME INTO DREAMS NOW!
WATANUKI!!!

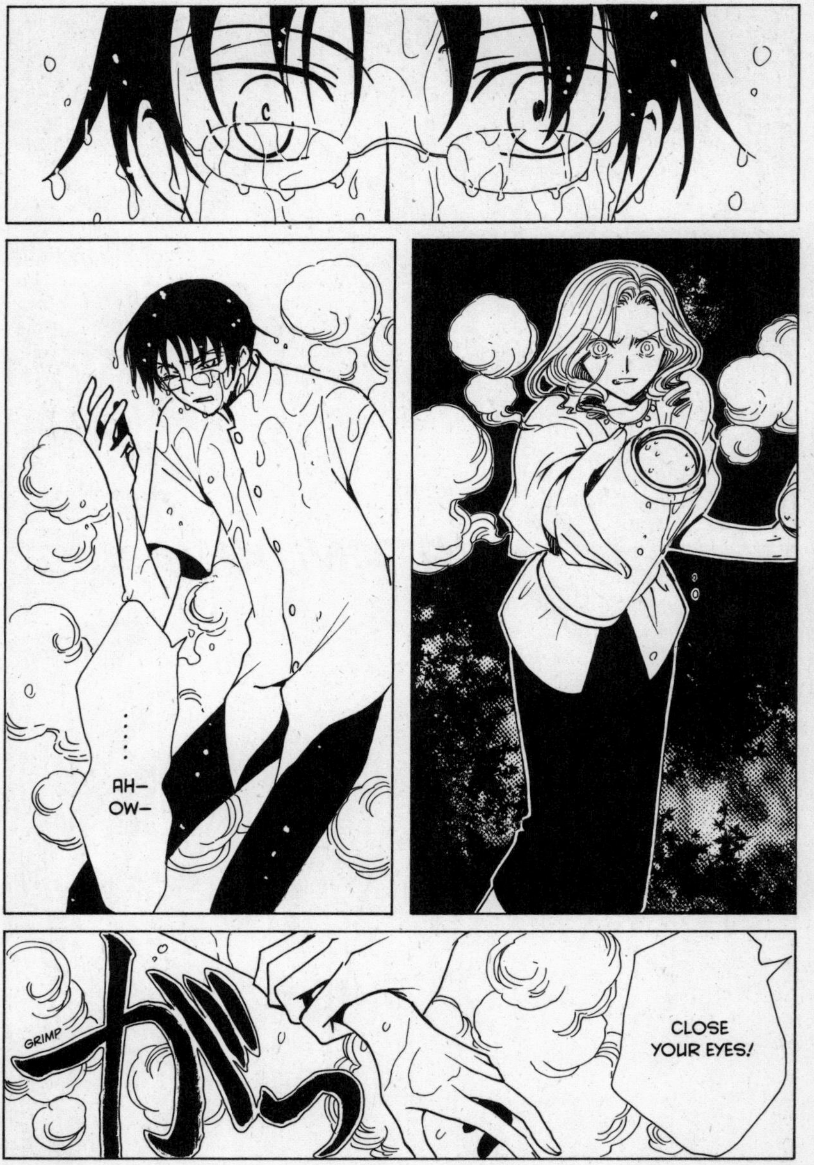
......
AH— OW—
CLOSE YOUR EYES!
GRIMP

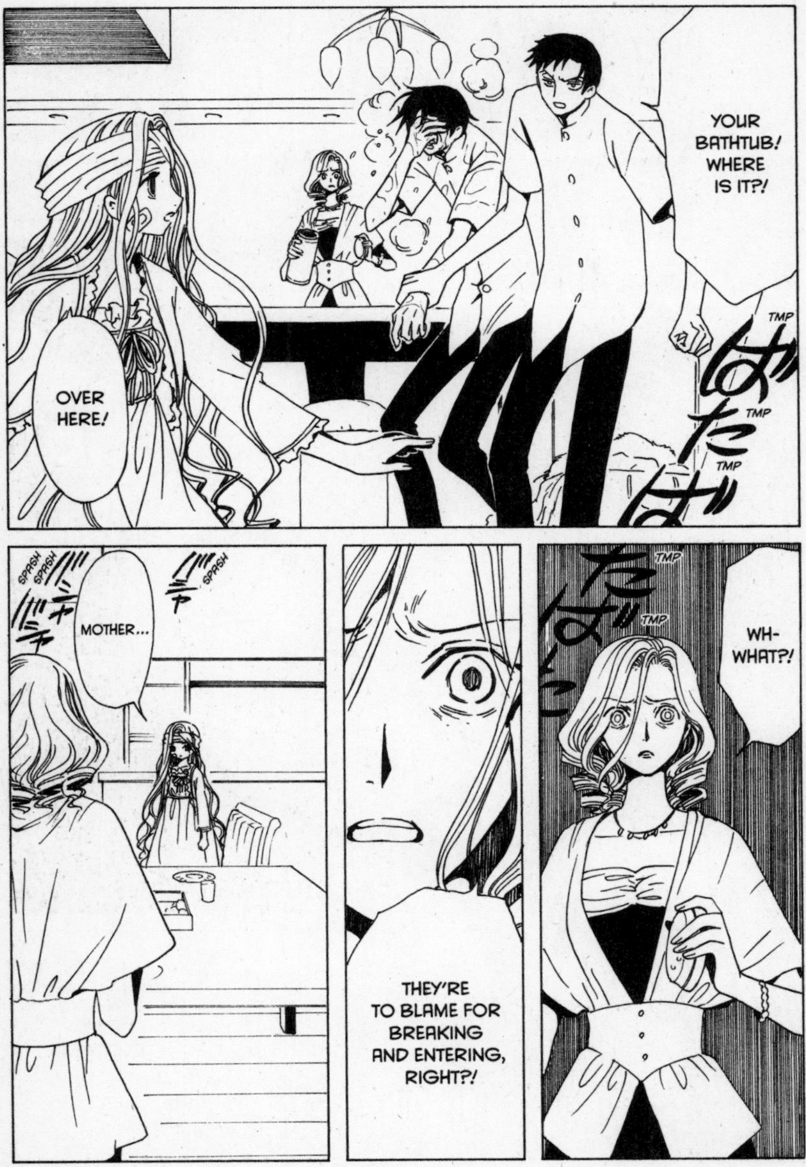
YOUR BATHTUB! WHERE IS IT?!
TMP
TMP
TMP
OVER HERE!
TMP
TMP
WH- WHAT?!
THEY'RE TO BLAME FOR BREAKING AND ENTERING, RIGHT?!
SPASH
SPASH
SPASH
MOTHER...

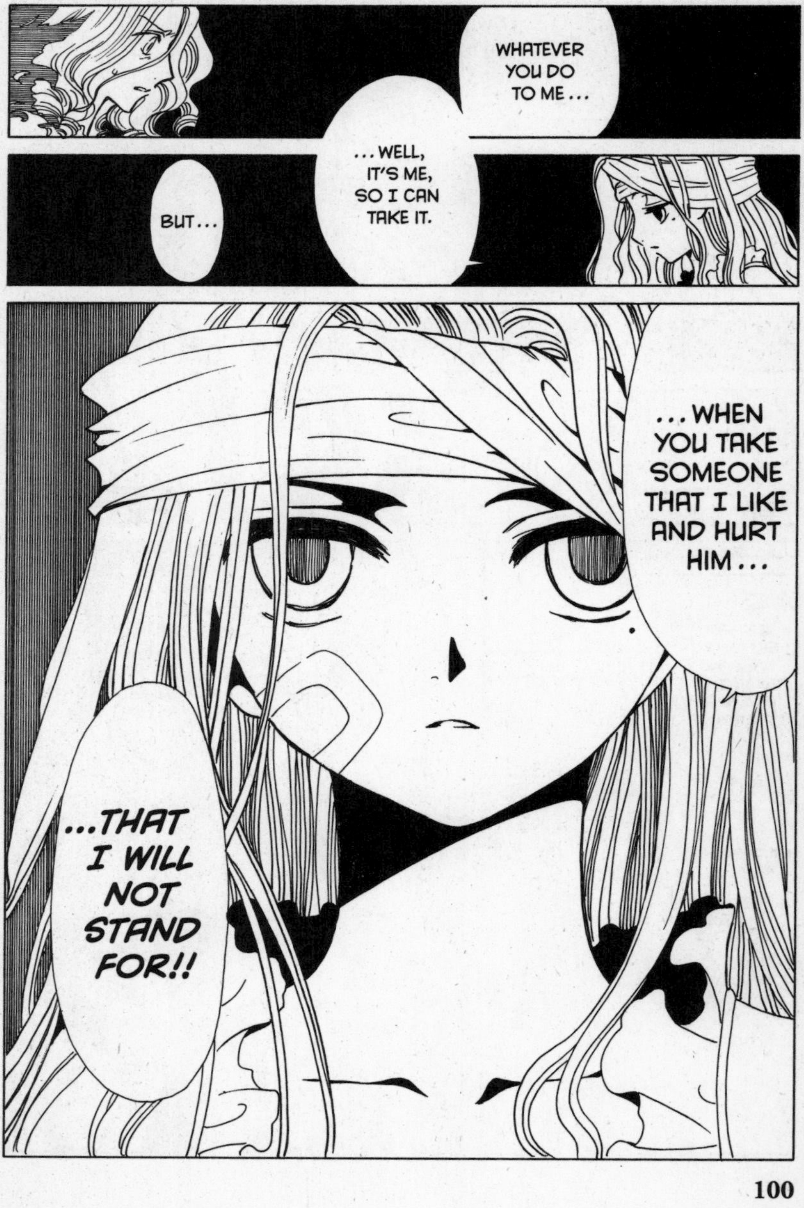
WHATEVER YOU DO TO ME...
...WELL, IT'S ME, SO I CAN TAKE IT.
BUT...
...WHEN YOU TAKE SOMEONE THAT I LIKE AND HURT HIM...
...THAT I WILL NOT STAND FOR!!

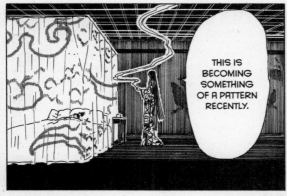

THIS IS BECOMING SOMETHING OF A PATTERN RECENTLY.
....
I CAN'T DENY IT.
YOU CAN THANK DÔMEKI-KUN'S QUICK FIRST AID. IT LOOKS LIKE IT WON'T EVEN LEAVE SCARS.
......
OH, DEAR! YOU'RE NOT DENYING THAT EITHER?
THANK GOODNESS, WATANUKI IS SPECTACLE-BOY!
IF IT HAD GOTTEN IN THE EYES! THAT WOULD HAVE BEEN DANGEROUS!
SPECTACLE-BOY?

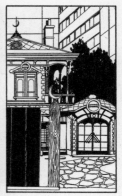

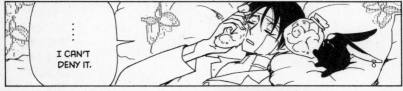

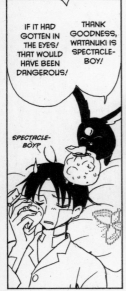

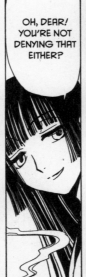

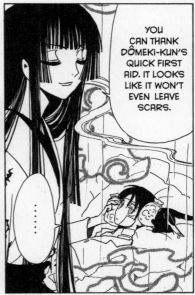

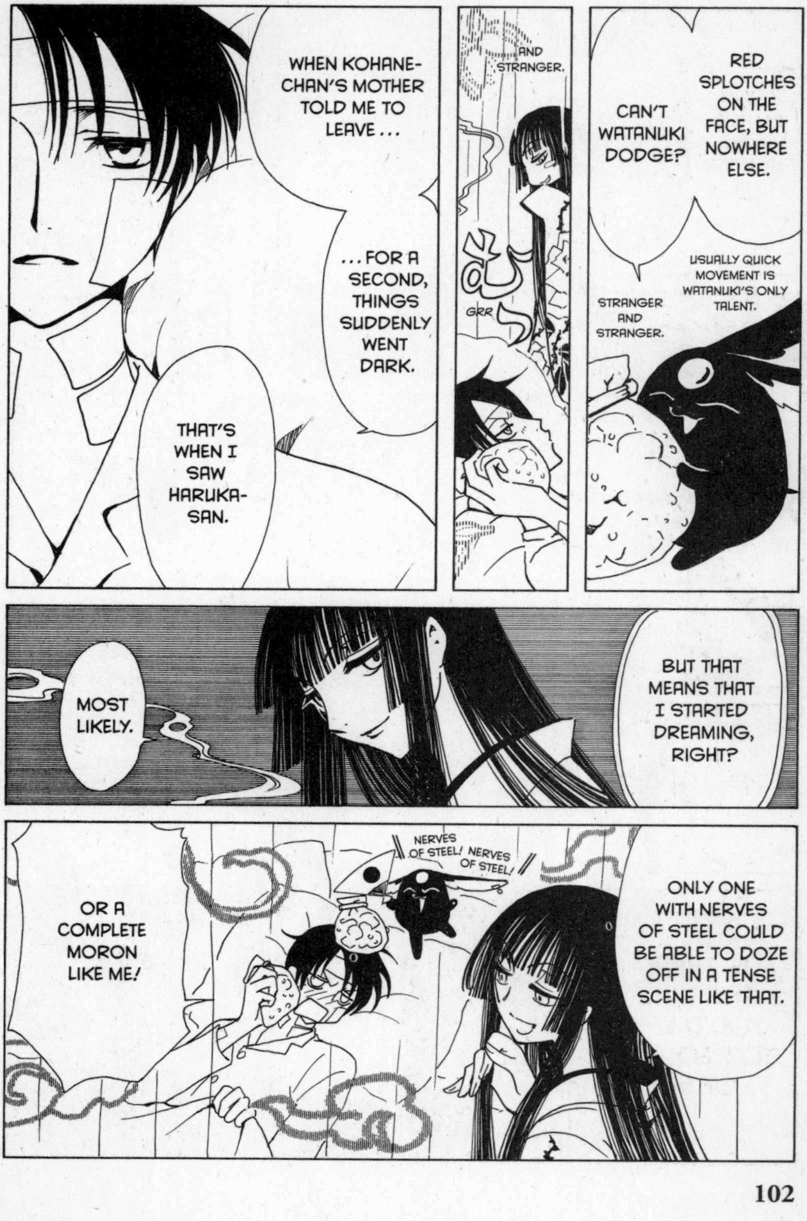
RED SPLOTCHES ON THE FACE, BUT NOWHERE ELSE.
CAN'T WATANUKI DODGE?
USUALLY QUICK MOVEMENT IS WATANUKI'S ONLY TALENT.
STRANGER AND STRANGER.
AND STRANGER.
GRR
WHEN KOHANE-CHAN'S MOTHER TOLD ME TO LEAVE...
...FOR A SECOND, THINGS SUDDENLY WENT DARK.
THAT'S WHEN I SAW HARUKA-SAN.
BUT THAT MEANS THAT I STARTED DREAMING, RIGHT?
MOST LIKELY.
ONLY ONE WITH NERVES OF STEEL COULD BE ABLE TO DOZE OFF IN A TENSE SCENE LIKE THAT.
NERVES OF STEEL! NERVES OF STEEL!
OR A COMPLETE MORON LIKE ME!

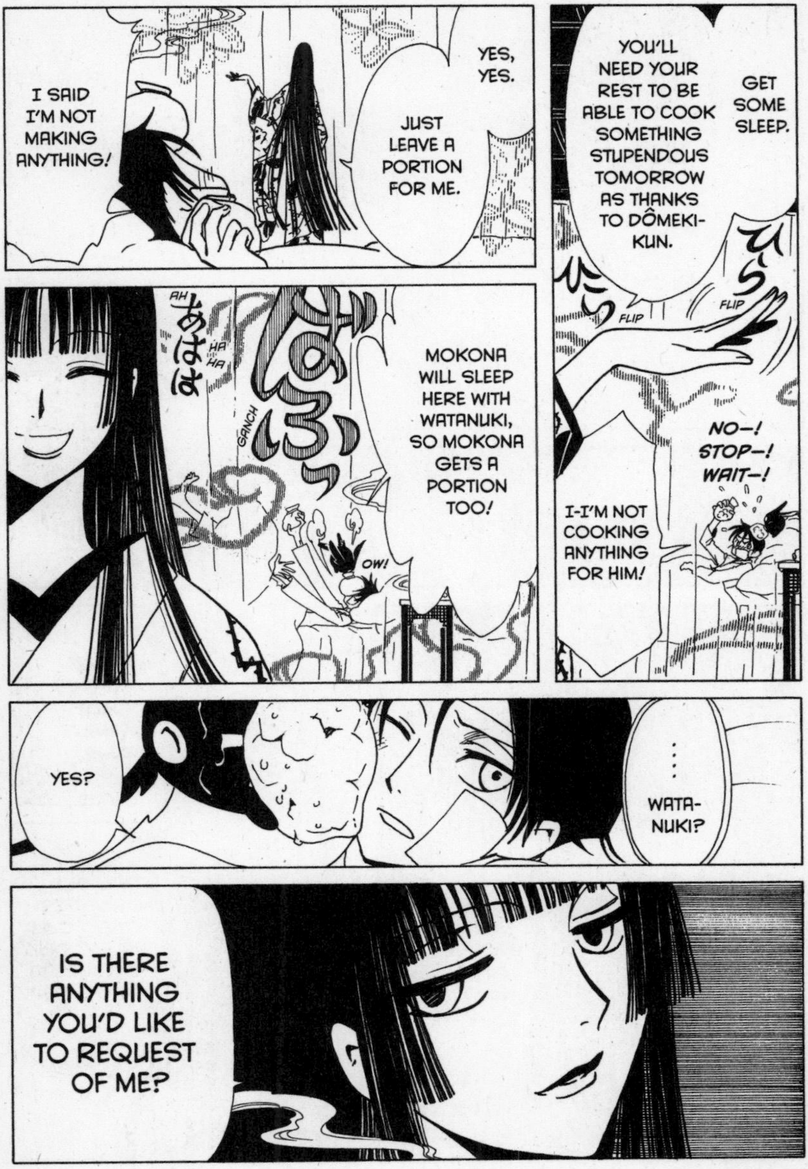
GET SOME SLEEP.
YOU'LL NEED YOUR REST TO BE ABLE TO COOK SOMETHING STUPENDOUS TOMORROW AS THANKS TO DÔMEKI-KUN.
ひら
FLIP
ひら
FLIP
NO—! STOP—! WAIT—!
I-I'M NOT COOKING ANYTHING FOR HIM!
YES, YES.
JUST LEAVE A PORTION FOR ME.
I SAID I'M NOT MAKING ANYTHING!
MOKONA WILL SLEEP HERE WITH WATANUKI, SO MOKONA GETS A PORTION TOO!
ぱふっ
GANCH
OW!
あはは
AH HA HA
......
WATA-NUKI?
YES?
IS THERE ANYTHING YOU'D LIKE TO REQUEST OF ME?

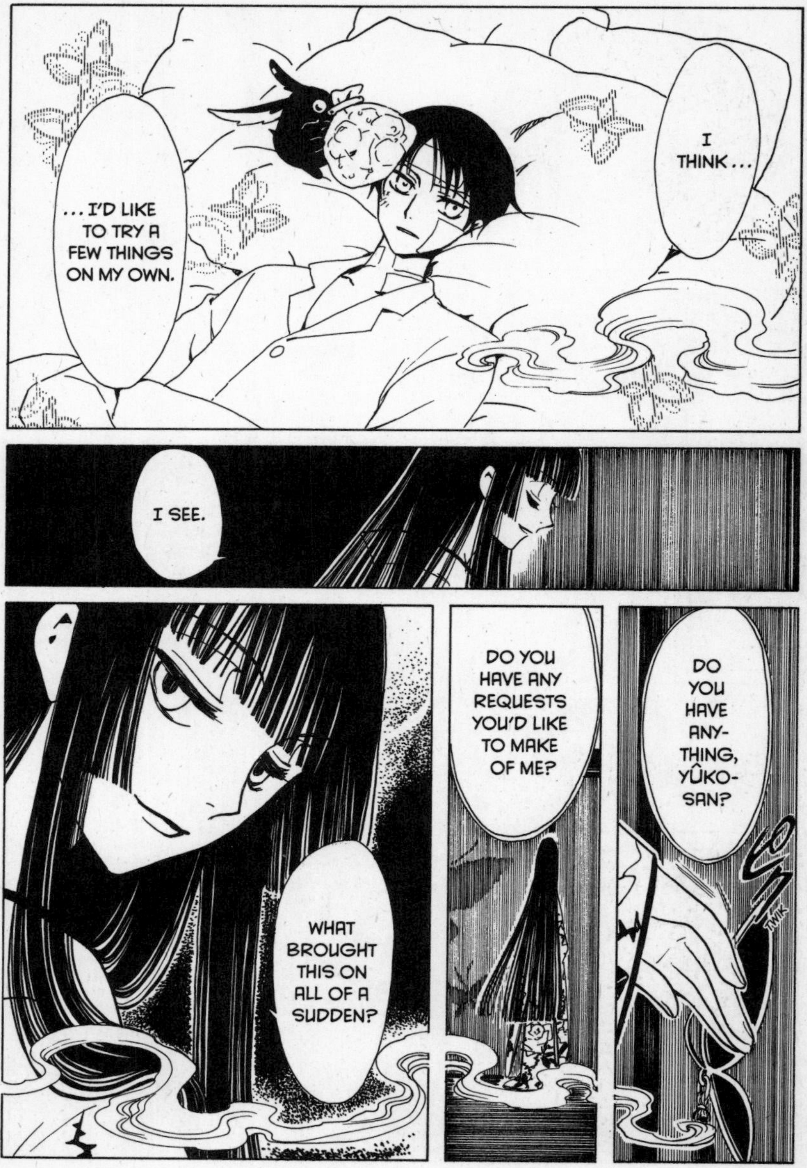
I THINK...
...I'D LIKE TO TRY A FEW THINGS ON MY OWN.
I SEE.
DO YOU HAVE ANY-THING, YÛKO-SAN?
TWIK
DO YOU HAVE ANY REQUESTS YOU'D LIKE TO MAKE OF ME?
WHAT BROUGHT THIS ON ALL OF A SUDDEN?

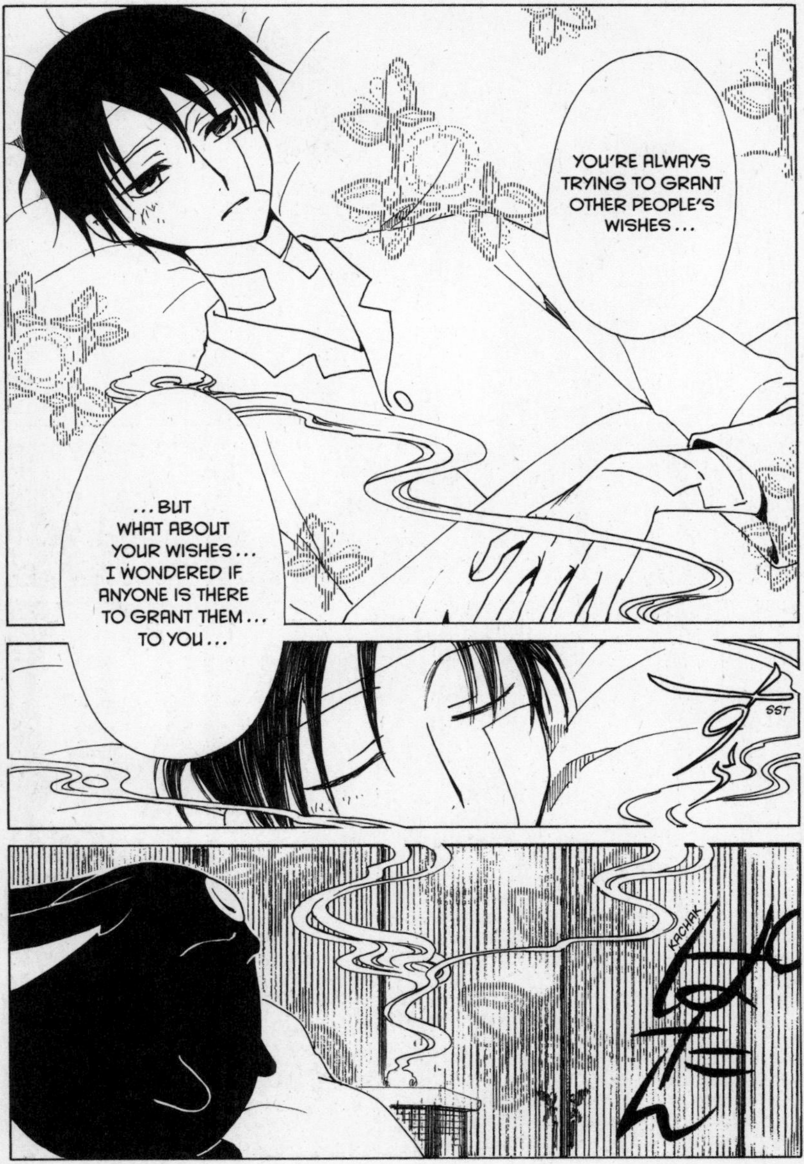
YOU'RE ALWAYS TRYING TO GRANT OTHER PEOPLE'S WISHES...
...BUT WHAT ABOUT YOUR WISHES... I WONDERED IF ANYONE IS THERE TO GRANT THEM... TO YOU...
SST
KACHAK

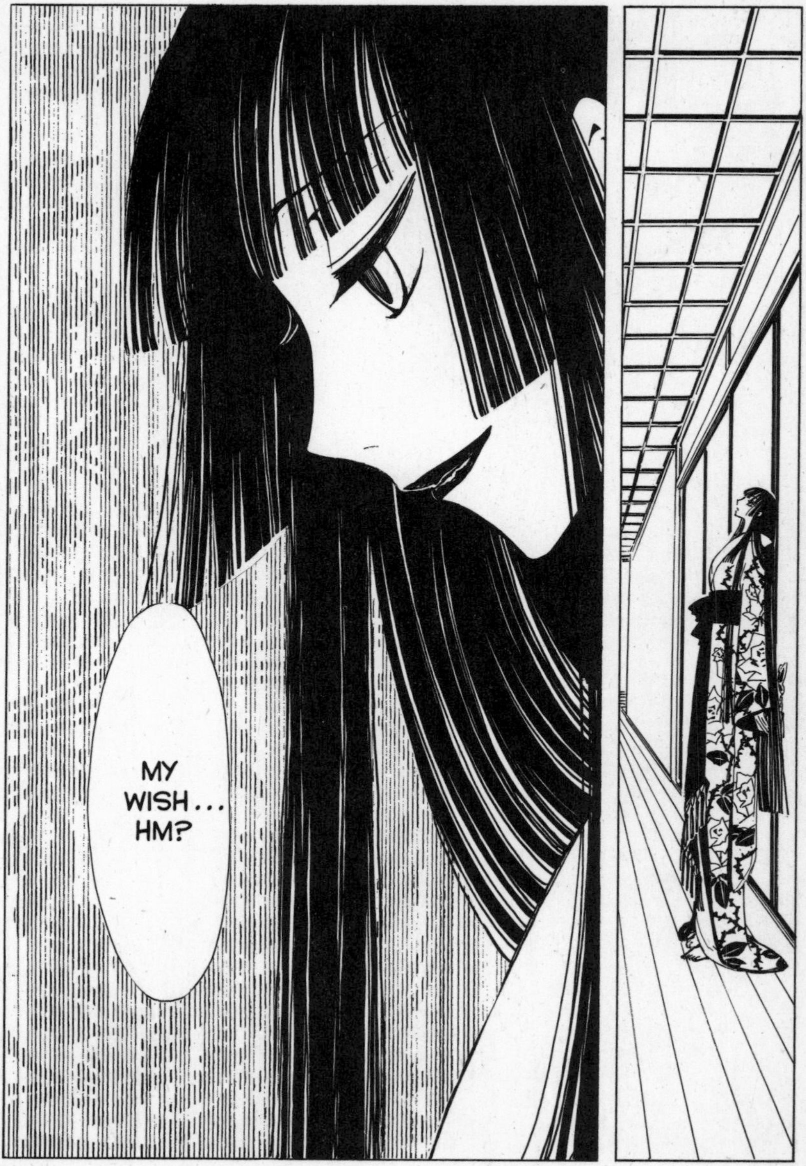
MY WISH... HM?

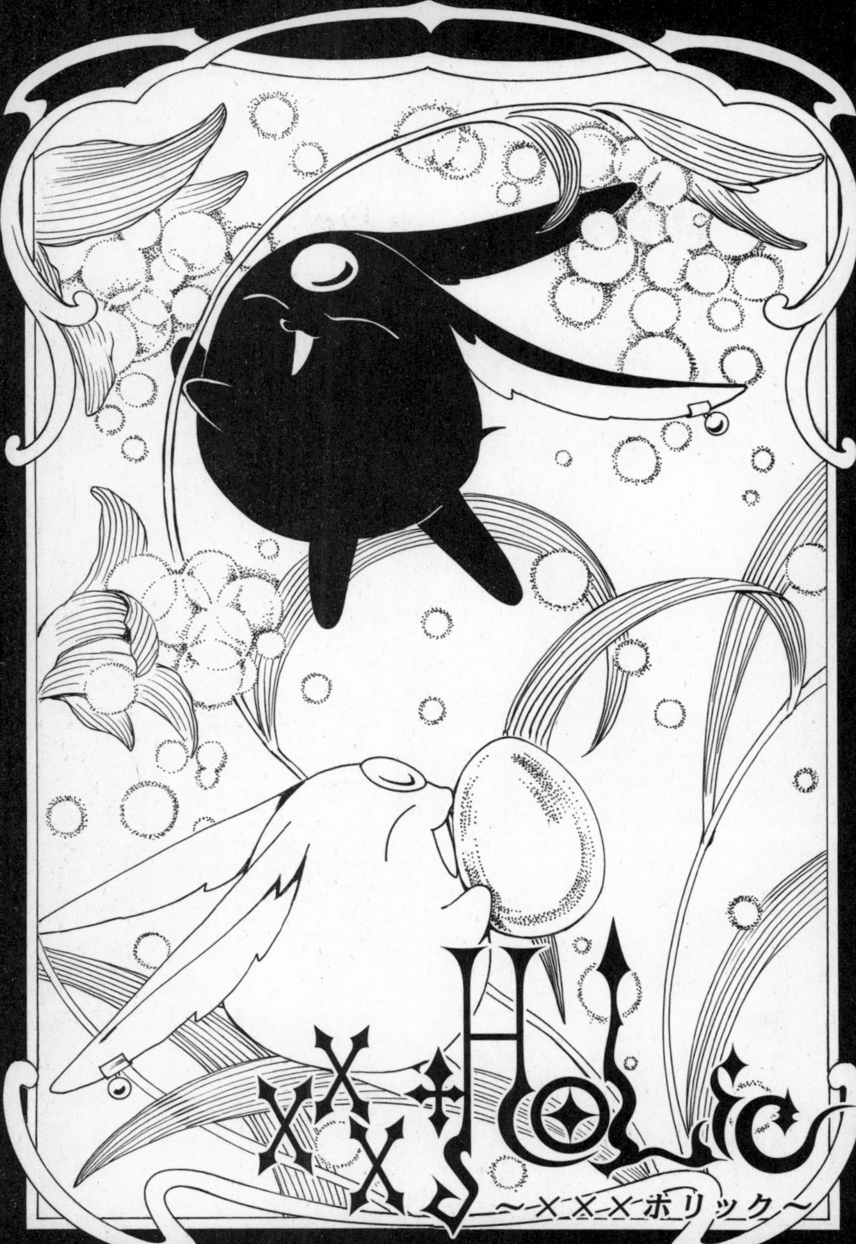
xxxHOLiC
~×××ホリック~

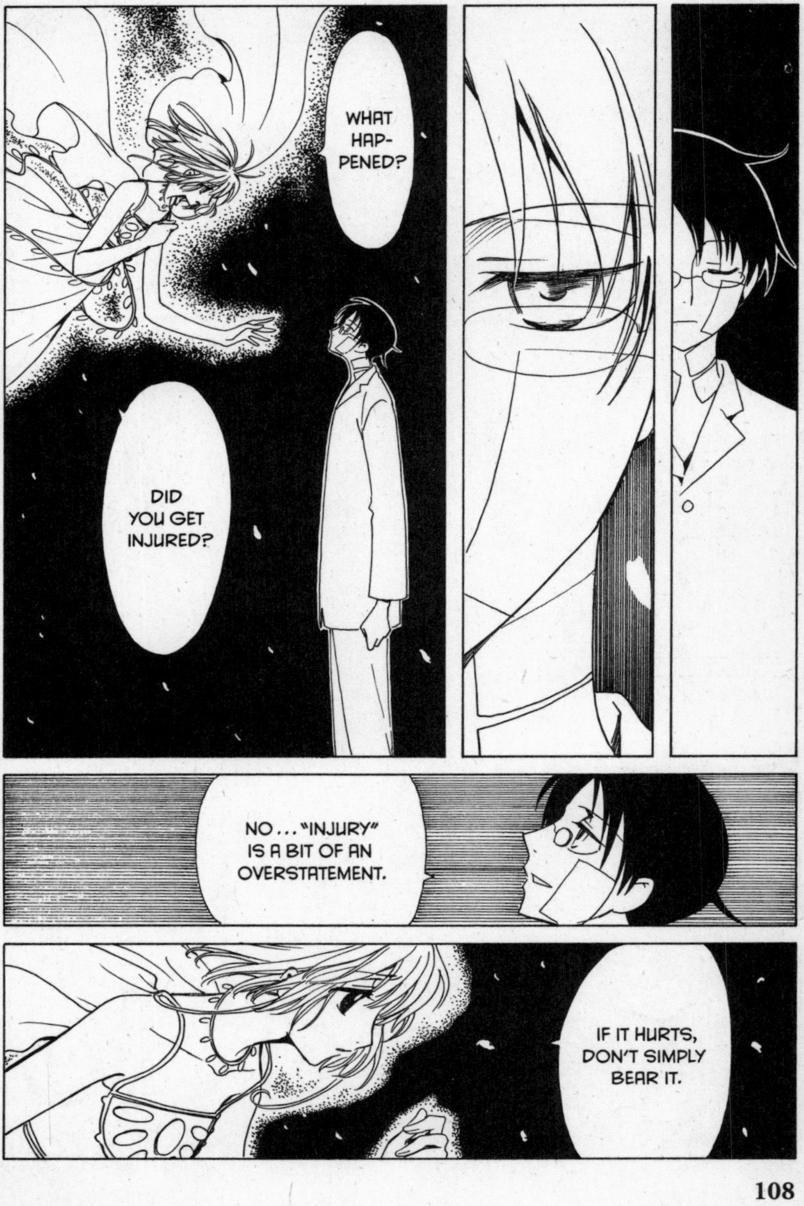
WHAT HAP-PENED?
DID YOU GET INJURED?
NO . . . "INJURY" IS A BIT OF AN OVERSTATEMENT.
IF IT HURTS, DON'T SIMPLY BEAR IT.

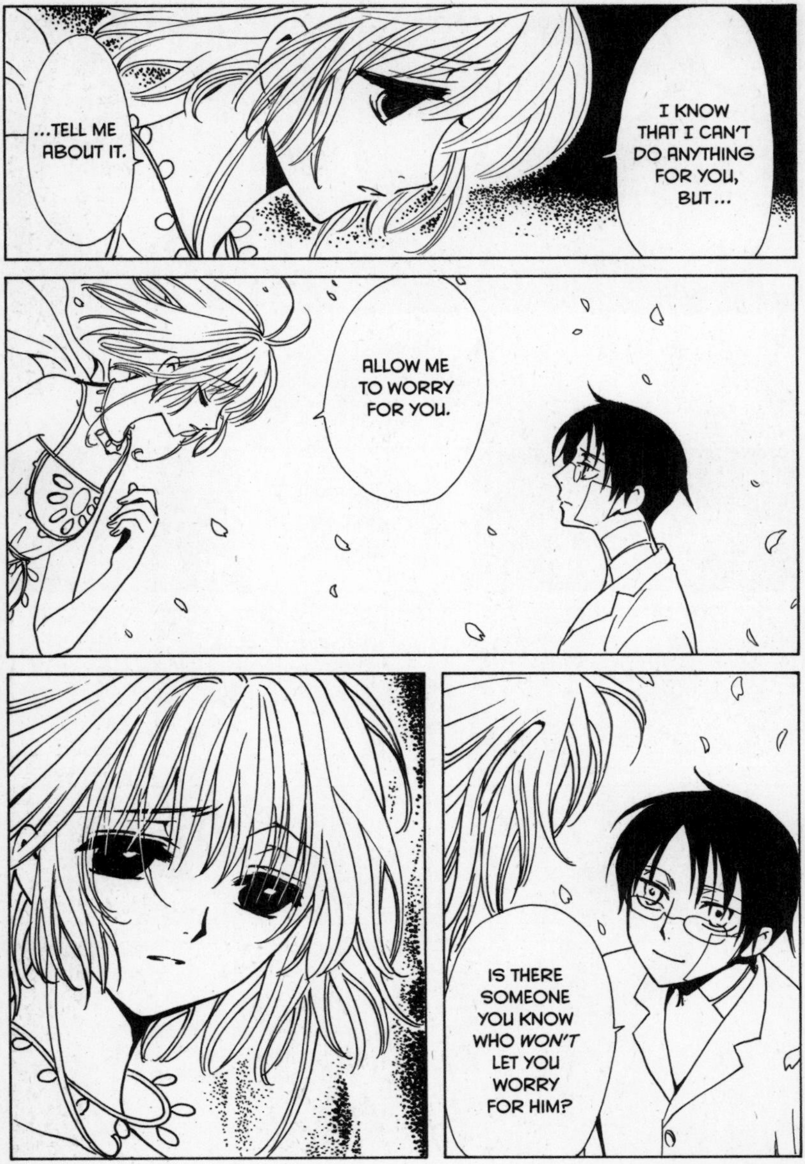
I KNOW THAT I CAN'T DO ANYTHING FOR YOU, BUT...
...TELL ME ABOUT IT.
ALLOW ME TO WORRY FOR YOU.
IS THERE SOMEONE YOU KNOW WHO *WON'T* LET YOU WORRY FOR HIM?

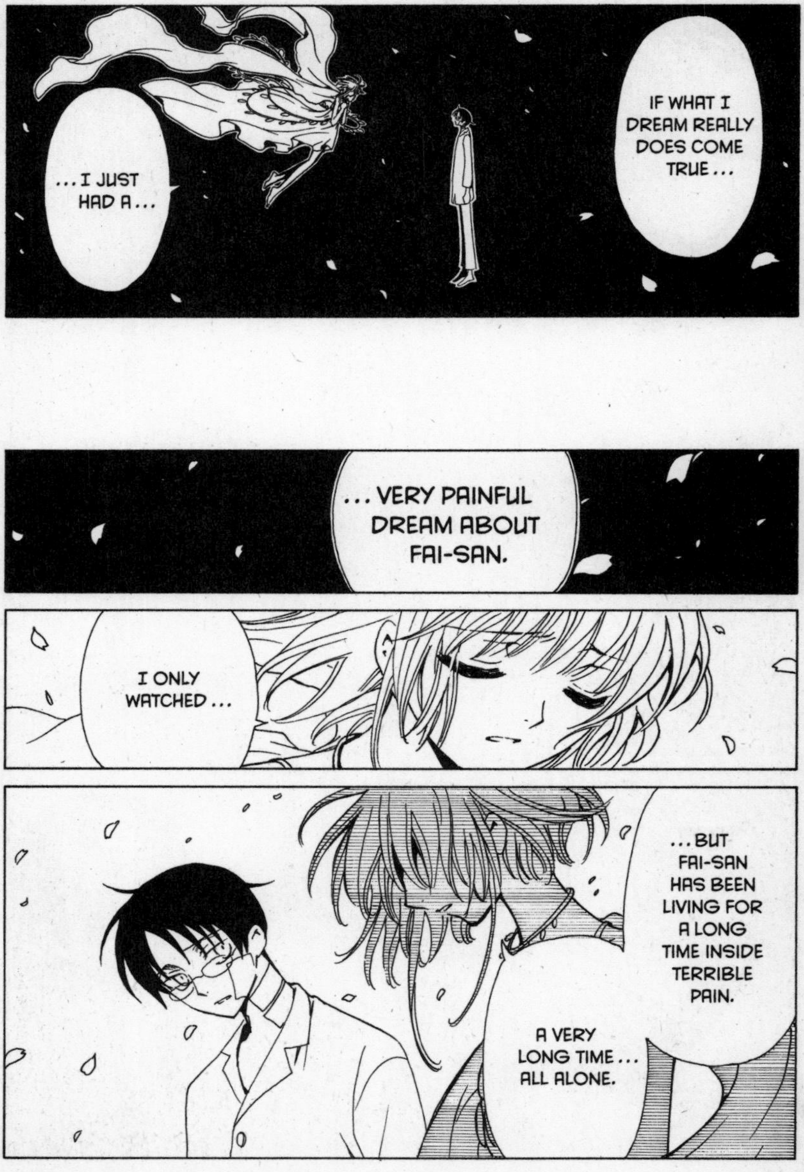
IF WHAT I DREAM REALLY DOES COME TRUE...
...I JUST HAD A...
...VERY PAINFUL DREAM ABOUT FAI-SAN.
I ONLY WATCHED...
...BUT FAI-SAN HAS BEEN LIVING FOR A LONG TIME INSIDE TERRIBLE PAIN.
A VERY LONG TIME... ALL ALONE.

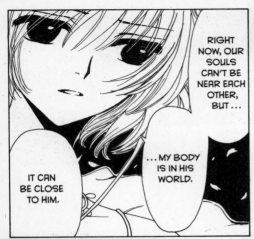

THERE WERE A LOT OF THINGS THAT FAI-SAN COULDN'T TELL US.
BUT HIS LIE COMES FROM HIS GENTILITY. AND I BELIEVE IN HIM.
RIGHT NOW, OUR SOULS CAN'T BE NEAR EACH OTHER, BUT . . .
. . . MY BODY IS IN HIS WORLD.
IT CAN BE CLOSE TO HIM.
IF ONE'S FUTURE CAN BE CHANGED BY CHOICE . . .
. . . THEN MY FALLEN BODY MIGHT BECOME A CHANCE FOR FAI-SAN . . .
. . . TO REMEMBER HIS LOST PAST.

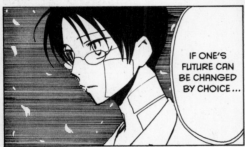

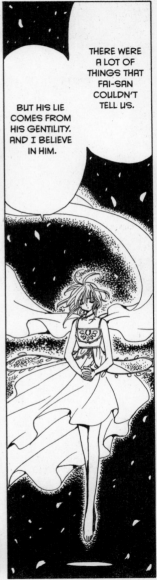

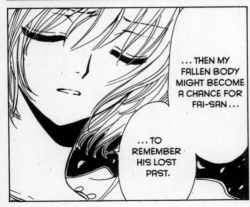

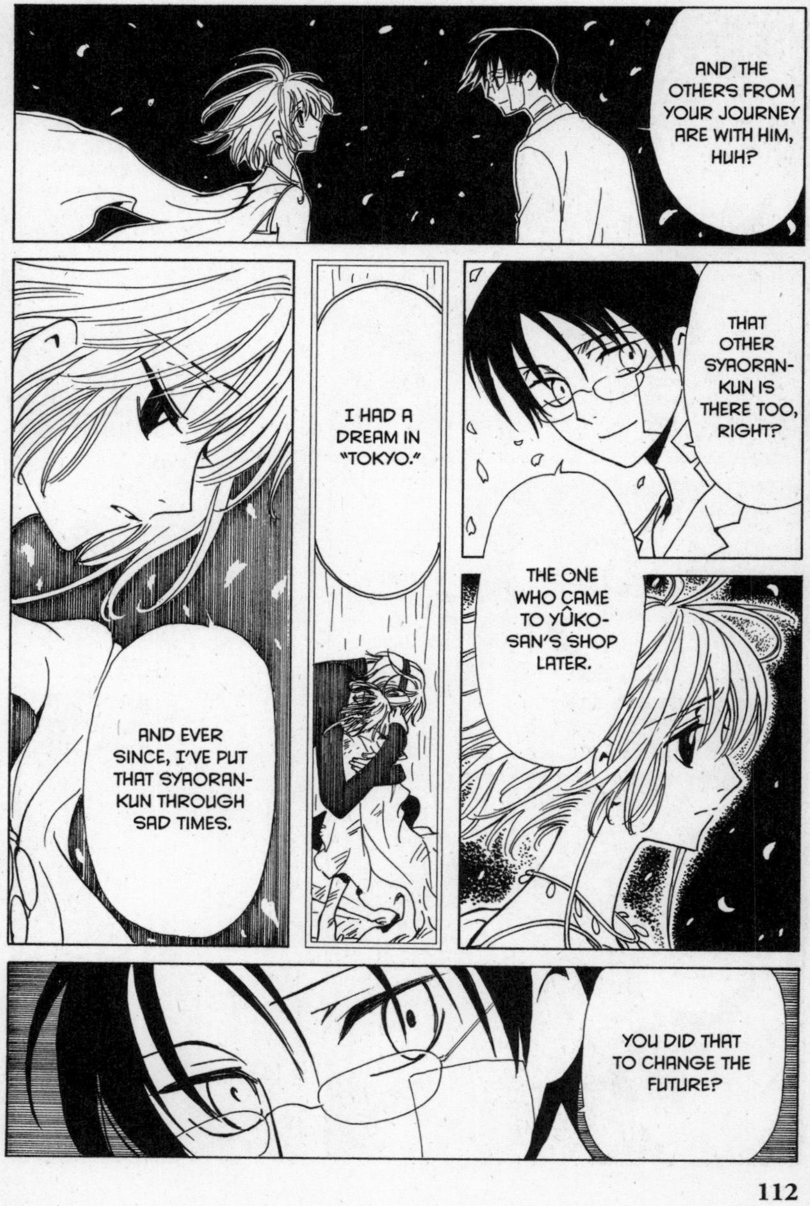
AND THE OTHERS FROM YOUR JOURNEY ARE WITH HIM, HUH?
THAT OTHER SYAORAN-KUN IS THERE TOO, RIGHT?
THE ONE WHO CAME TO YÛKO-SAN'S SHOP LATER.
I HAD A DREAM IN "TOKYO."
AND EVER SINCE, I'VE PUT THAT SYAORAN-KUN THROUGH SAD TIMES.
YOU DID THAT TO CHANGE THE FUTURE?

BUT...

...EVEN SO...

THE ONLY THING I COULD DO UNTIL THE "TIME" THAT I CHANGED THE FUTURE WAS TO ACT THROUGH THE PART I SAW IN THE DREAM.

...IT DOESN'T CHANGE THE FACT THAT I LEFT SCARS ON THAT SYAORAN-KUN.

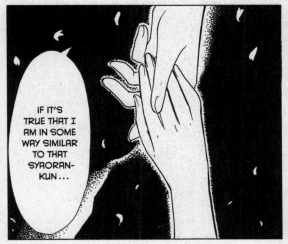

IF IT'S TRUE THAT I AM IN SOME WAY SIMILAR TO THAT SYAORAN-KUN...

...

SAKURA-CHAN...

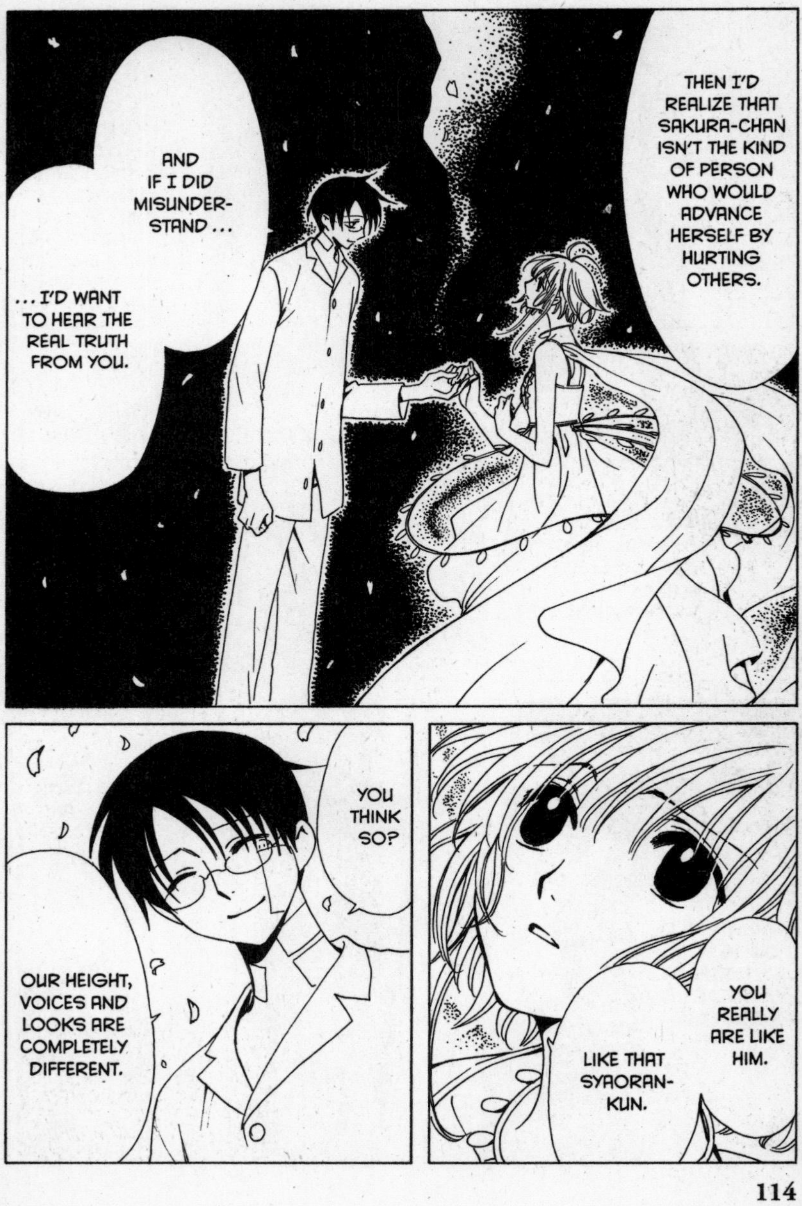
THEN I'D REALIZE THAT SAKURA-CHAN ISN'T THE KIND OF PERSON WHO WOULD ADVANCE HERSELF BY HURTING OTHERS.
AND IF I DID MISUNDERSTAND...
...I'D WANT TO HEAR THE REAL TRUTH FROM YOU.
YOU REALLY ARE LIKE HIM.
LIKE THAT SYAORAN-KUN.
YOU THINK SO?
OUR HEIGHT, VOICES AND LOOKS ARE COMPLETELY DIFFERENT.

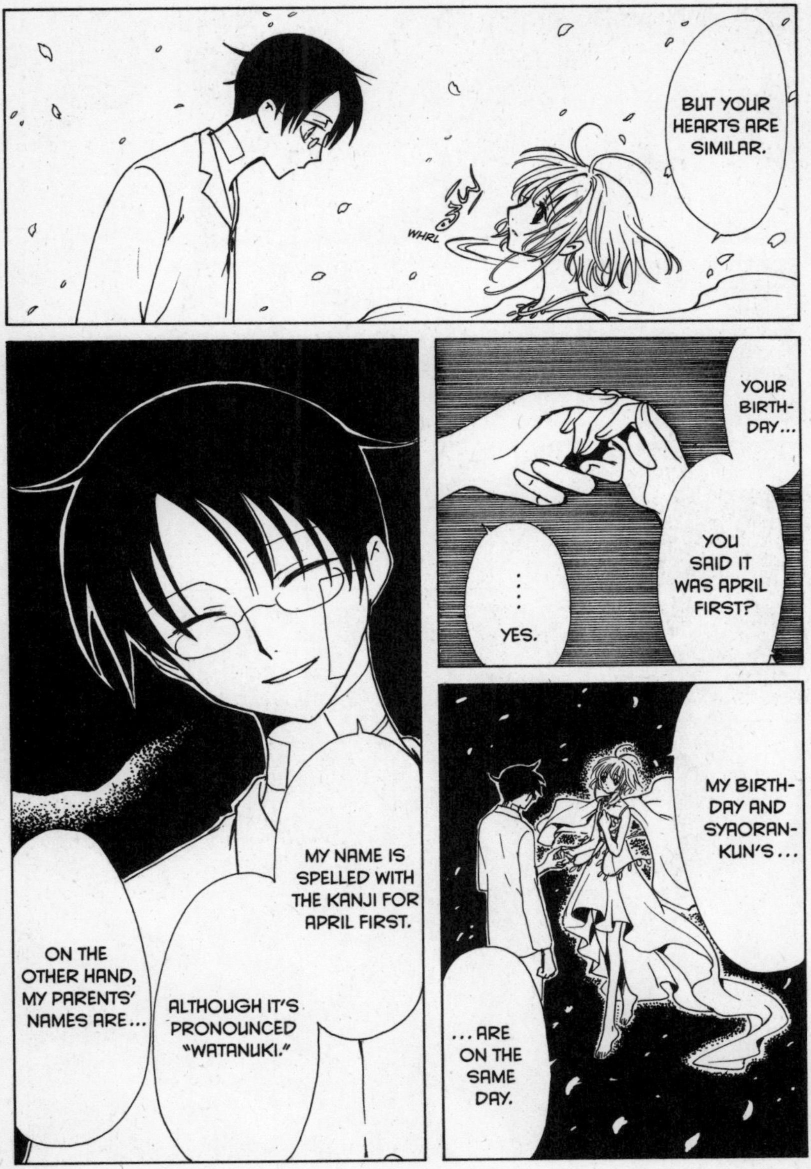
BUT YOUR HEARTS ARE SIMILAR.
WHRL
YOUR BIRTH-DAY...
YOU SAID IT WAS APRIL FIRST?
....
YES.
MY BIRTH-DAY AND SYAORAN-KUN'S...
...ARE ON THE SAME DAY.
MY NAME IS SPELLED WITH THE KANJI FOR APRIL FIRST.
ALTHOUGH IT'S PRONOUNCED "WATANUKI."
ON THE OTHER HAND, MY PARENTS' NAMES ARE...

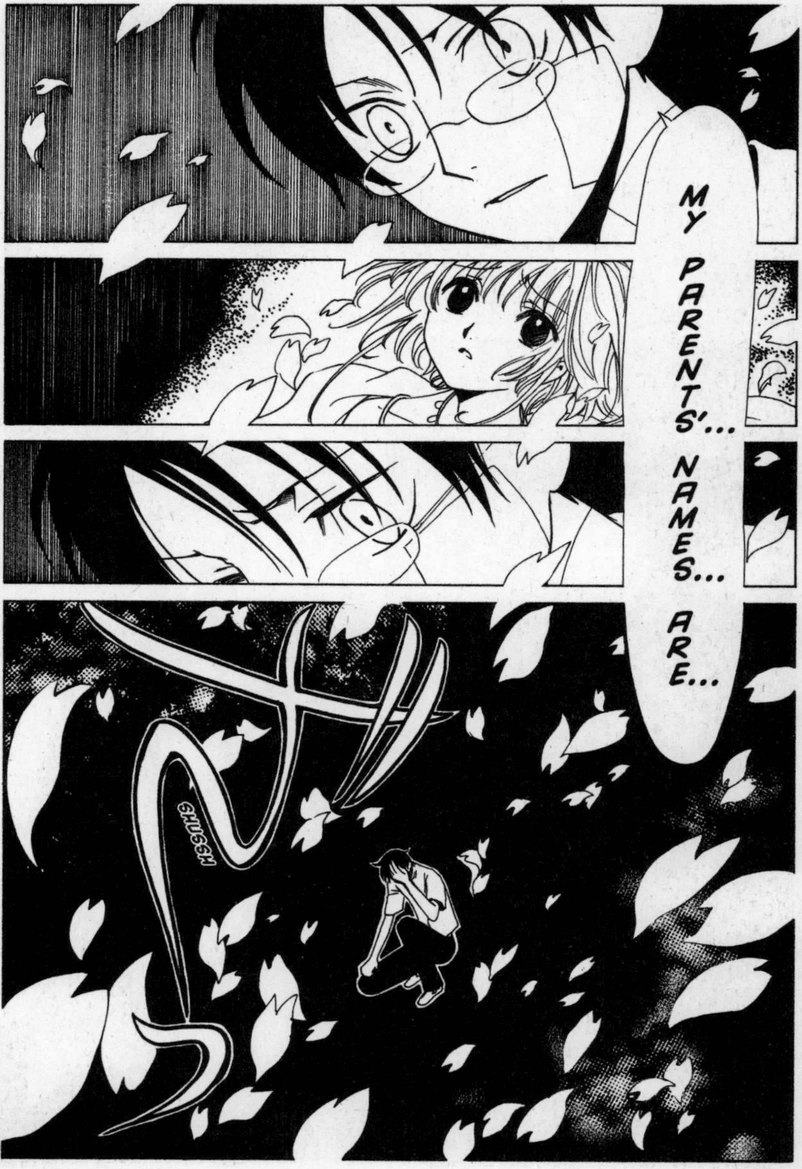
MY PARENTS'... NAMES... ARE...
SHUSSH

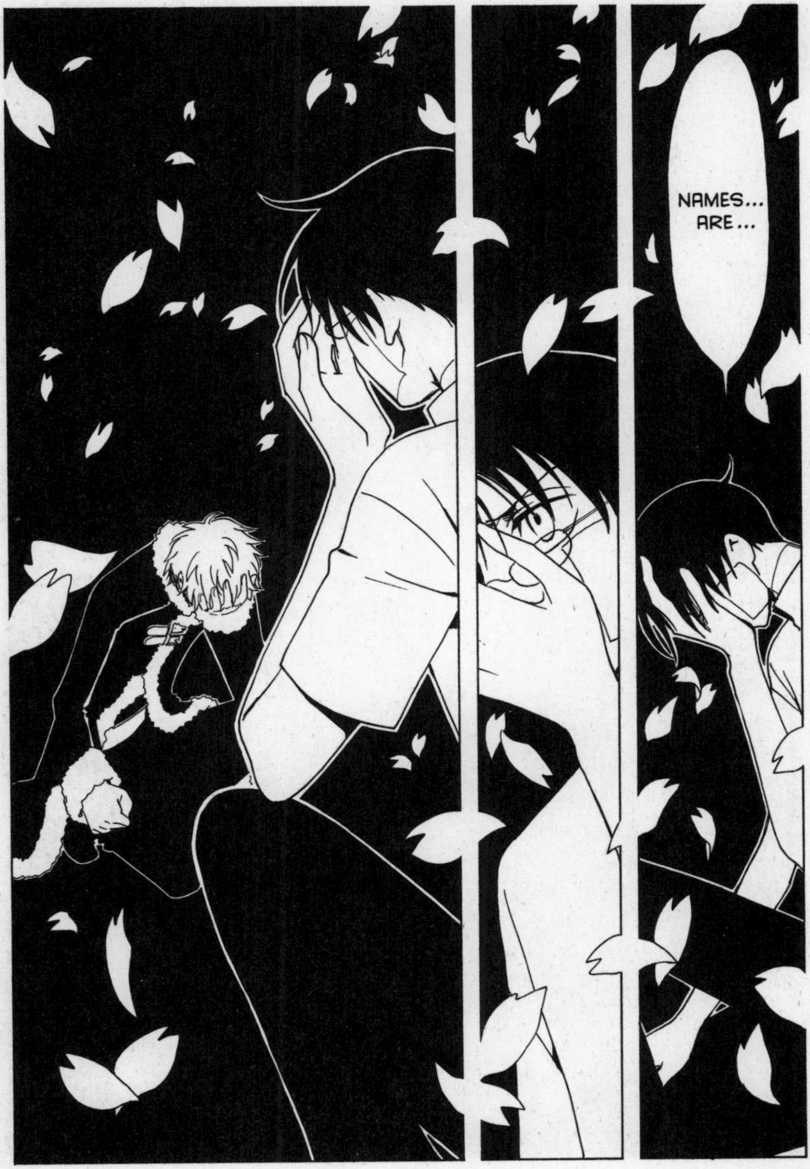
NAMES... ARE...

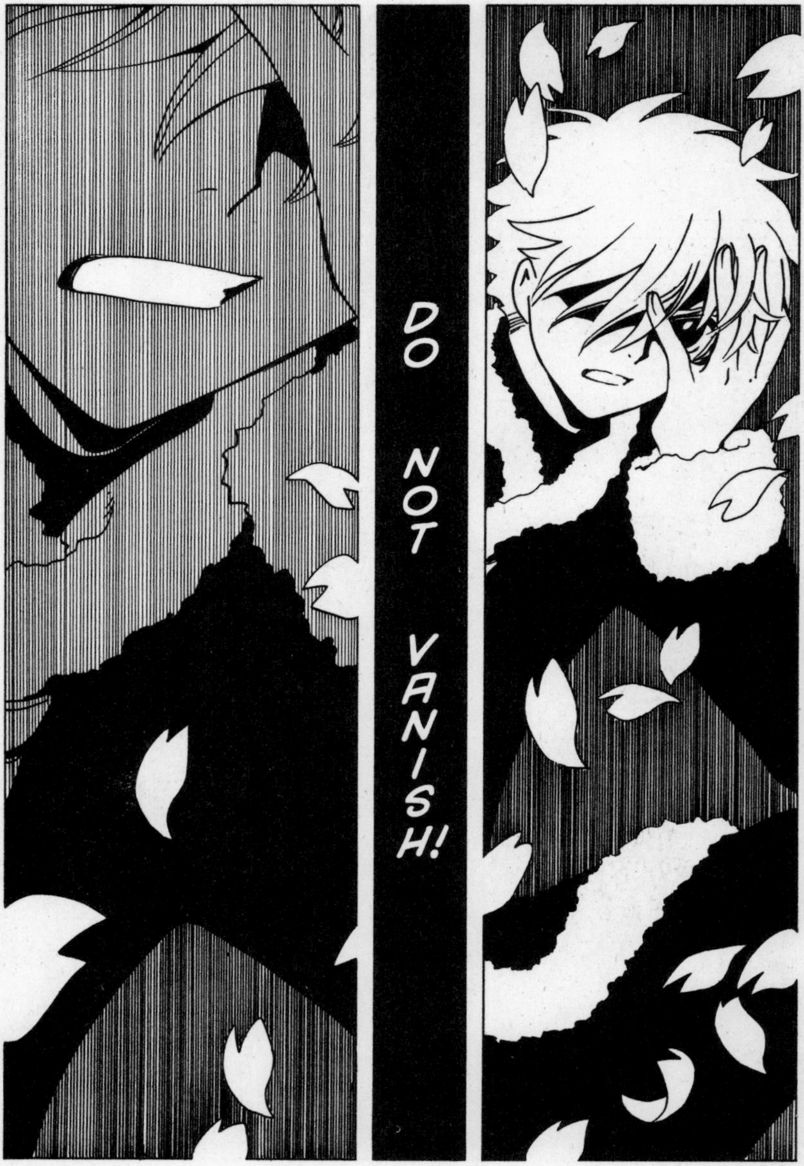
DO NOT VANISH!

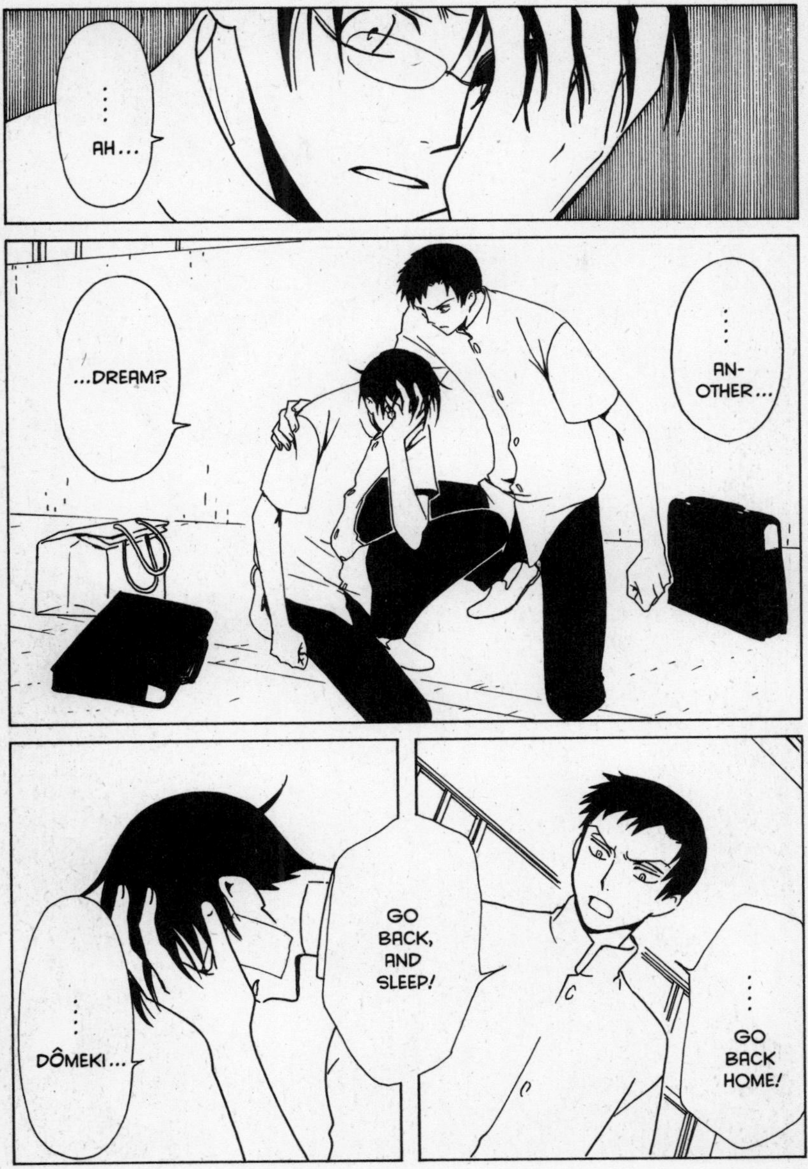

... AH...
... AN-OTHER...
...DREAM?
... GO BACK HOME!
GO BACK, AND SLEEP!
... DÔMEKI...

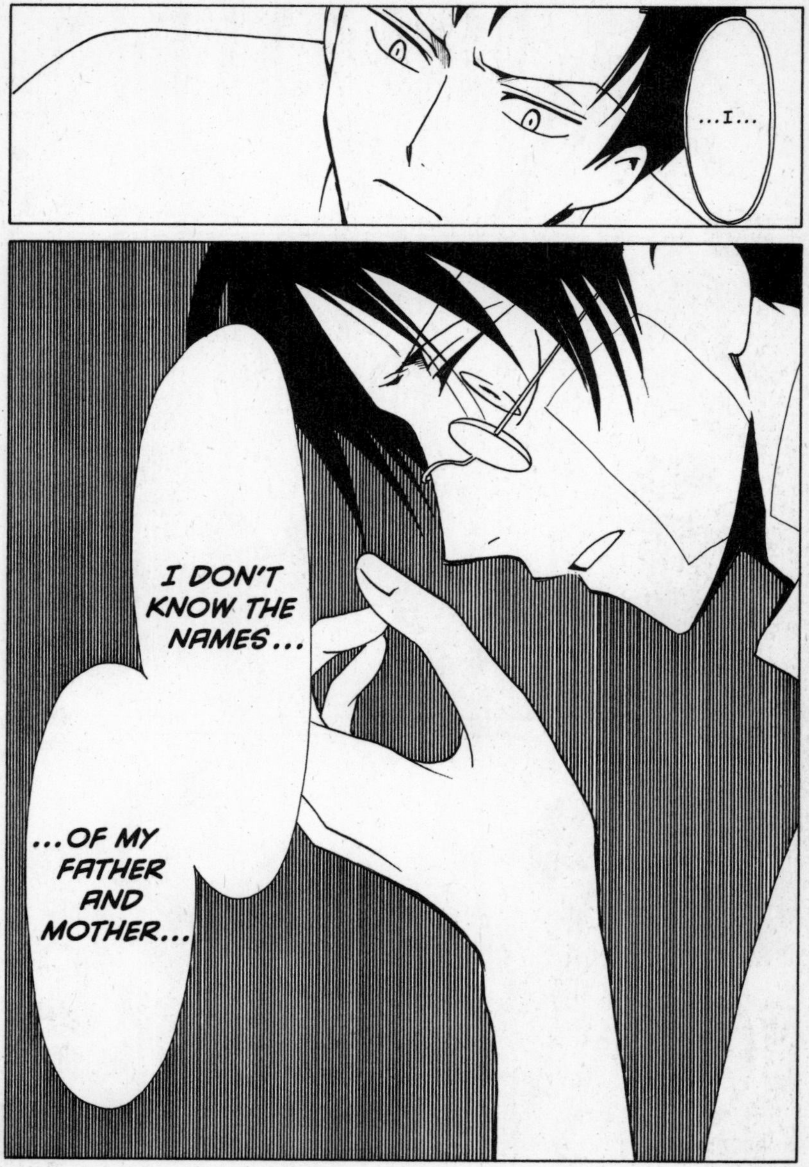
...I...
I DON'T KNOW THE NAMES...
...OF MY FATHER AND MOTHER...

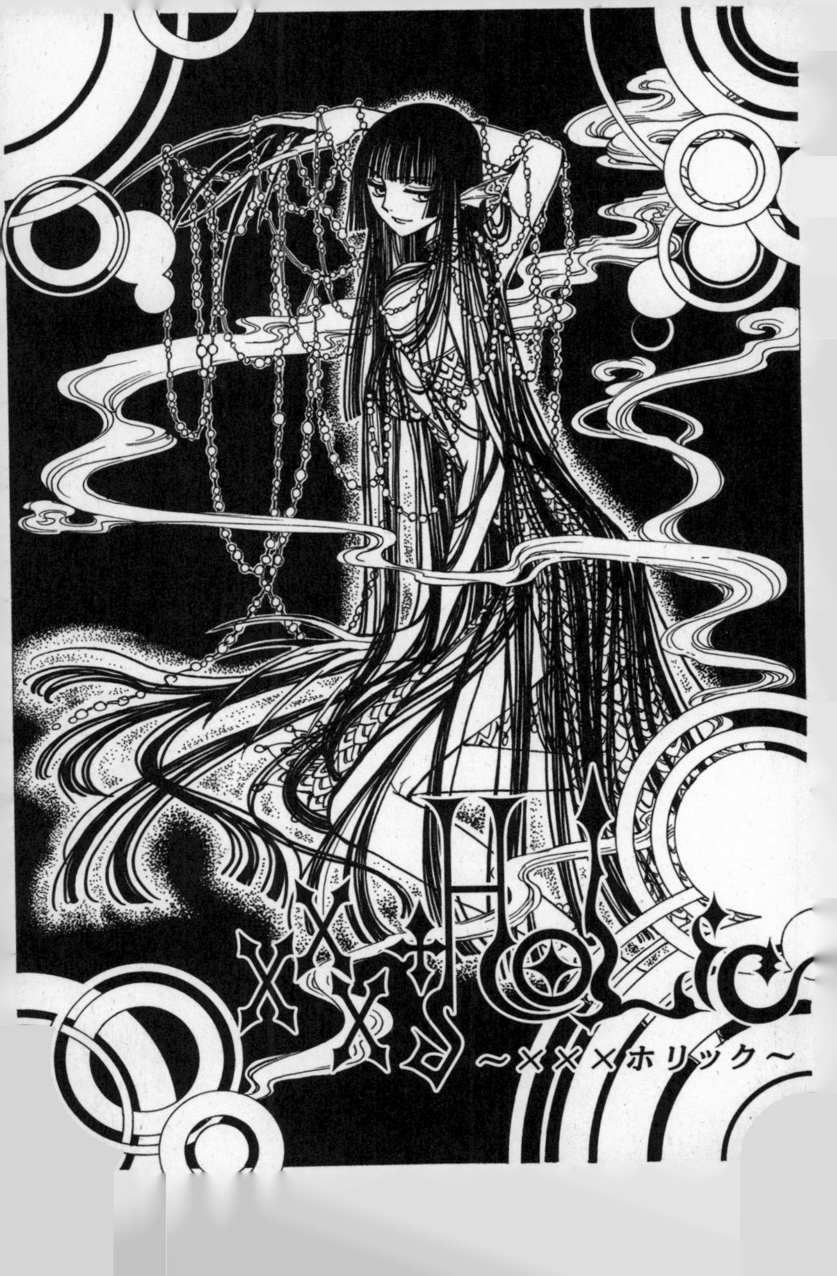
xxxHOLiC
〜×××ホリック〜

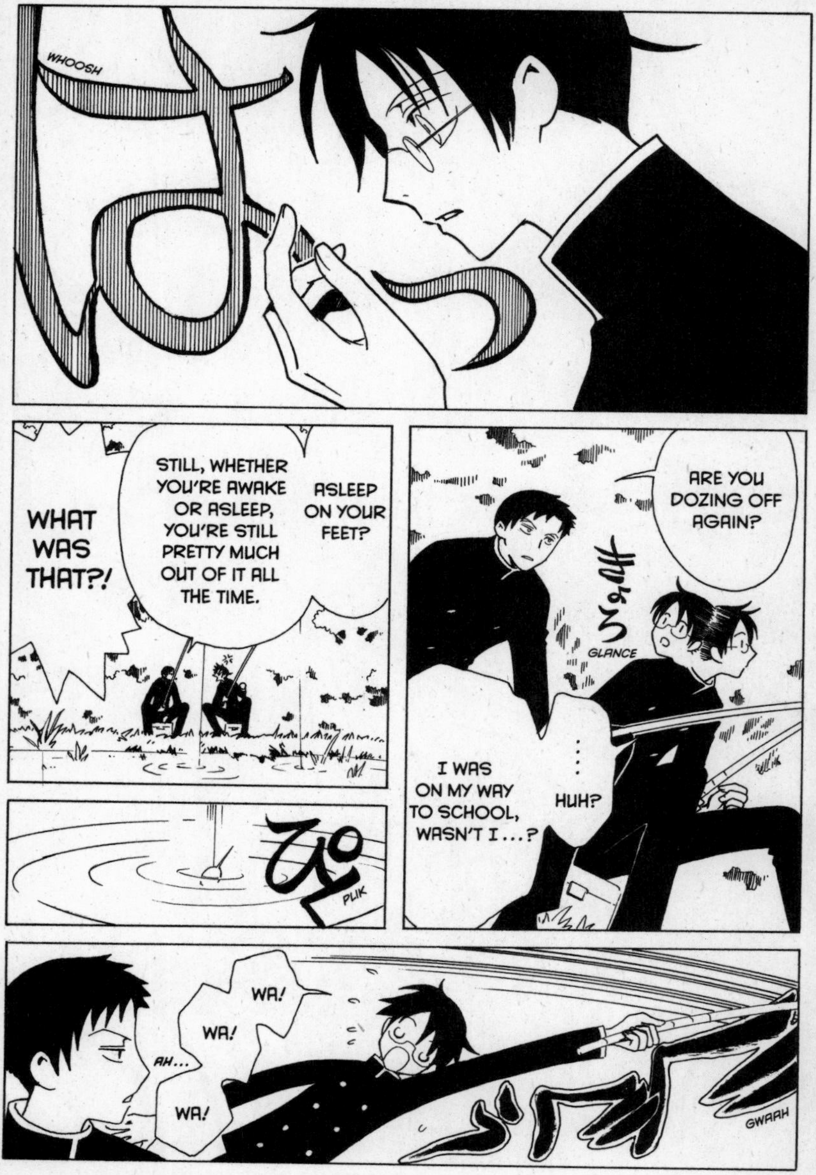
WHOOSH
ARE YOU DOZING OFF AGAIN?
GLANCE
. . .
HUH?
I WAS ON MY WAY TO SCHOOL, WASN'T I . . .?
ASLEEP ON YOUR FEET?
STILL, WHETHER YOU'RE AWAKE OR ASLEEP, YOU'RE STILL PRETTY MUCH OUT OF IT ALL THE TIME.
WHAT WAS THAT?!
PLIK
WA!
WA!
AH...
WA!
GWAAH

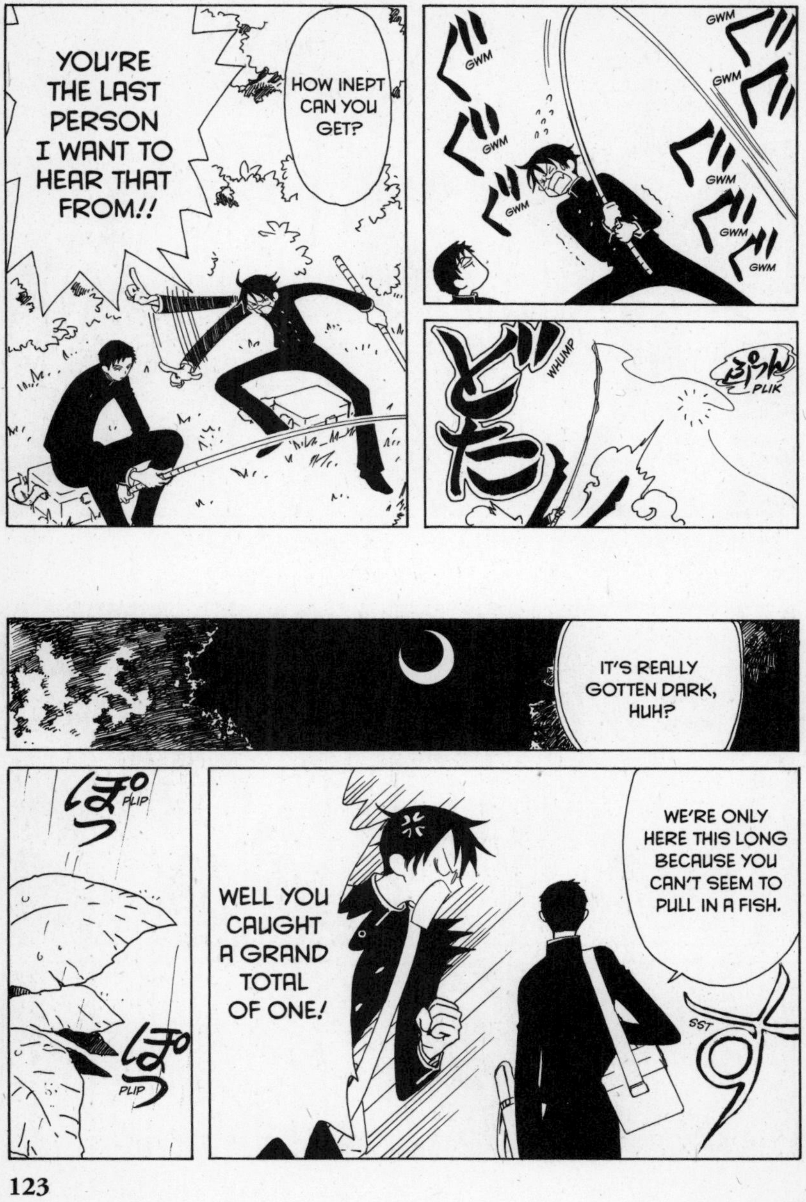
GWM
GWM
GWM
GWM
GWM
GWM
GWM
WHUMP
PLIK
HOW INEPT CAN YOU GET?
YOU'RE THE LAST PERSON I WANT TO HEAR THAT FROM!!
IT'S REALLY GOTTEN DARK, HUH?
WE'RE ONLY HERE THIS LONG BECAUSE YOU CAN'T SEEM TO PULL IN A FISH.
SST
WELL YOU CAUGHT A GRAND TOTAL OF ONE!
PLIP
PLIP

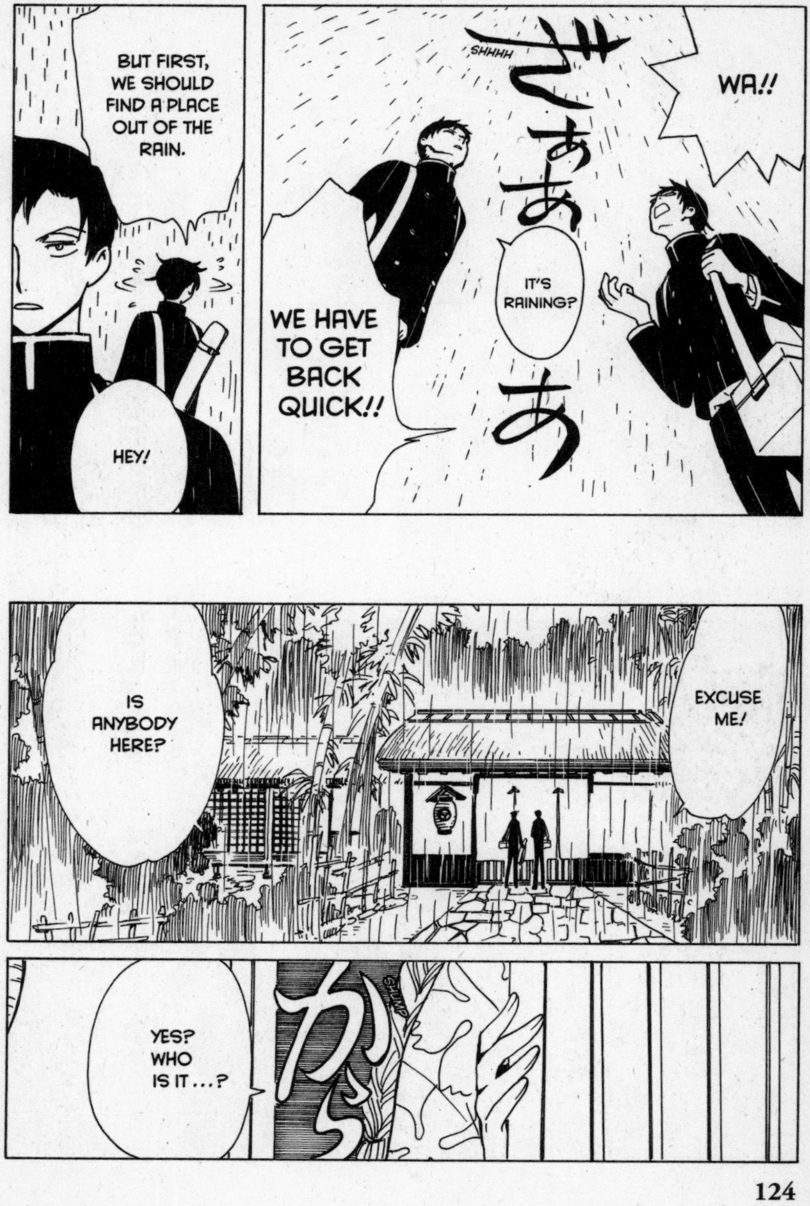
WA!!
SHHHH
ざあああ
IT'S RAINING?
WE HAVE TO GET BACK QUICK!!
BUT FIRST, WE SHOULD FIND A PLACE OUT OF THE RAIN.
HEY!
EXCUSE ME!
IS ANYBODY HERE?
SHUMP
から
YES? WHO IS IT...?

I'M SORRY FOR BARG-ING IN LIKE THIS...

...BUT IT SUDDENLY STARTED TO RAIN, AND...

?   ?

DO WE HAVE A GUEST?

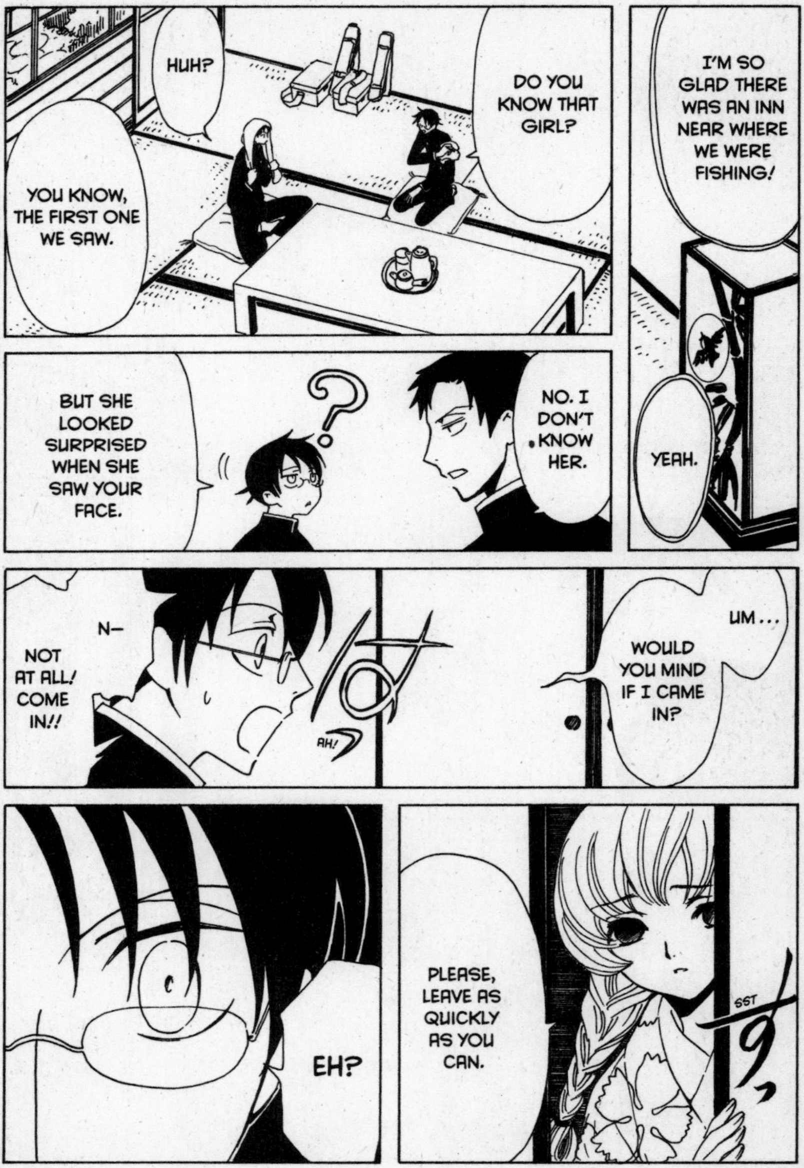

I'M SO GLAD THERE WAS AN INN NEAR WHERE WE WERE FISHING!
YEAH.
DO YOU KNOW THAT GIRL?
HUH?
YOU KNOW, THE FIRST ONE WE SAW.
NO. I DON'T KNOW HER.
BUT SHE LOOKED SURPRISED WHEN SHE SAW YOUR FACE.
UM...
WOULD YOU MIND IF I CAME IN?
AH!
N—
NOT AT ALL! COME IN!!
SST
PLEASE, LEAVE AS QUICKLY AS YOU CAN.
EH?

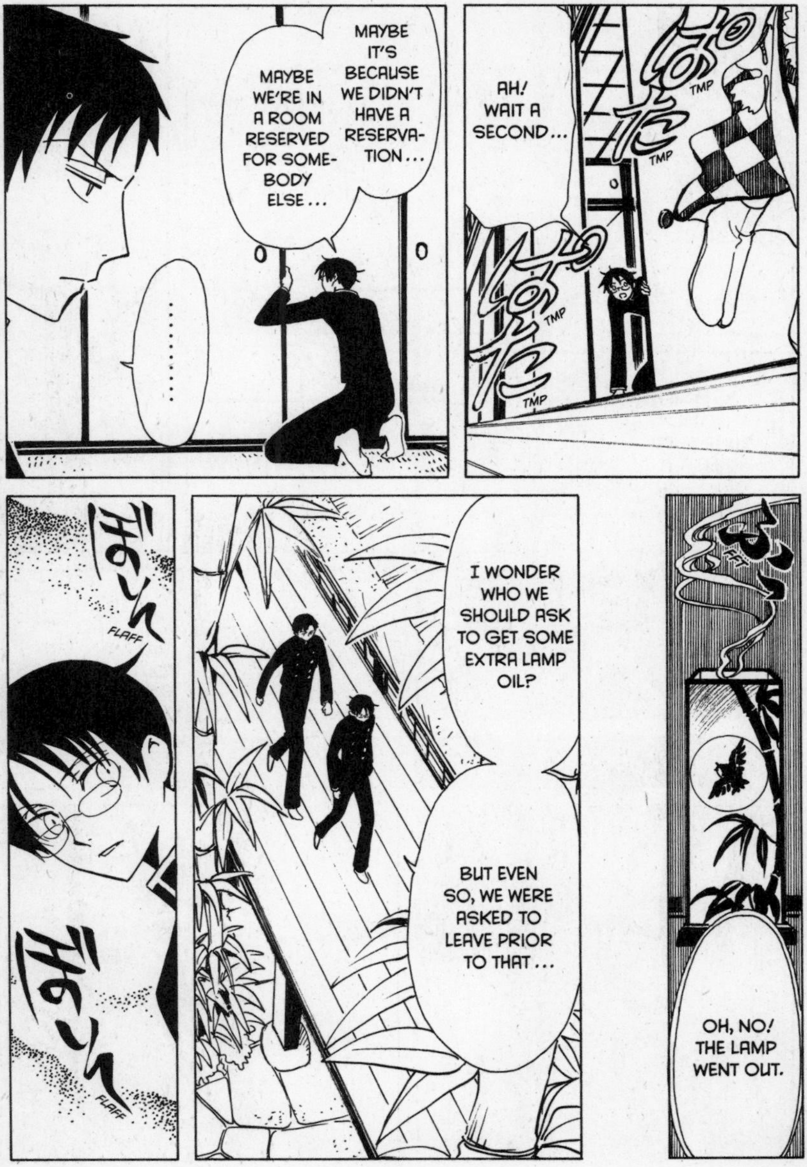
TMP
TMP
AH! WAIT A SECOND...
TMP
TMP
MAYBE IT'S BECAUSE WE DIDN'T HAVE A RESERVA-TION...
MAYBE WE'RE IN A ROOM RESERVED FOR SOME-BODY ELSE...
......
FFT
OH, NO! THE LAMP WENT OUT.
I WONDER WHO WE SHOULD ASK TO GET SOME EXTRA LAMP OIL?
BUT EVEN SO, WE WERE ASKED TO LEAVE PRIOR TO THAT...
FLAFF
FLAFF

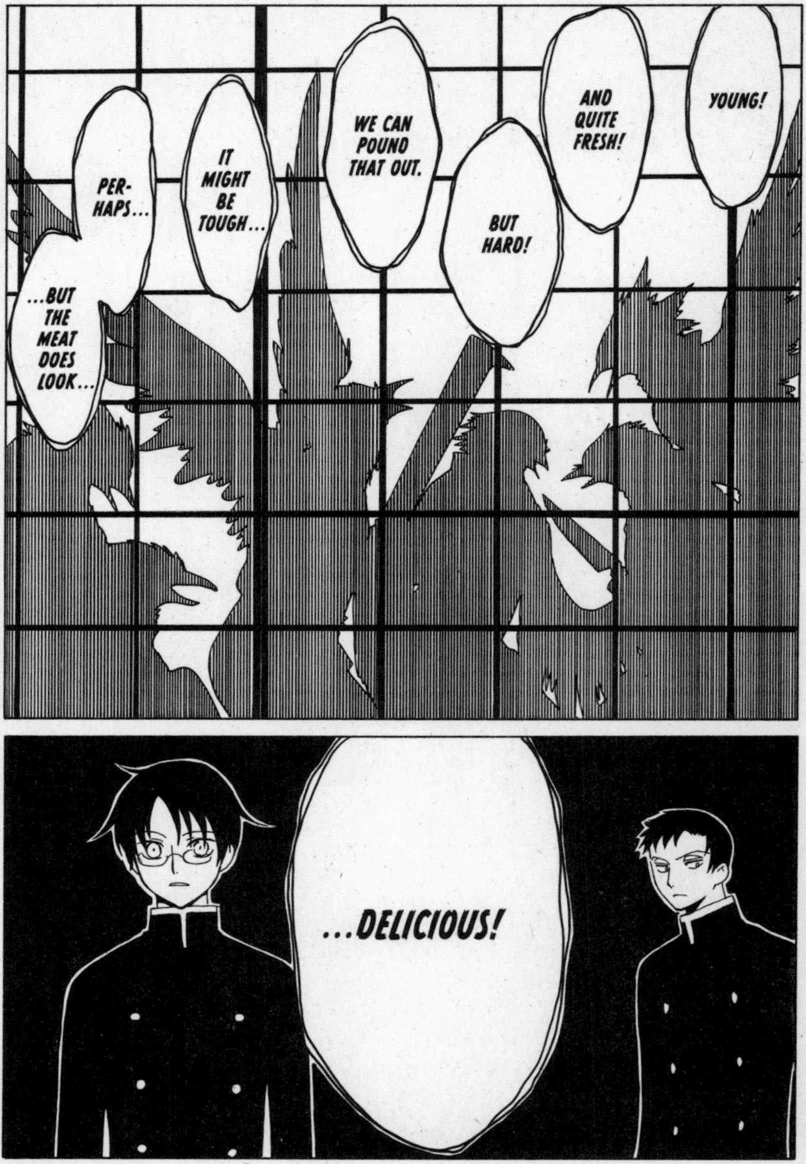
YOUNG!
AND QUITE FRESH!
BUT HARD!
WE CAN POUND THAT OUT.
IT MIGHT BE TOUGH...
PER-HAPS...
...BUT THE MEAT DOES LOOK...
...DELICIOUS!

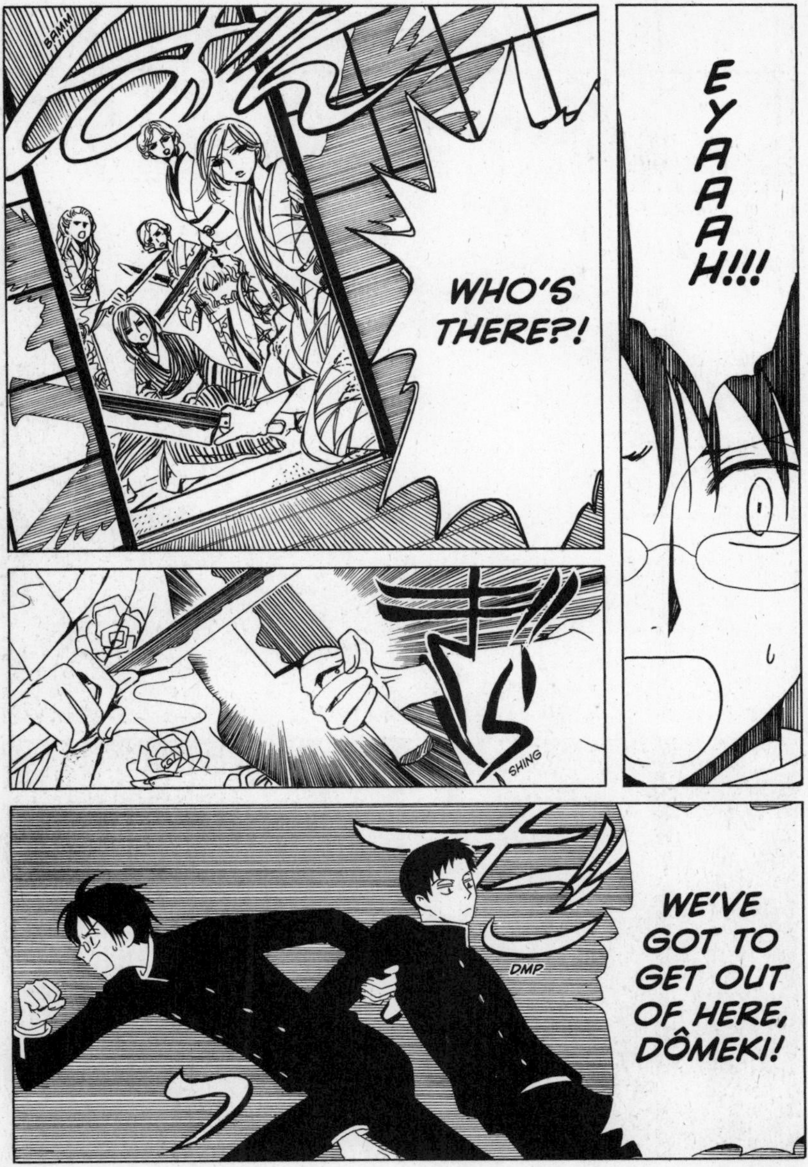
EYAAAAH!!!
BAMM
WHO'S THERE?!
SHING
WE'VE GOT TO GET OUT OF HERE, DÔMEKI!
DMP

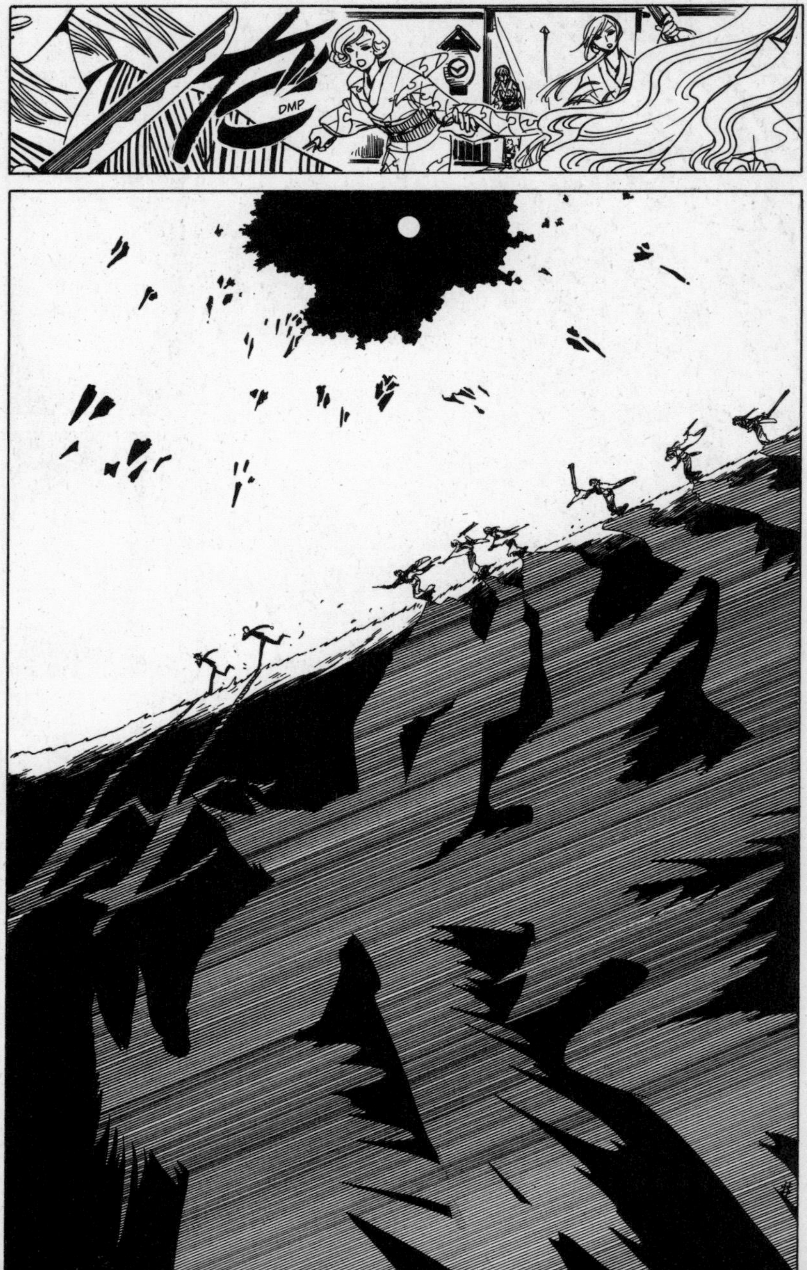
DMP

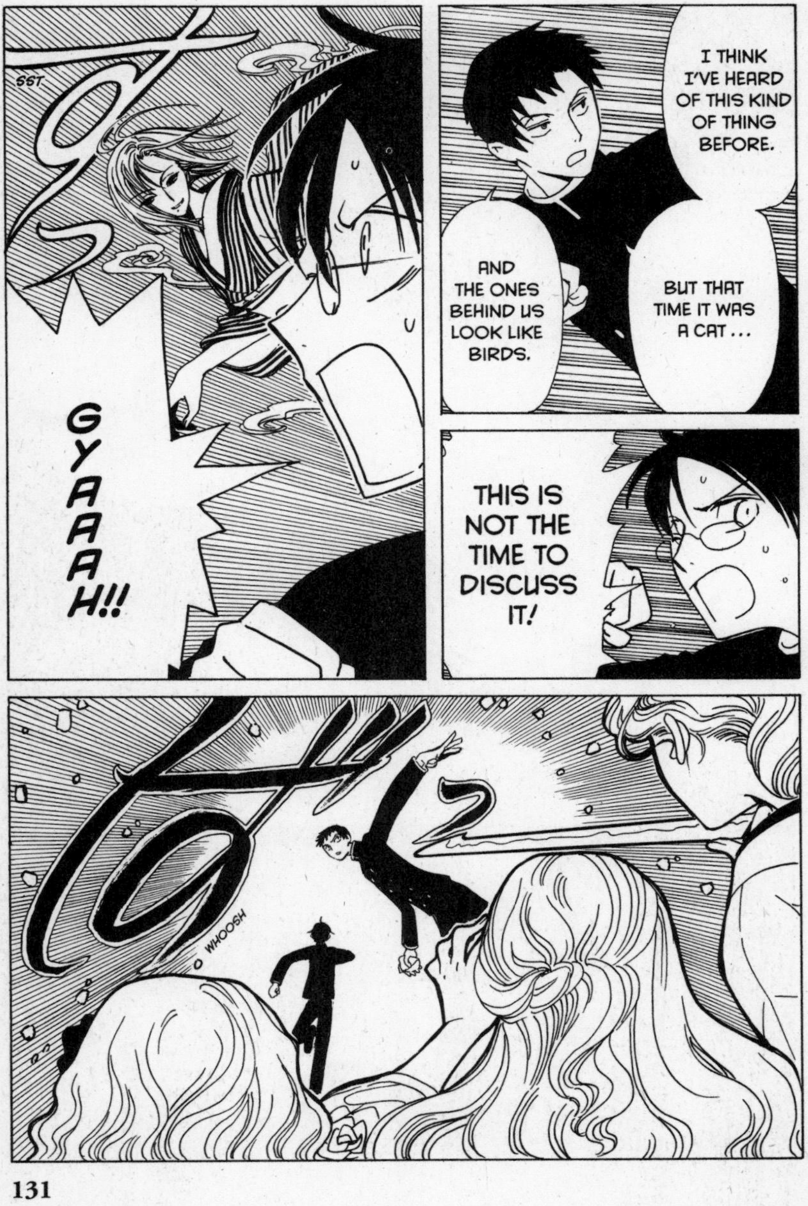
I THINK I'VE HEARD OF THIS KIND OF THING BEFORE.
BUT THAT TIME IT WAS A CAT...
AND THE ONES BEHIND US LOOK LIKE BIRDS.
THIS IS NOT THE TIME TO DISCUSS IT!
SST
GYAAAAH!!
WHOOSH

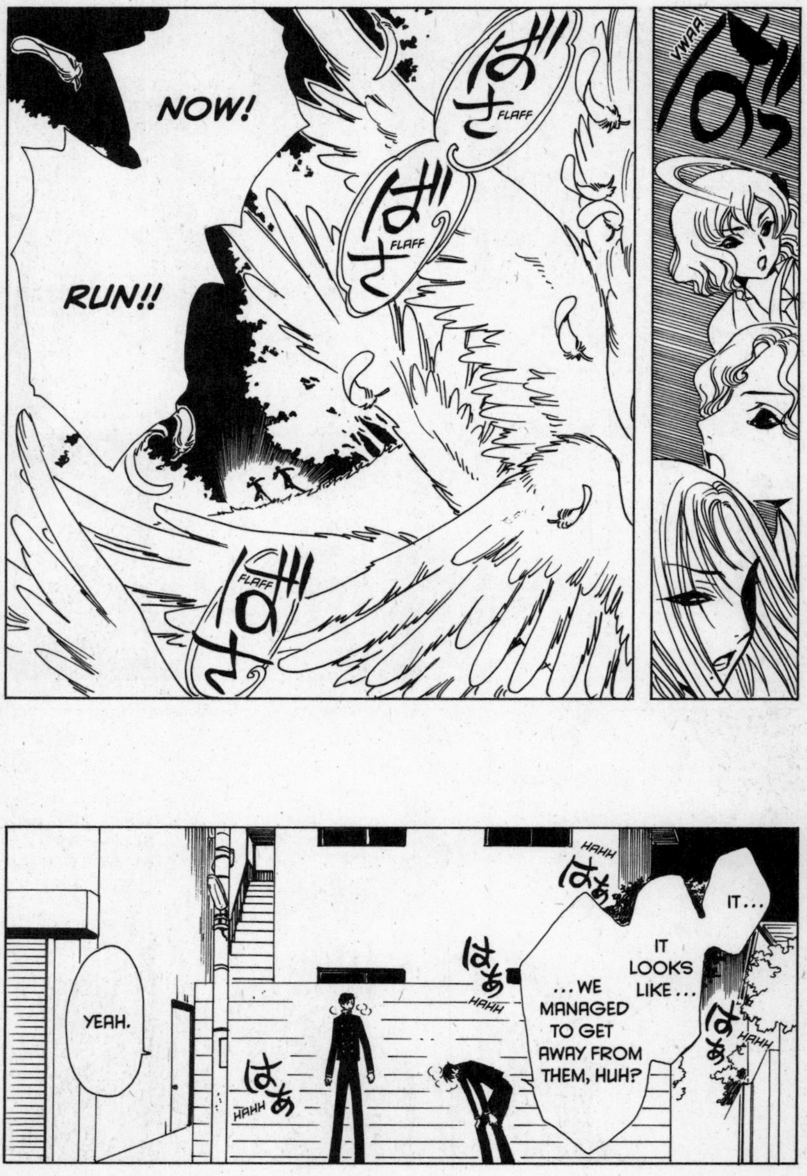
VWAA
ぱっ
ばさ
FLAFF
ばさ
FLAFF
NOW!
RUN!!
ばさ
FLAFF
IT...
IT LOOKS LIKE...
はぁ
HAHH
...WE MANAGED TO GET AWAY FROM THEM, HUH?
はぁ
HAHH
はぁ
HAHH
はぁ
HAHH
YEAH.

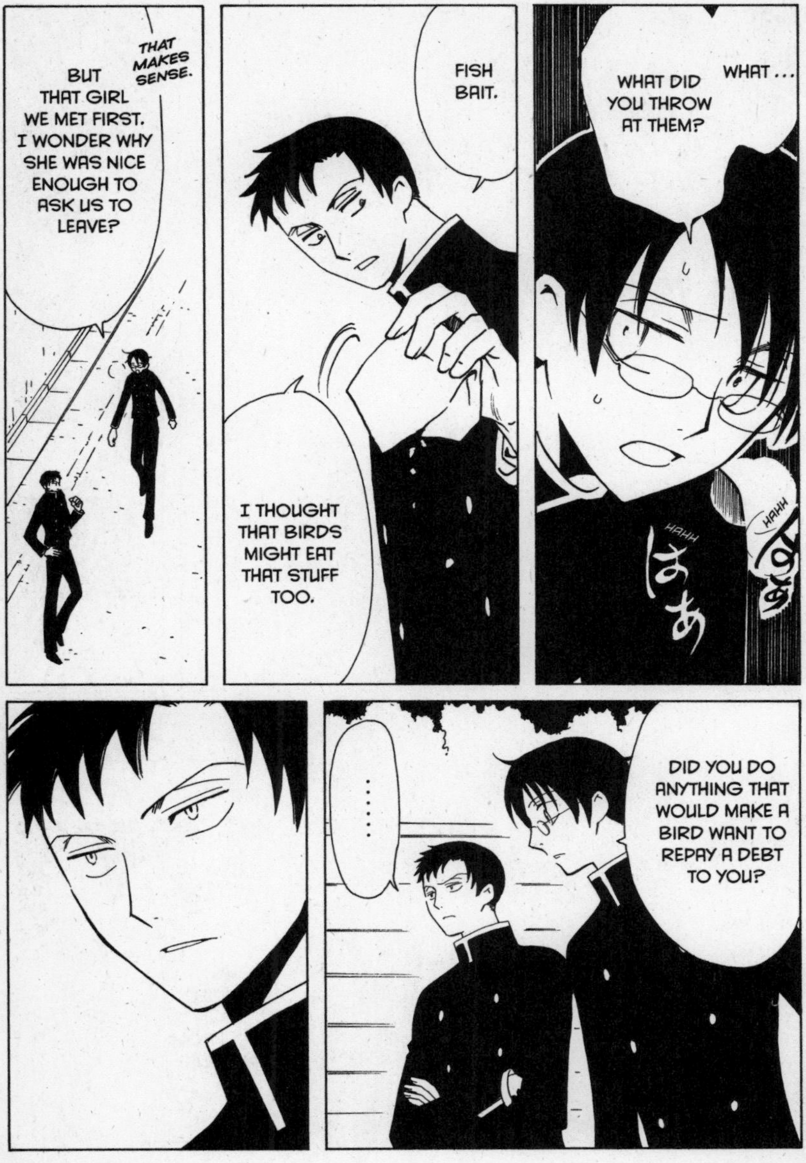
WHAT...
WHAT DID YOU THROW AT THEM?
HAHH
HAHH
はあ
はあ
FISH BAIT.
I THOUGHT THAT BIRDS MIGHT EAT THAT STUFF TOO.
THAT MAKES SENSE.
BUT THAT GIRL WE MET FIRST. I WONDER WHY SHE WAS NICE ENOUGH TO ASK US TO LEAVE?
DID YOU DO ANYTHING THAT WOULD MAKE A BIRD WANT TO REPAY A DEBT TO YOU?
......

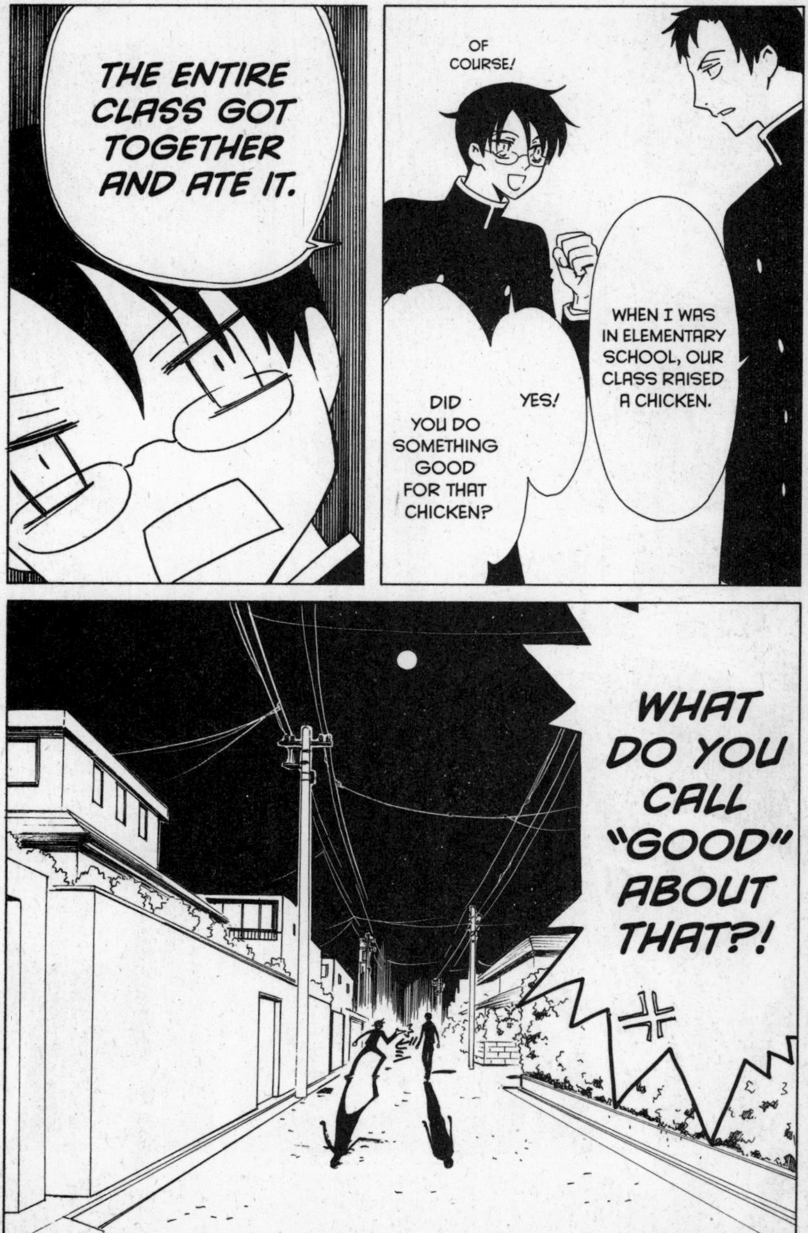
WHEN I WAS IN ELEMENTARY SCHOOL, OUR CLASS RAISED A CHICKEN.
DID YOU DO SOMETHING GOOD FOR THAT CHICKEN?
YES!
OF COURSE!
THE ENTIRE CLASS GOT TOGETHER AND ATE IT.
WHAT DO YOU CALL "GOOD" ABOUT THAT?!

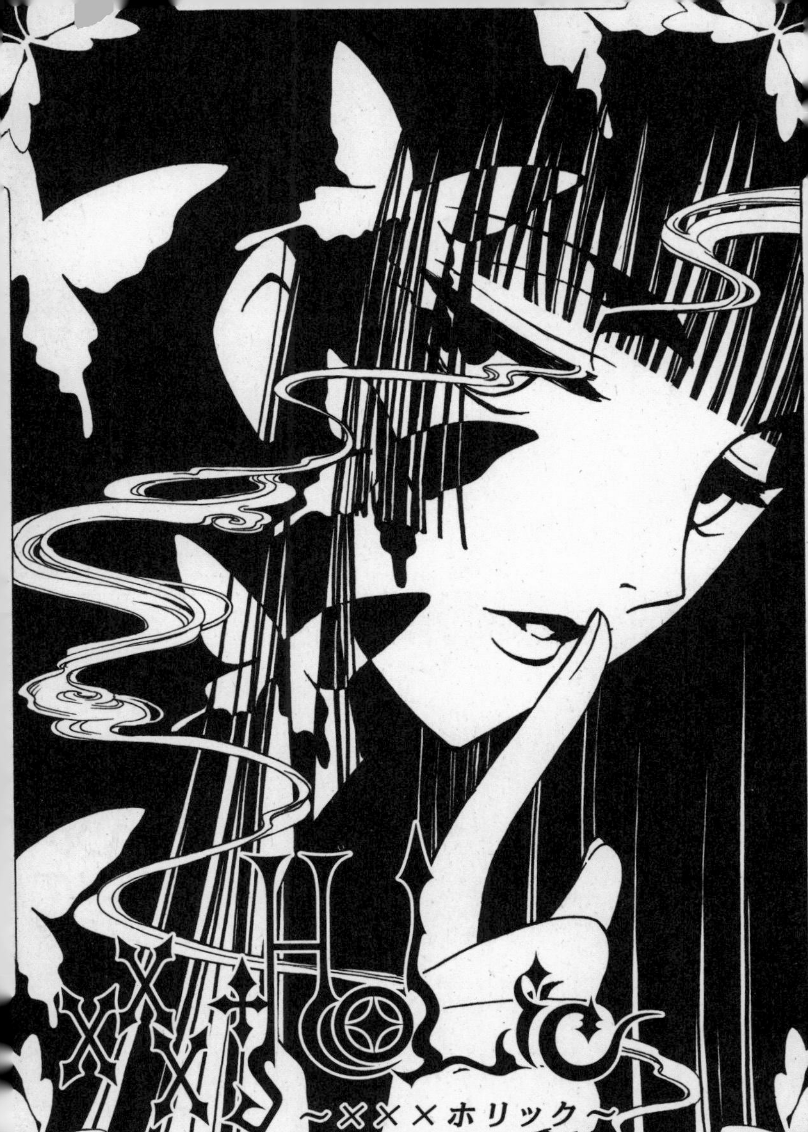
xxxHOLiC
~×××ホリック~

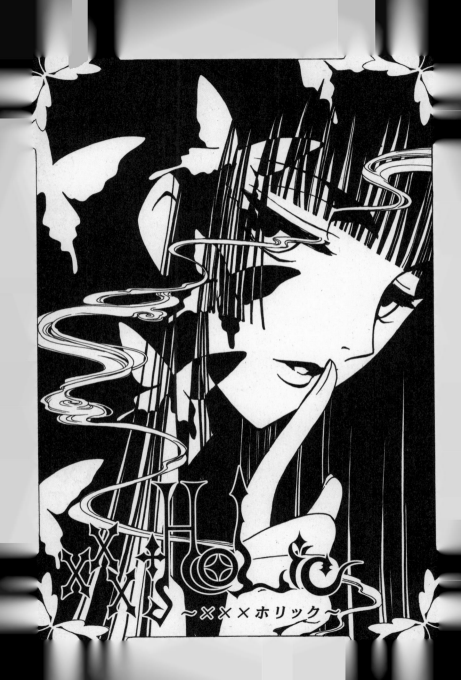

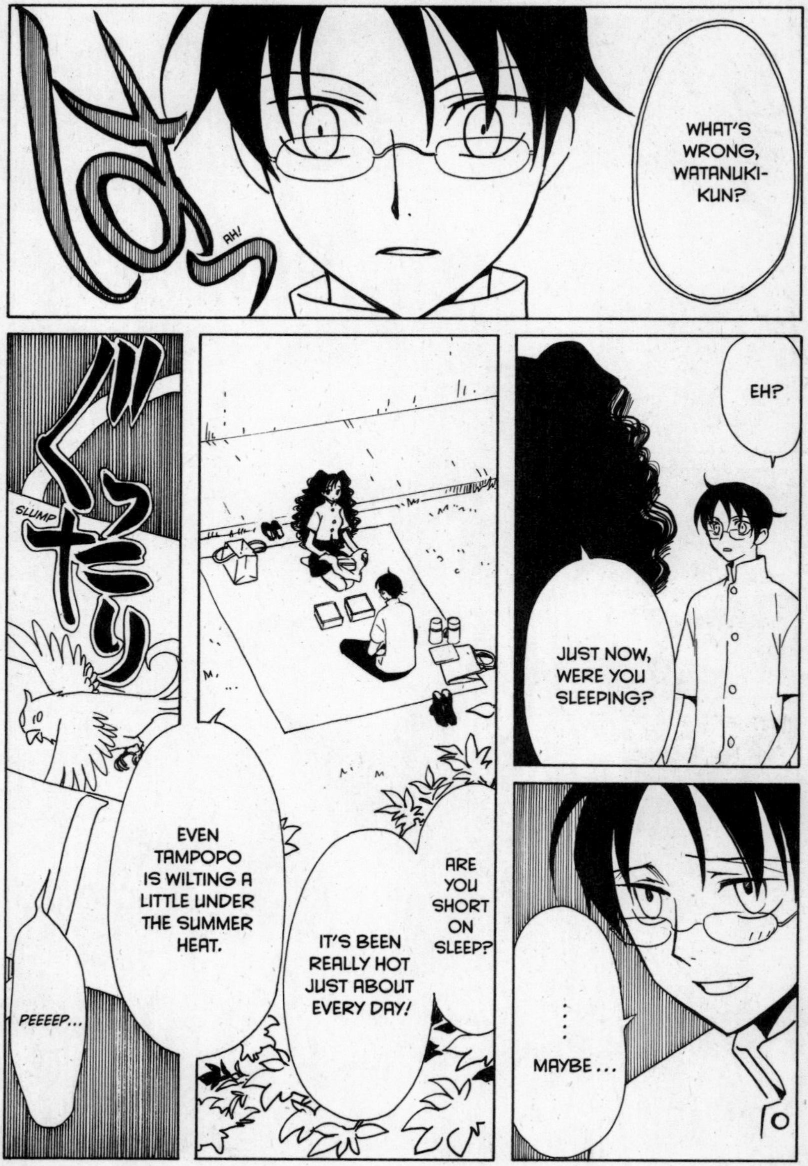
WHAT'S WRONG, WATANUKI-KUN?
AH!
EH?
JUST NOW, WERE YOU SLEEPING?
...
MAYBE...
ARE YOU SHORT ON SLEEP?
IT'S BEEN REALLY HOT JUST ABOUT EVERY DAY!
EVEN TAMPOPO IS WILTING A LITTLE UNDER THE SUMMER HEAT.
SLUMP
PEEEEP...

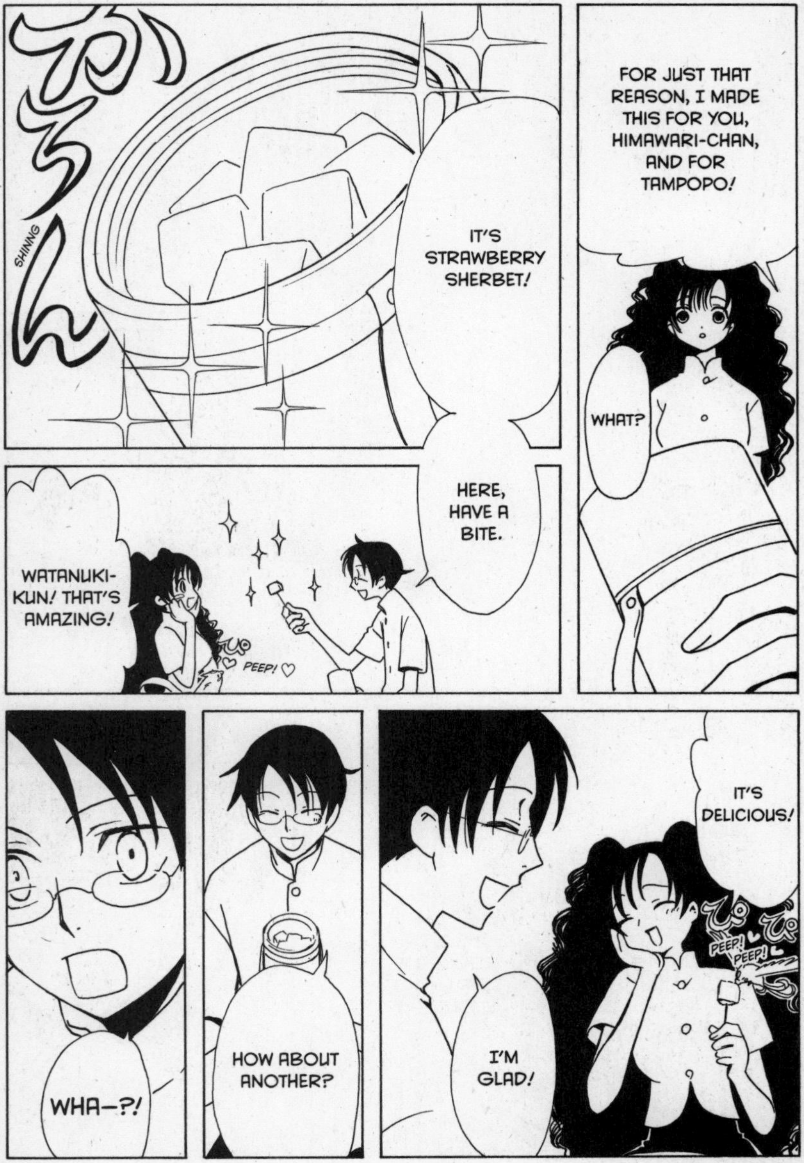

FOR JUST THAT REASON, I MADE THIS FOR YOU, HIMAWARI-CHAN, AND FOR TAMPOPO!
WHAT?
SHINING
IT'S STRAWBERRY SHERBET!
HERE, HAVE A BITE.
WATANUKI-KUN! THAT'S AMAZING!
PEEP! ♡
IT'S DELICIOUS!
PEEP! PEEP!
I'M GLAD!
HOW ABOUT ANOTHER?
WHA—?!

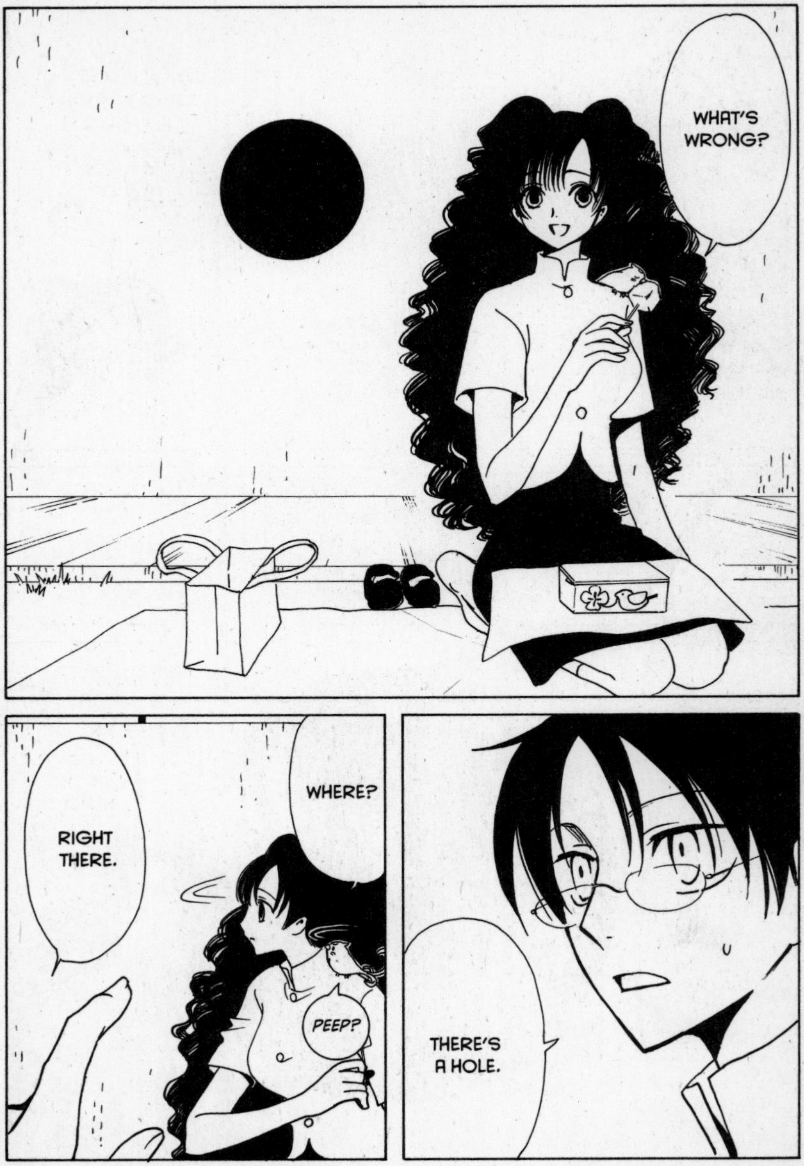
WHAT'S WRONG?
THERE'S A HOLE.
WHERE?
RIGHT THERE.
PEEP?

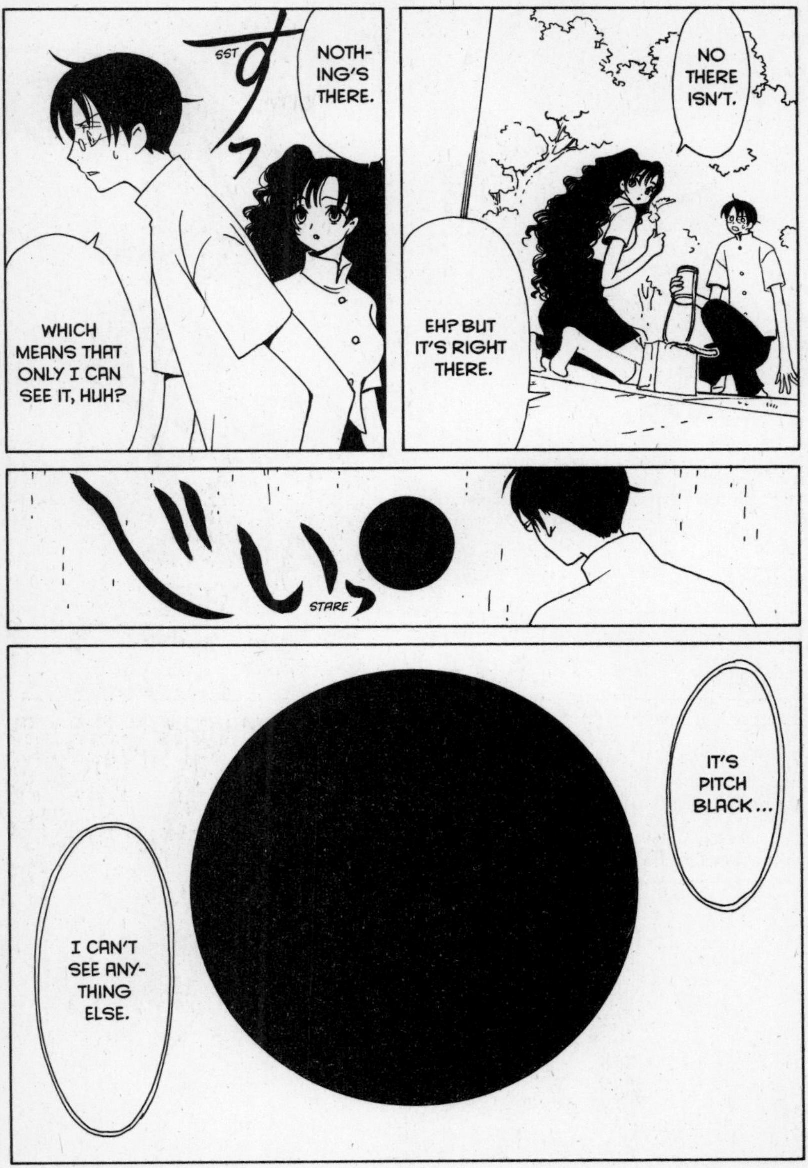
NO THERE ISN'T.
EH? BUT IT'S RIGHT THERE.
SST
NOTHING'S THERE.
WHICH MEANS THAT ONLY I CAN SEE IT, HUH?
STARE
IT'S PITCH BLACK...
I CAN'T SEE ANYTHING ELSE.

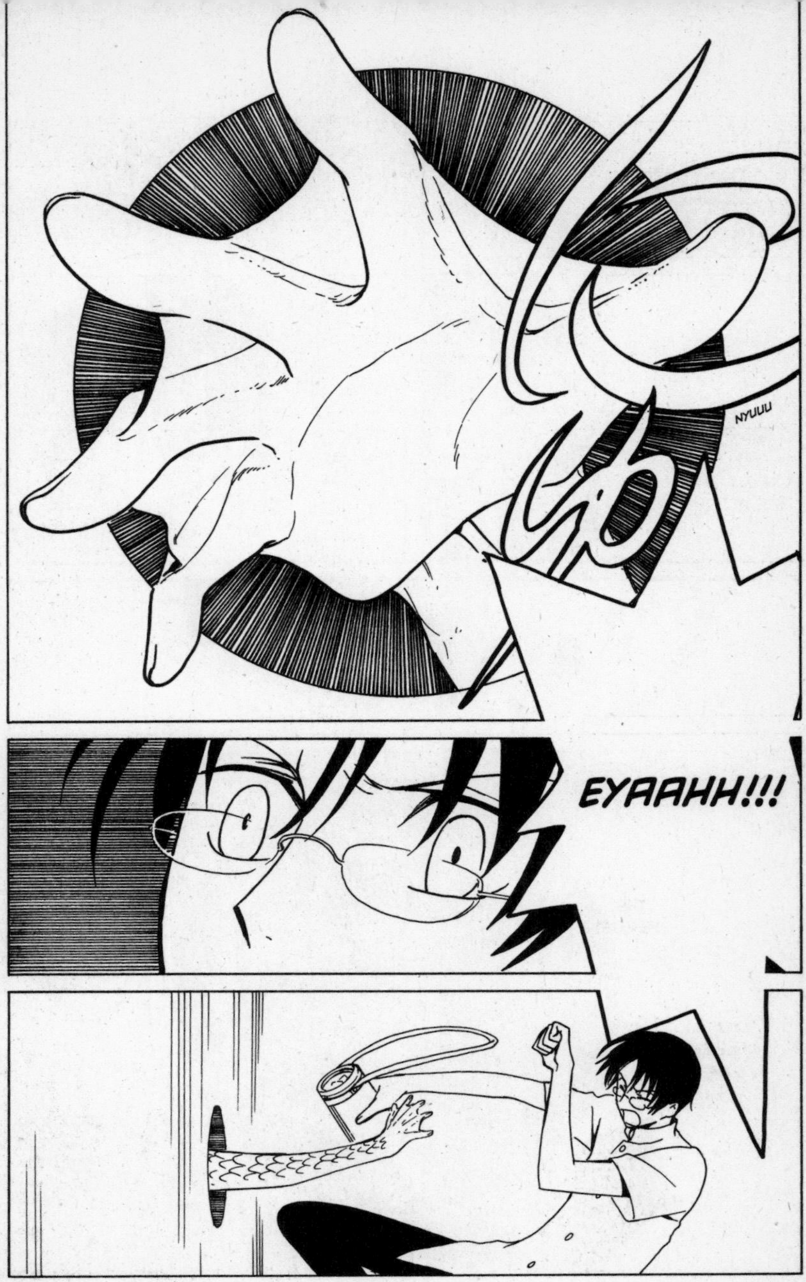
NYUUU
EYAAHH!!!

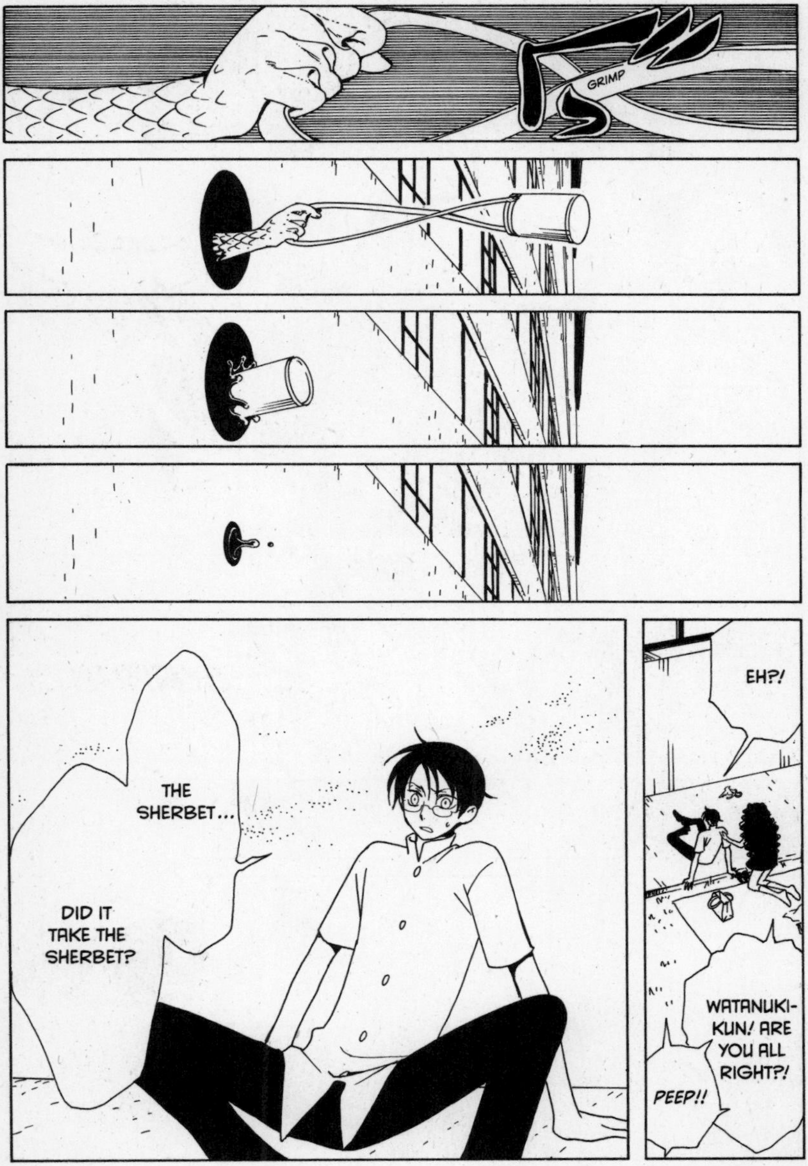
GRIMP
EH?!
WATANUKI-KUN! ARE YOU ALL RIGHT?!
PEEP!!
THE SHERBET...
DID IT TAKE THE SHERBET?

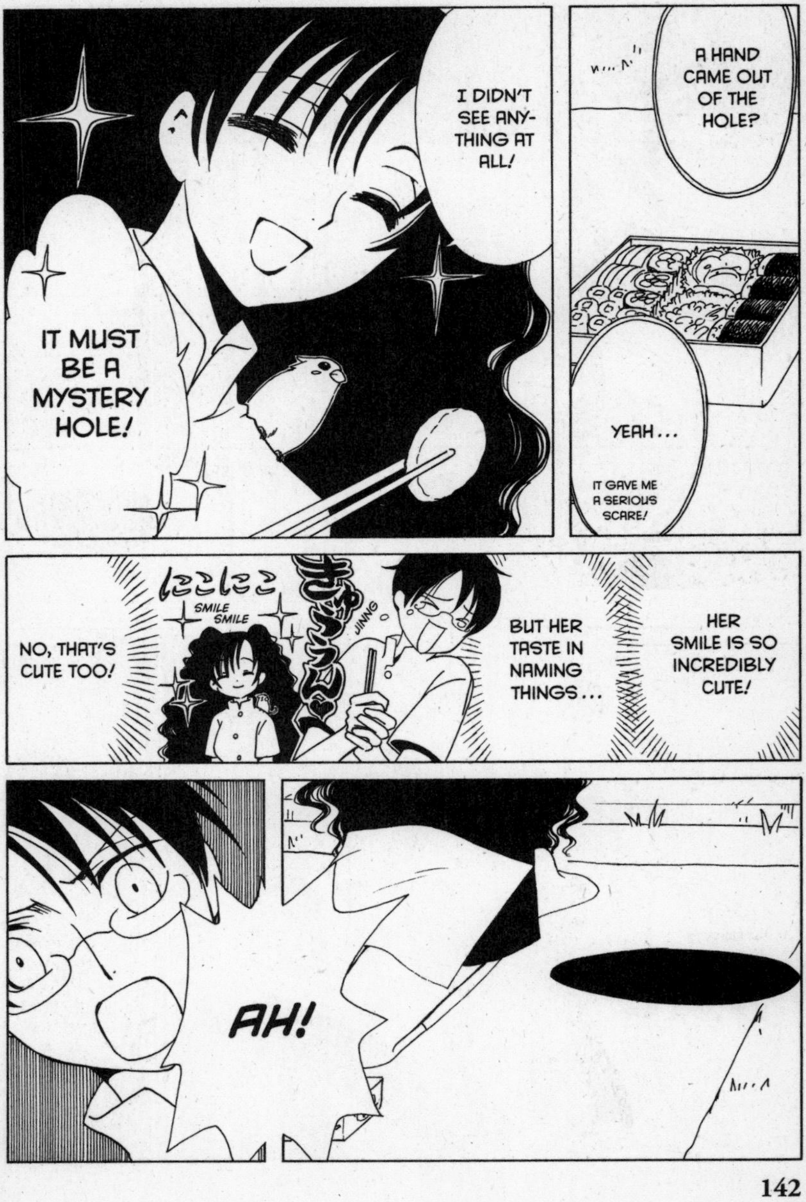
A HAND CAME OUT OF THE HOLE?
YEAH...
IT GAVE ME A SERIOUS SCARE!
I DIDN'T SEE ANY-THING AT ALL!
IT MUST BE A MYSTERY HOLE!
HER SMILE IS SO INCREDIBLY CUTE!
BUT HER TASTE IN NAMING THINGS...
JINNG
にこにこ
SMILE SMILE
NO, THAT'S CUTE TOO!
AH!

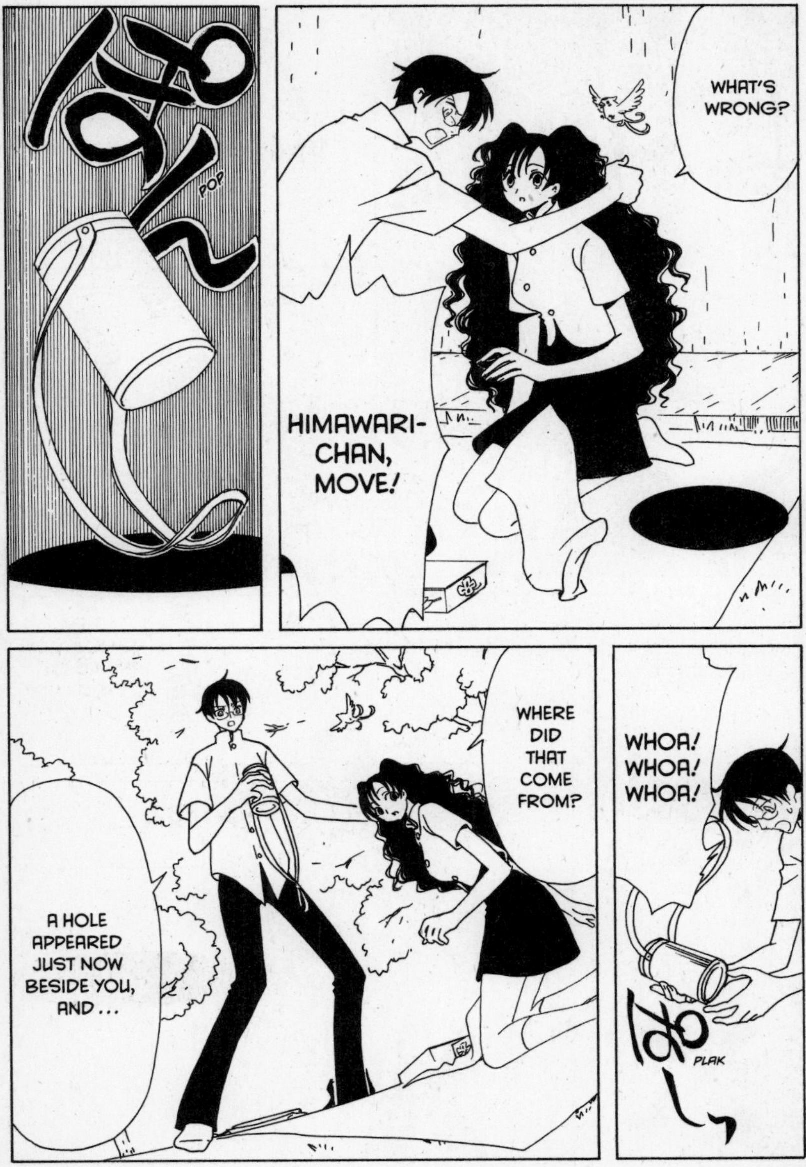
WHAT'S WRONG?
HIMAWARI-CHAN, MOVE!
POP
WHOA! WHOA! WHOA!
PLAK
WHERE DID THAT COME FROM?
A HOLE APPEARED JUST NOW BESIDE YOU, AND...

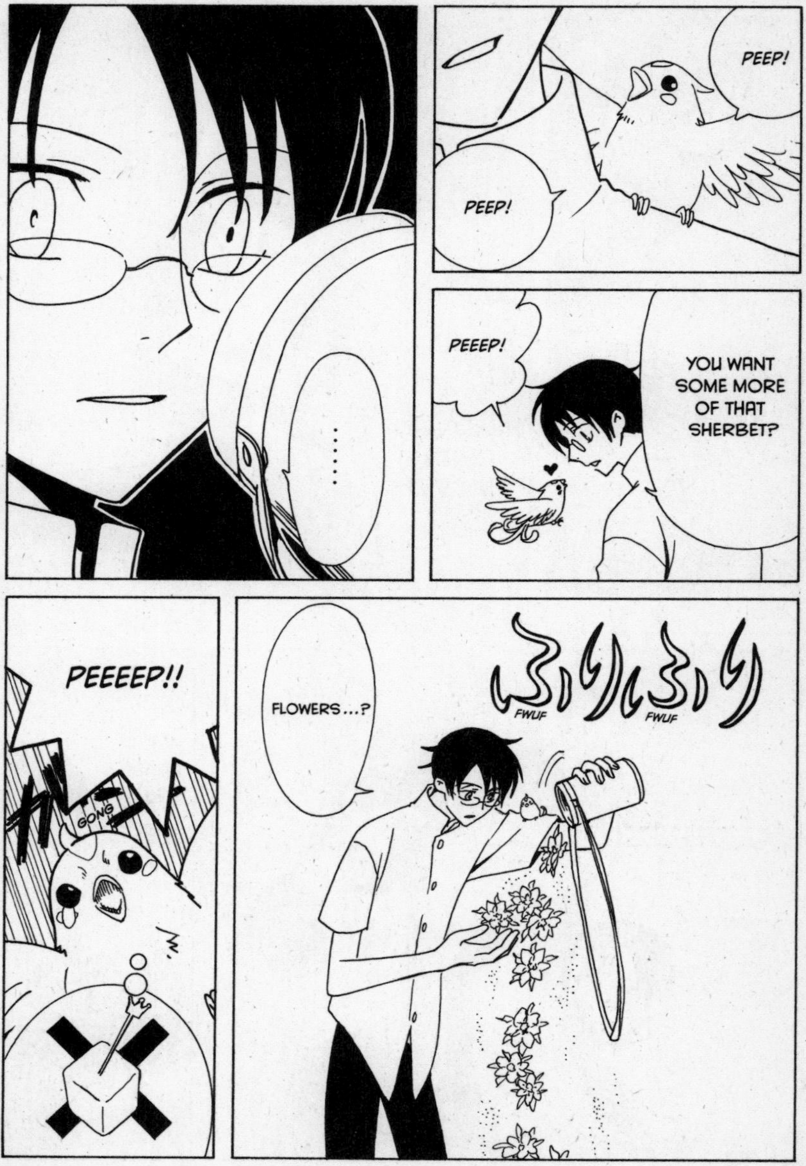
PEEP!
PEEP!
YOU WANT SOME MORE OF THAT SHERBET?
PEEEP!
......
ふりふり
FWUF FWUF
FLOWERS...?
PEEEEP!!
GONG

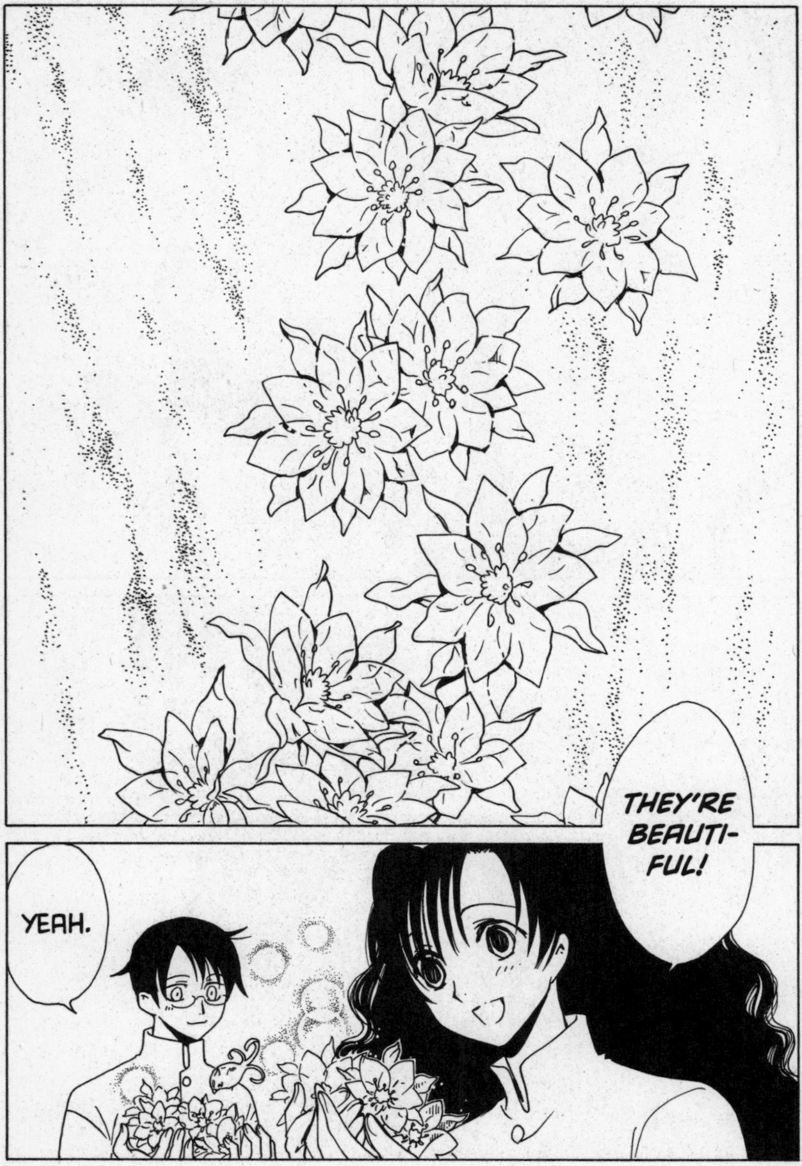
THEY'RE BEAUTI-FUL!
YEAH.

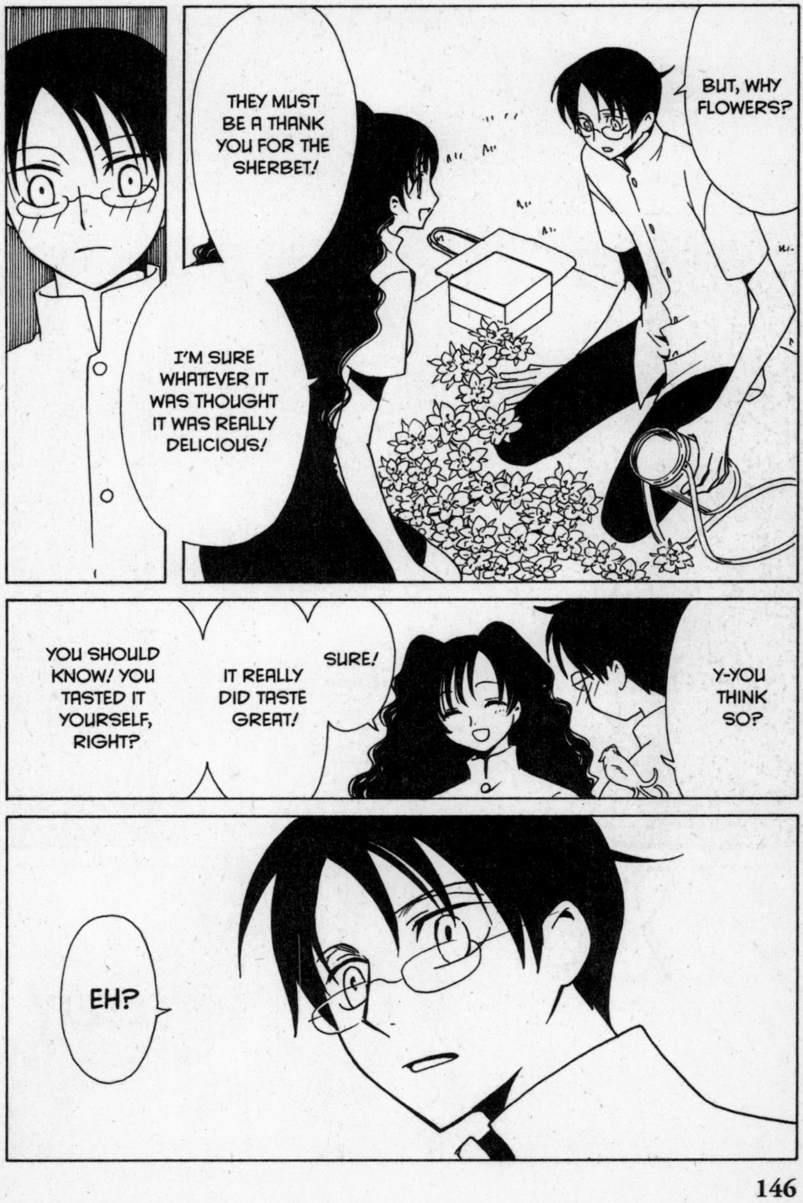
BUT, WHY FLOWERS?
THEY MUST BE A THANK YOU FOR THE SHERBET!
I'M SURE WHATEVER IT WAS THOUGHT IT WAS REALLY DELICIOUS!
Y-YOU THINK SO?
SURE!
IT REALLY DID TASTE GREAT!
YOU SHOULD KNOW! YOU TASTED IT YOURSELF, RIGHT?
EH?

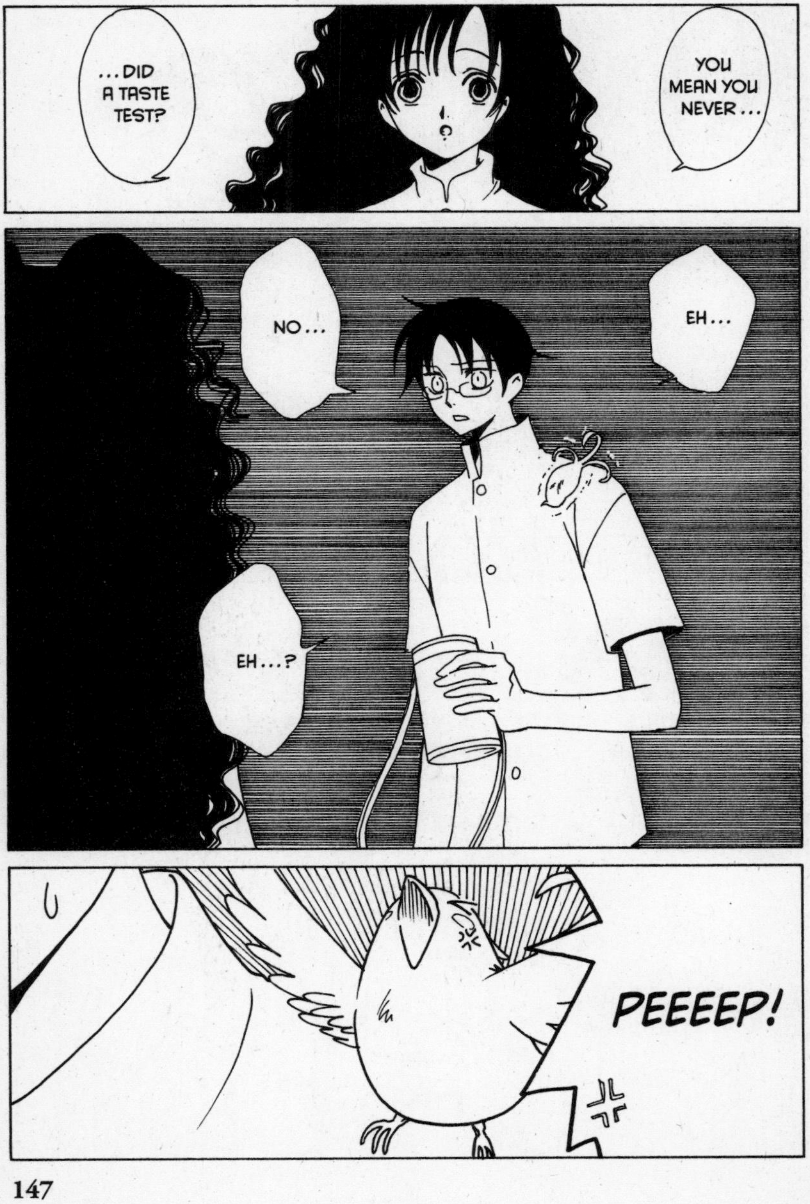
YOU MEAN YOU NEVER...
...DID A TASTE TEST?
EH...
NO...
EH...?
PEEEEP!

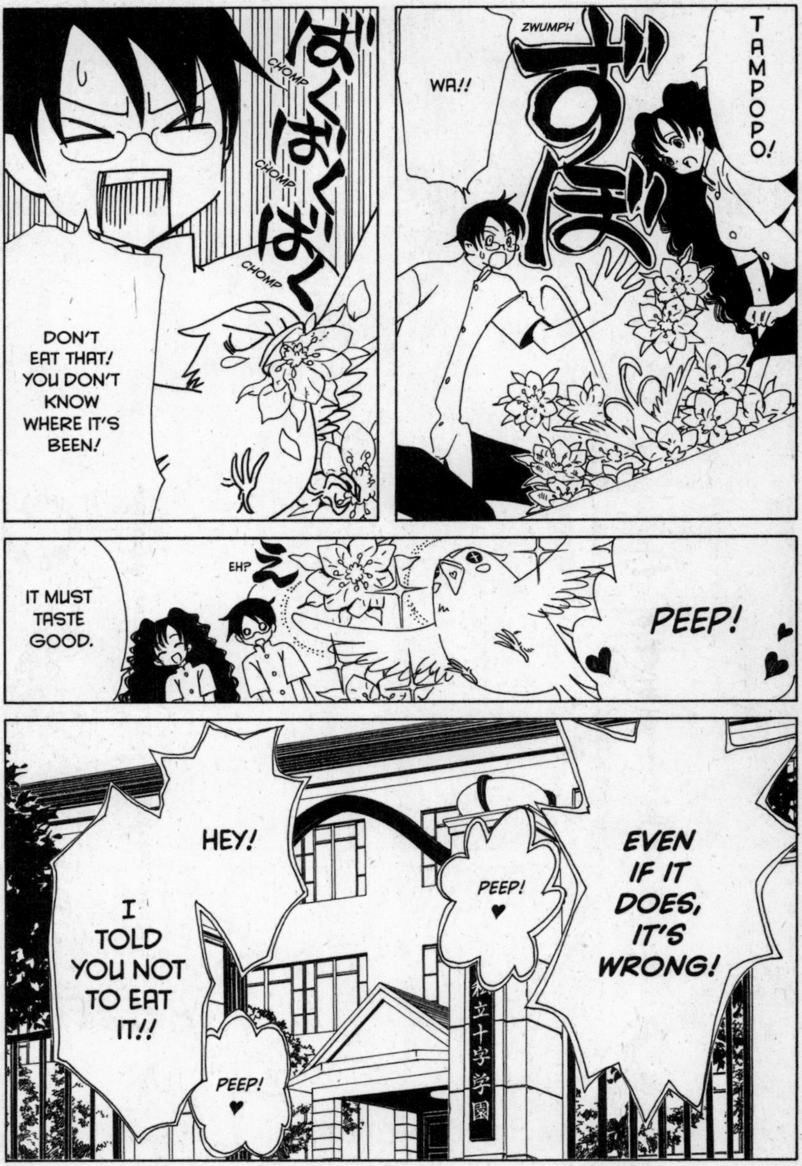
TAMPOPO!
WA!!
ずぼ
ZWUMPH
ぱくぱくぱく
CHOMP
CHOMP
CHOMP
DON'T EAT THAT! YOU DON'T KNOW WHERE IT'S BEEN!
PEEP!
え
EH?
IT MUST TASTE GOOD.
EVEN IF IT DOES, IT'S WRONG!
PEEP!
HEY!
I TOLD YOU NOT TO EAT IT!!
PEEP!

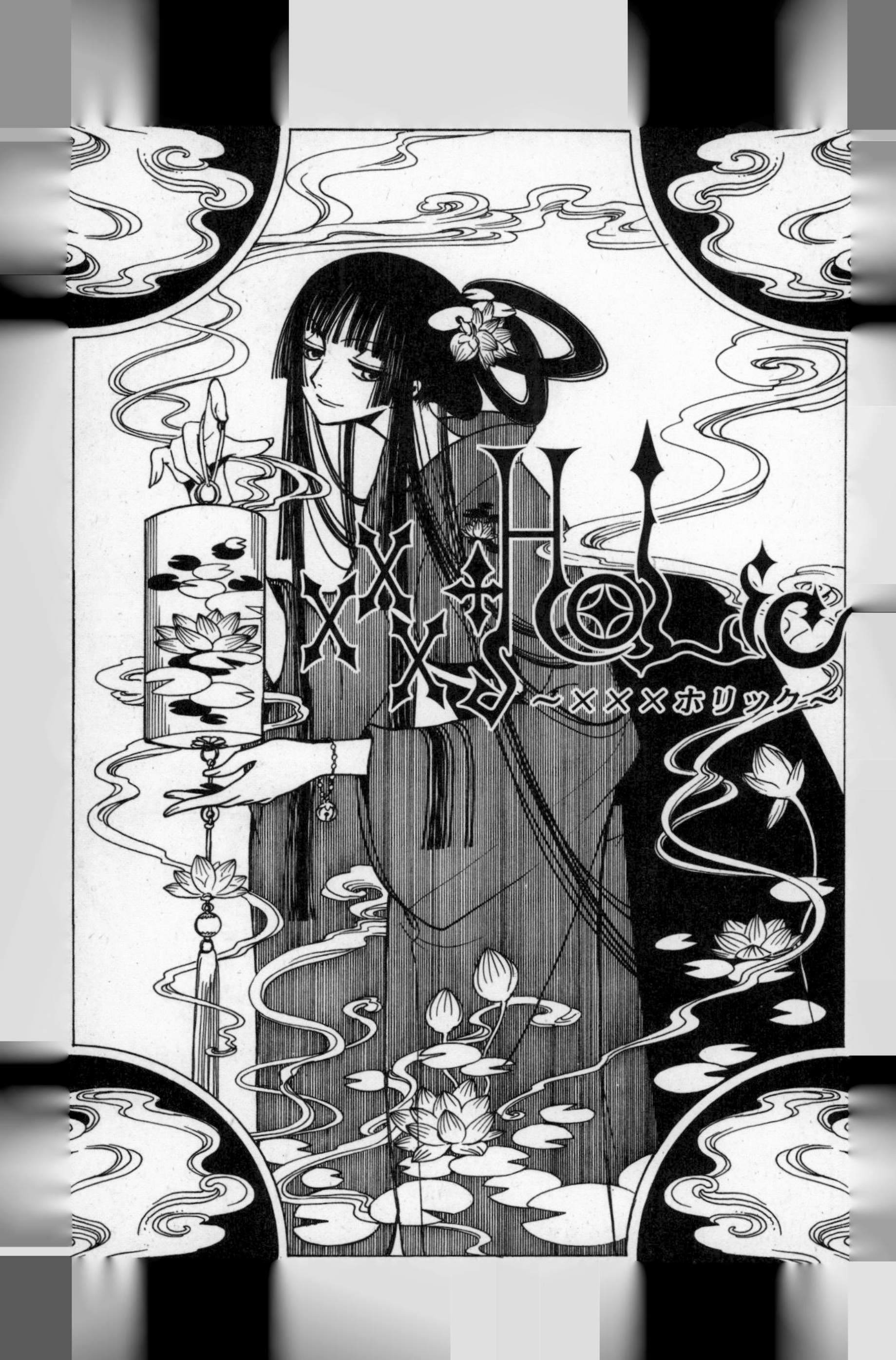
xxxHolic
~×××ホリック~

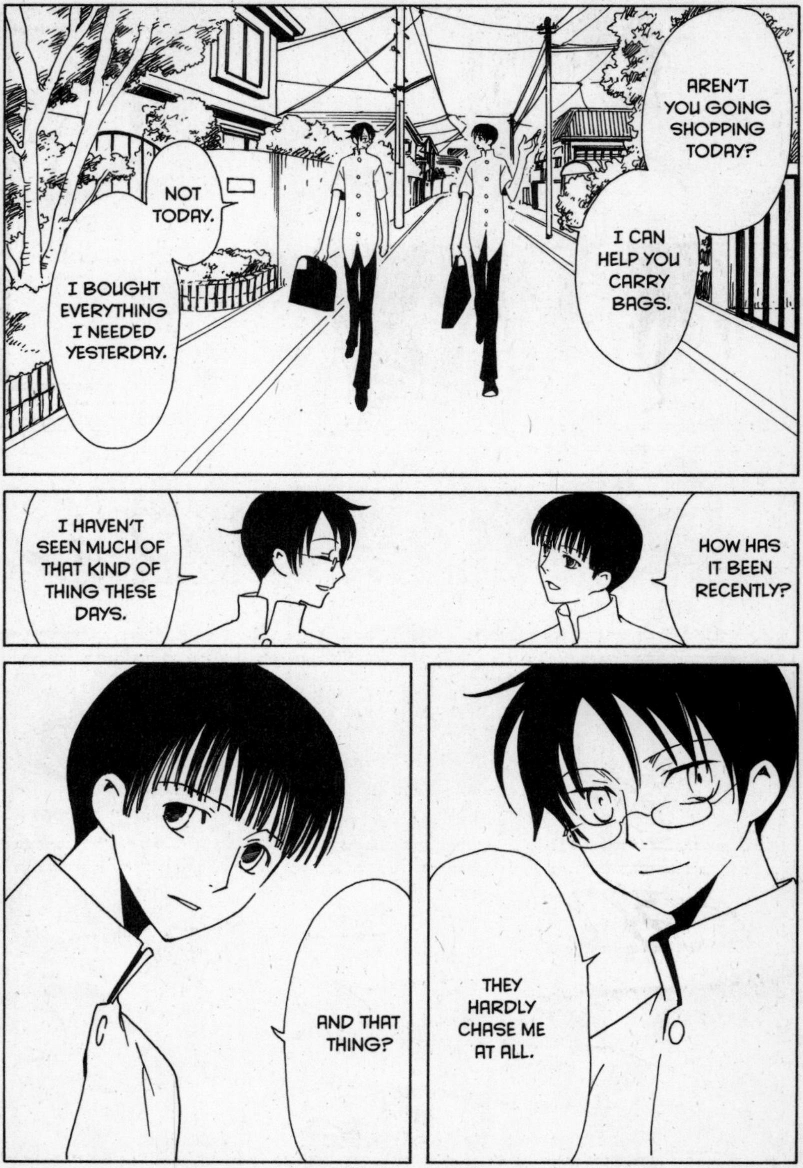
AREN'T YOU GOING SHOPPING TODAY?
I CAN HELP YOU CARRY BAGS.
NOT TODAY.
I BOUGHT EVERYTHING I NEEDED YESTERDAY.
HOW HAS IT BEEN RECENTLY?
I HAVEN'T SEEN MUCH OF THAT KIND OF THING THESE DAYS.
THEY HARDLY CHASE ME AT ALL.
AND THAT THING?

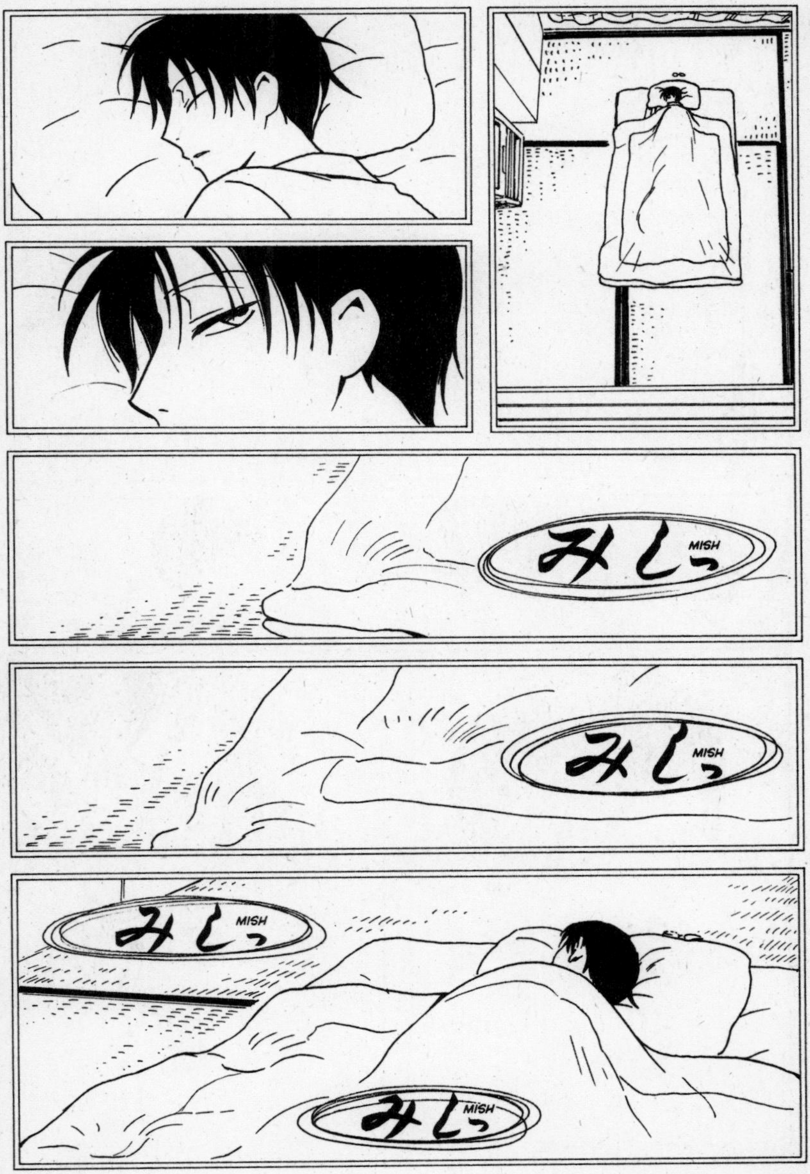
みしっ
MISH
みしっ
MISH
みしっ
MISH
みしっ
MISH

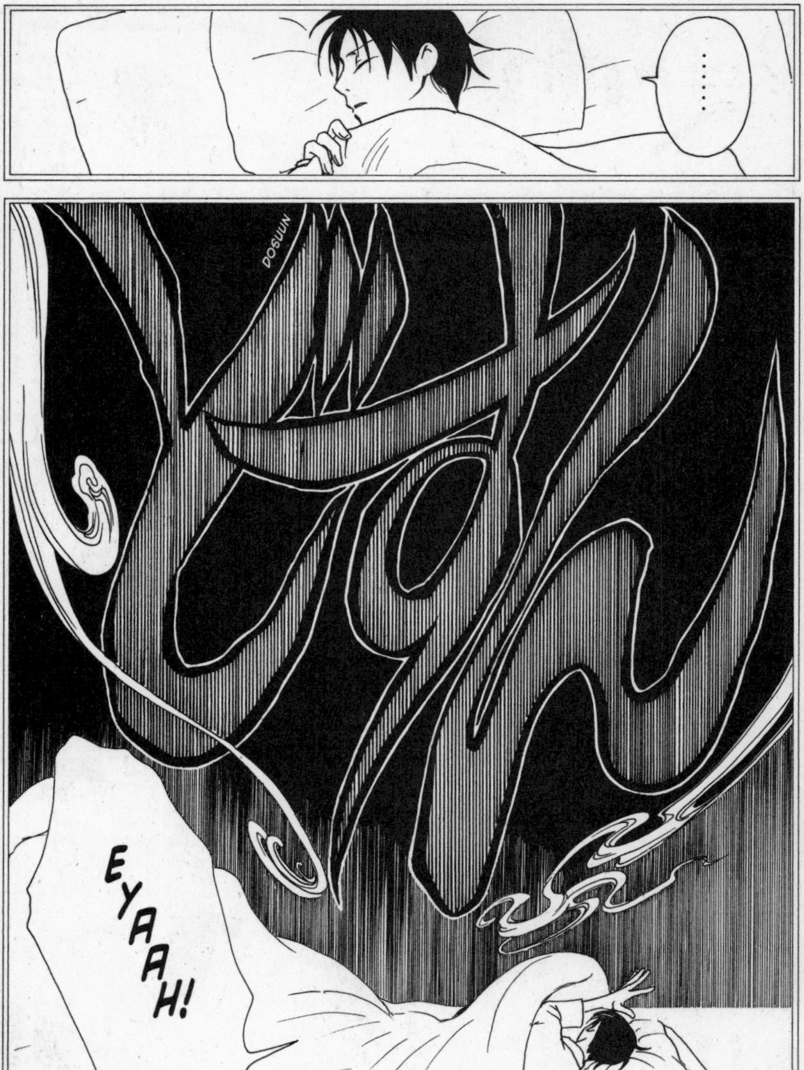
……
DOSUUN
EYAAH!

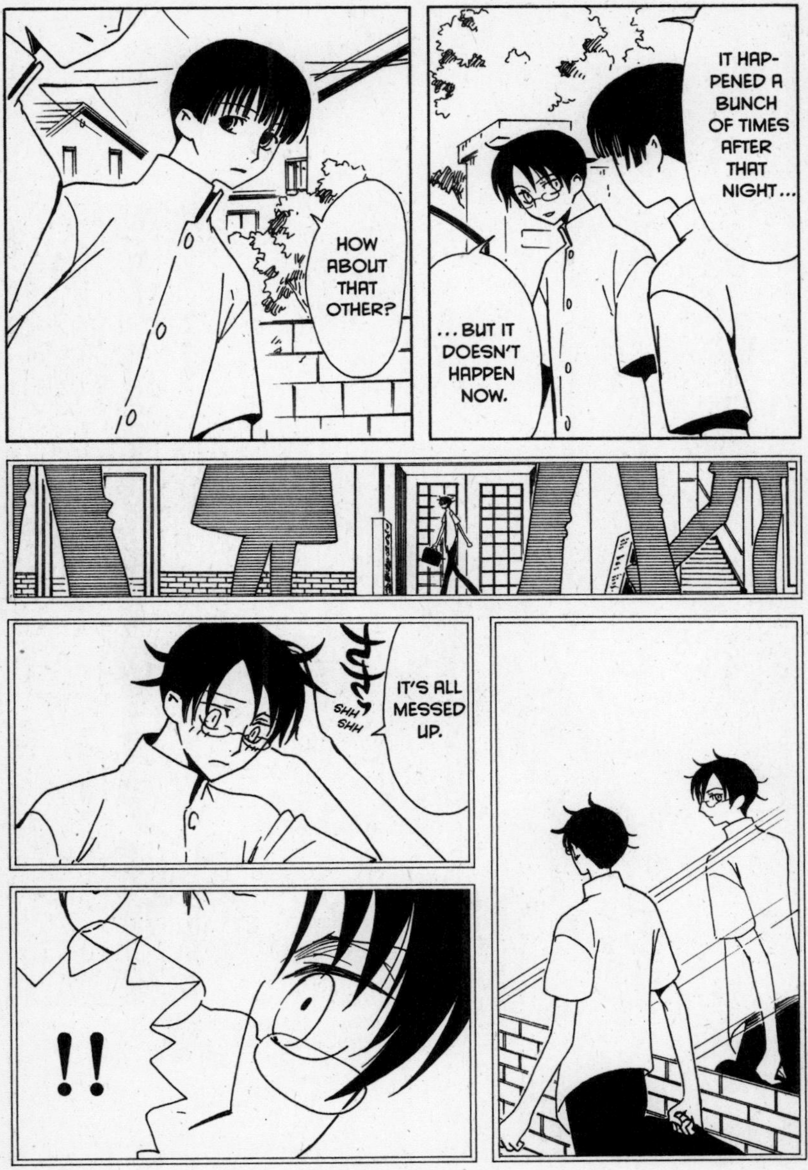
IT HAPPENED A BUNCH OF TIMES AFTER THAT NIGHT...
...BUT IT DOESN'T HAPPEN NOW.
HOW ABOUT THAT OTHER?
IT'S ALL MESSED UP.
SHH SHH
!!

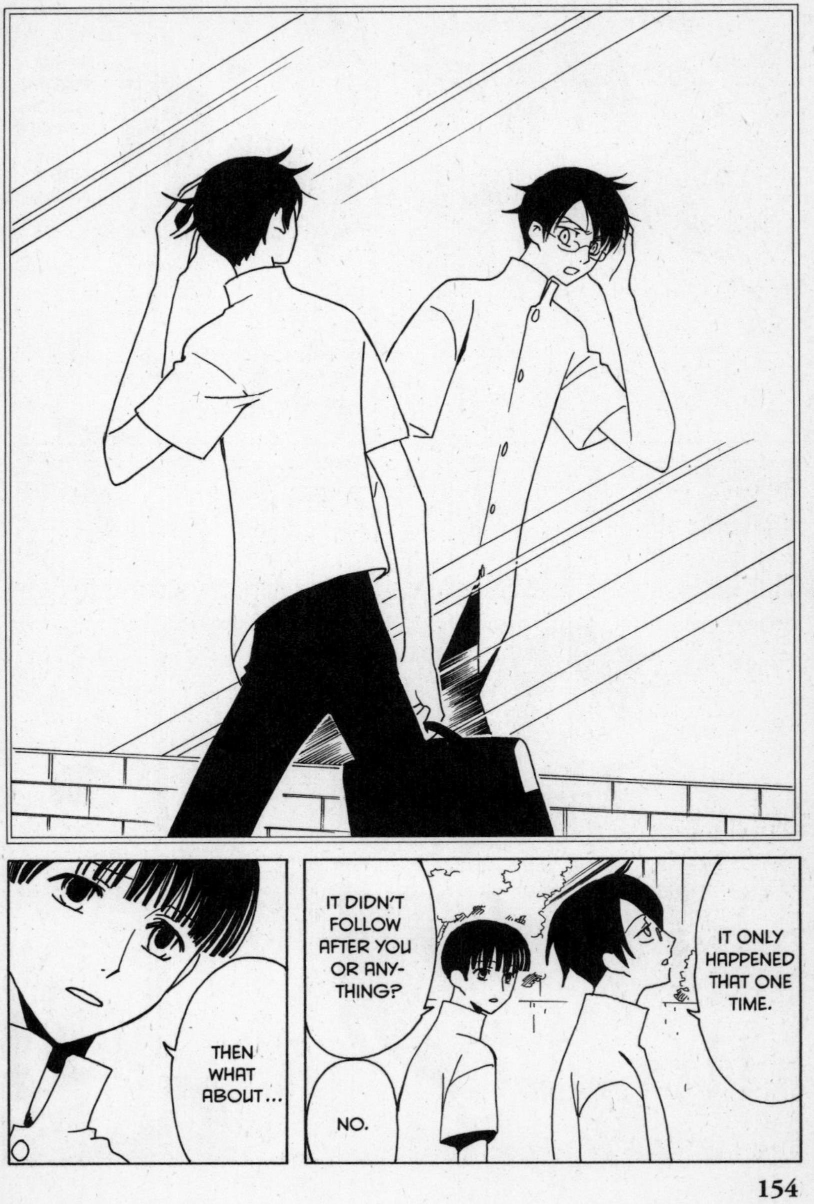
IT ONLY HAPPENED THAT ONE TIME.
IT DIDN'T FOLLOW AFTER YOU OR ANY-THING?
NO.
THEN WHAT ABOUT...

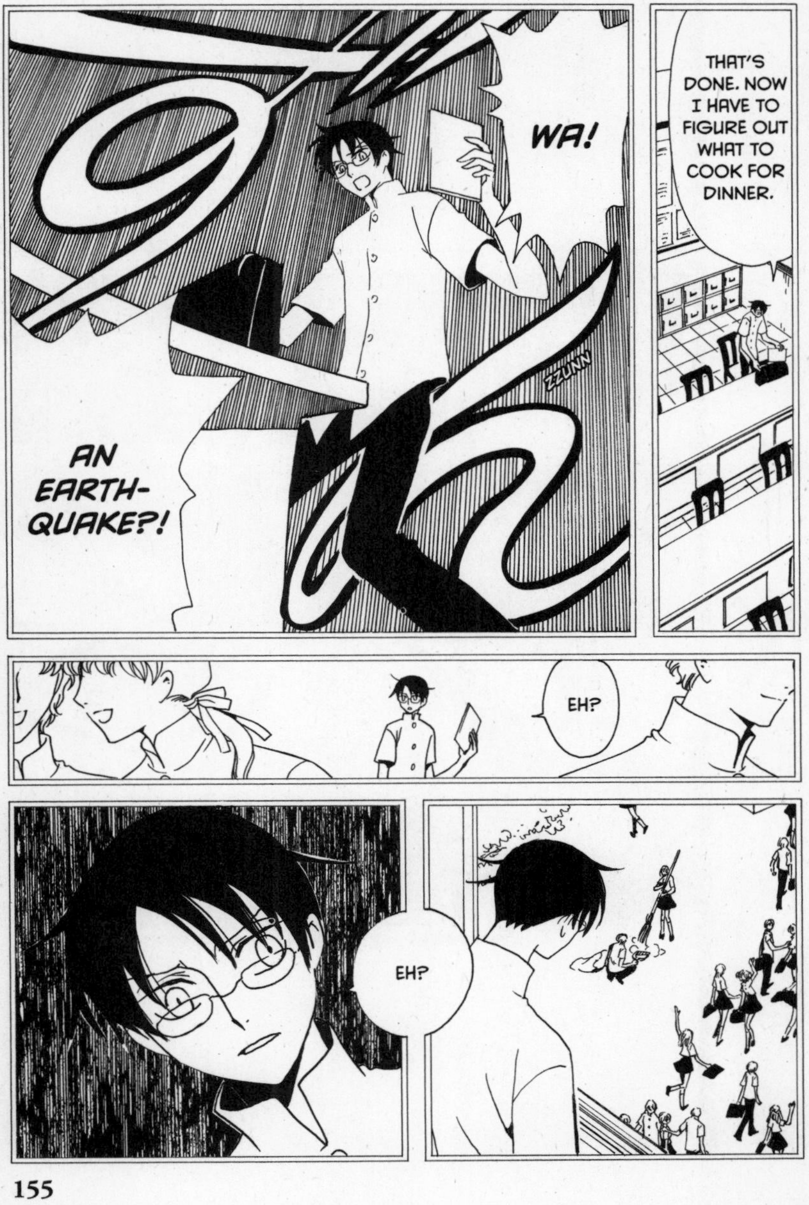
THAT'S DONE. NOW I HAVE TO FIGURE OUT WHAT TO COOK FOR DINNER.
WA!
ZZUNN
AN EARTH-QUAKE?!
EH?
EH?

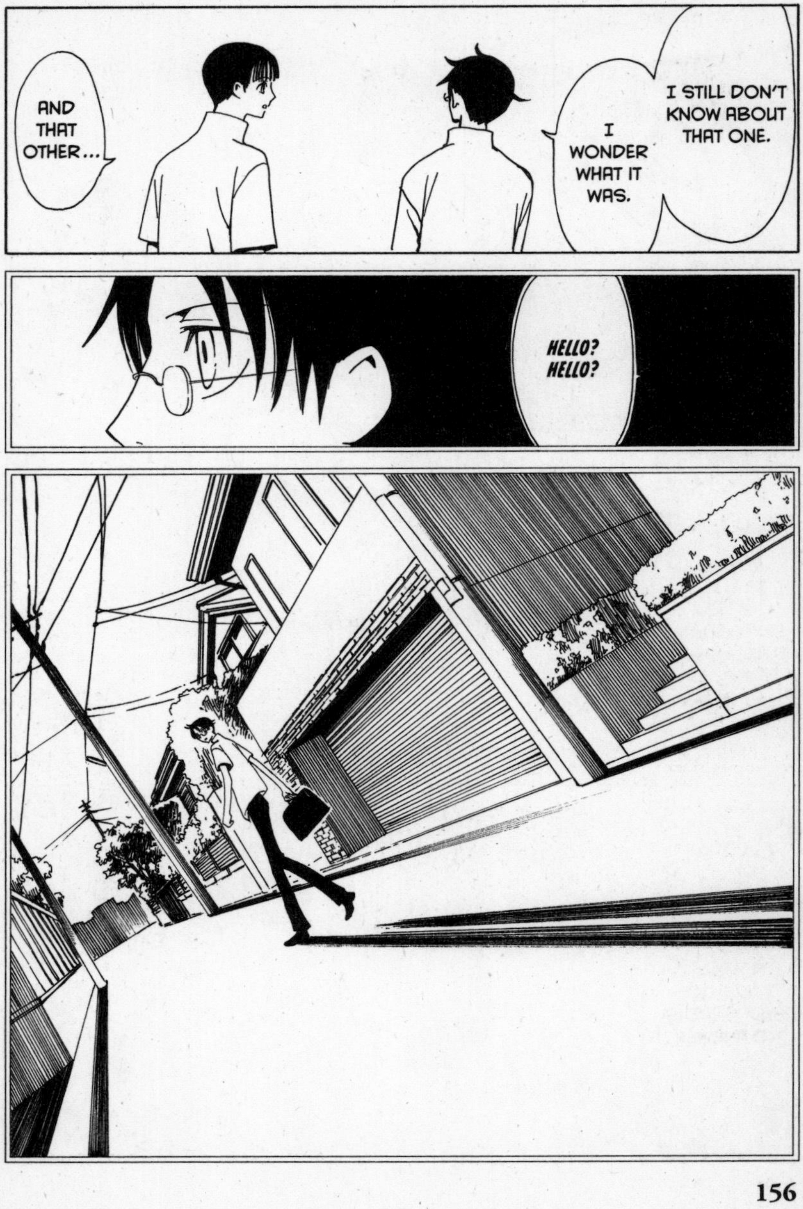
I STILL DON'T KNOW ABOUT THAT ONE.
I WONDER WHAT IT WAS.
AND THAT OTHER...
HELLO? HELLO?

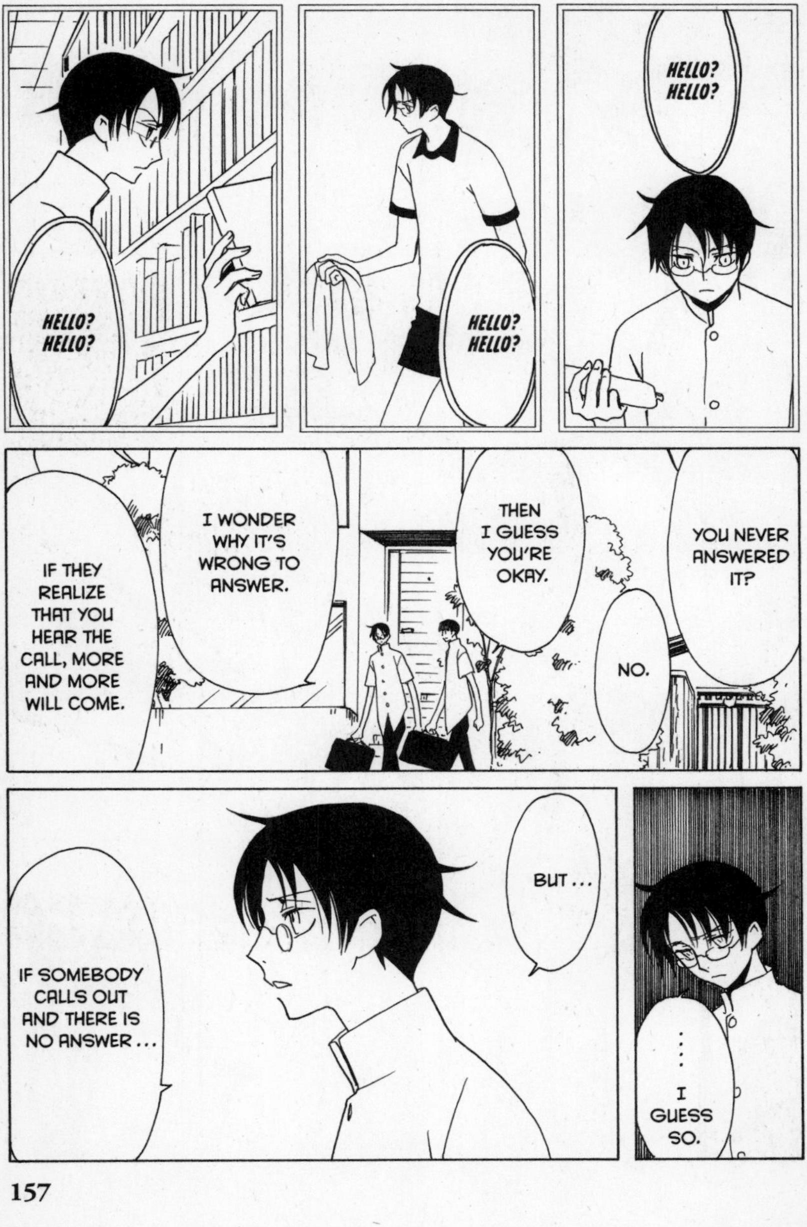
HELLO? HELLO?
HELLO? HELLO?
HELLO? HELLO?
YOU NEVER ANSWERED IT?
NO.
THEN I GUESS YOU'RE OKAY.
I WONDER WHY IT'S WRONG TO ANSWER.
IF THEY REALIZE THAT YOU HEAR THE CALL, MORE AND MORE WILL COME.
.... I GUESS SO.
BUT ...
IF SOMEBODY CALLS OUT AND THERE IS NO ANSWER ...

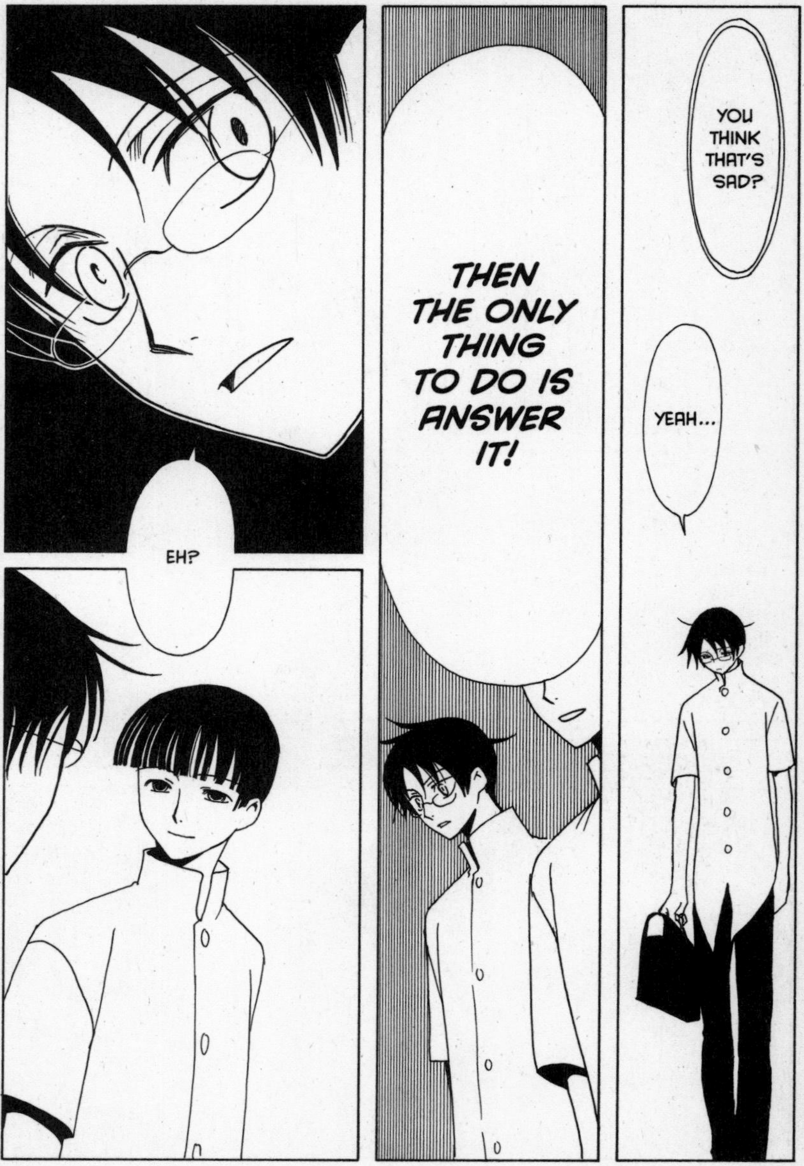
YOU THINK THAT'S SAD?
YEAH...
THEN THE ONLY THING TO DO IS ANSWER IT!
EH?

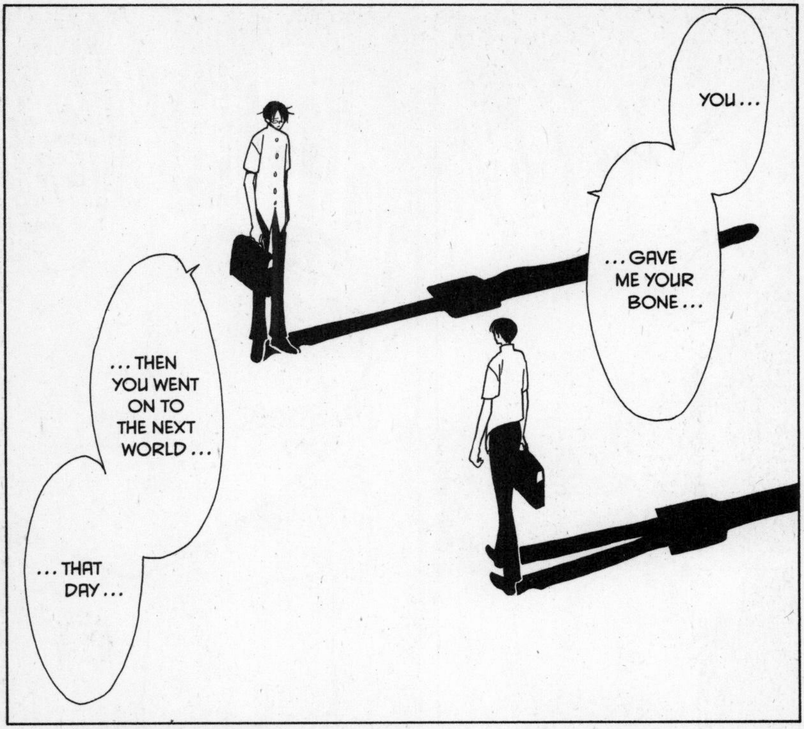
YOU...
...GAVE ME YOUR BONE...
...THEN YOU WENT ON TO THE NEXT WORLD...
...THAT DAY...

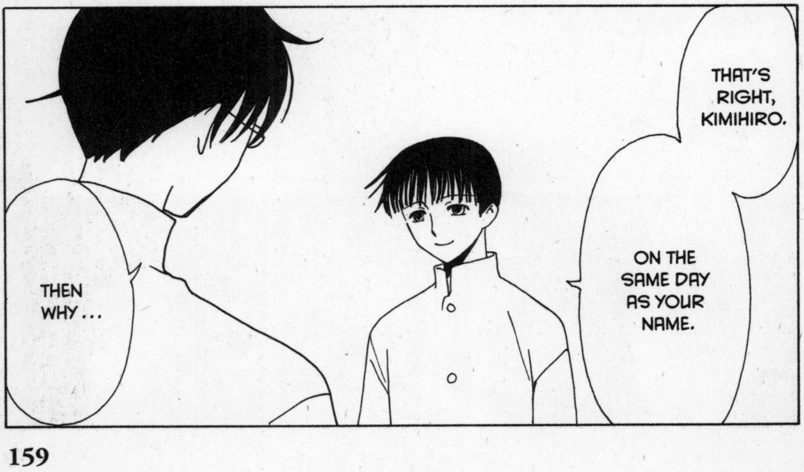
THAT'S RIGHT, KIMIHIRO.
ON THE SAME DAY AS YOUR NAME.
THEN WHY...

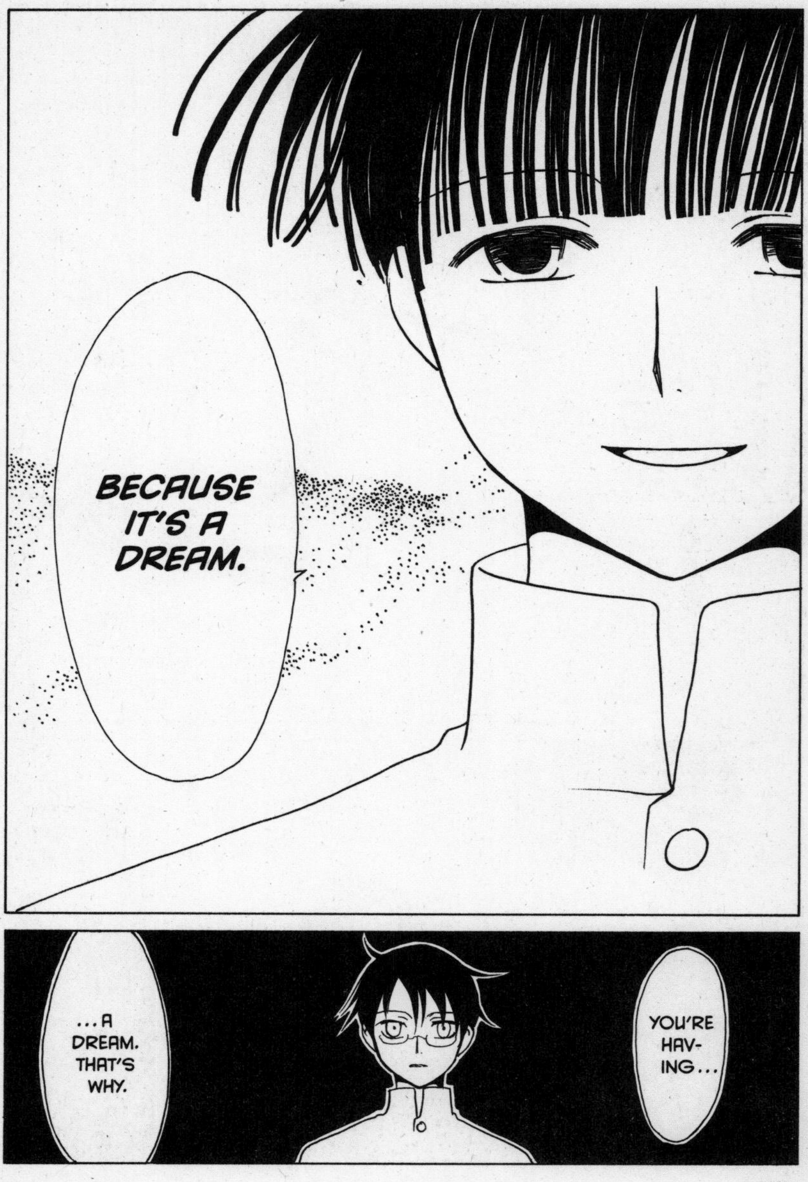
BECAUSE IT'S A DREAM.
YOU'RE HAV-ING...
...A DREAM. THAT'S WHY.

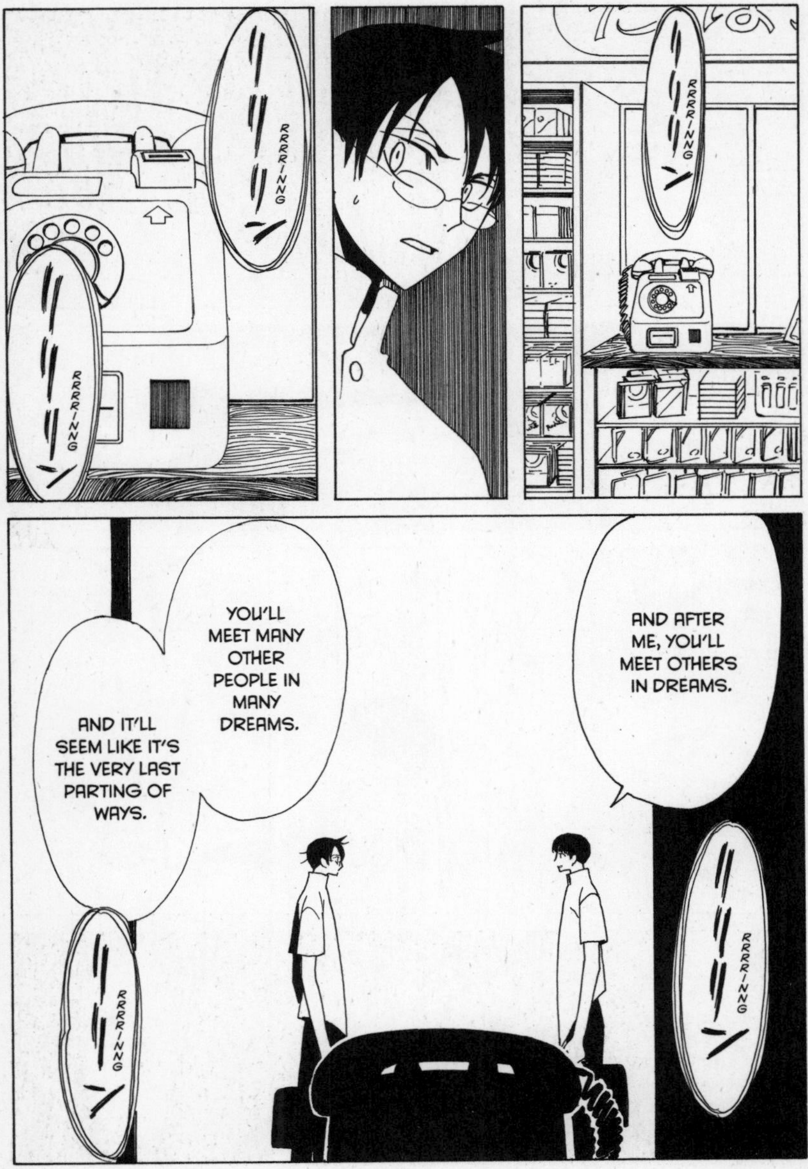
RRRRINNG
RRRRINNG
RRRRINNG
AND AFTER ME, YOU'LL MEET OTHERS IN DREAMS.
RRRRINNG
YOU'LL MEET MANY OTHER PEOPLE IN MANY DREAMS.
AND IT'LL SEEM LIKE IT'S THE VERY LAST PARTING OF WAYS.
RRRRINNG

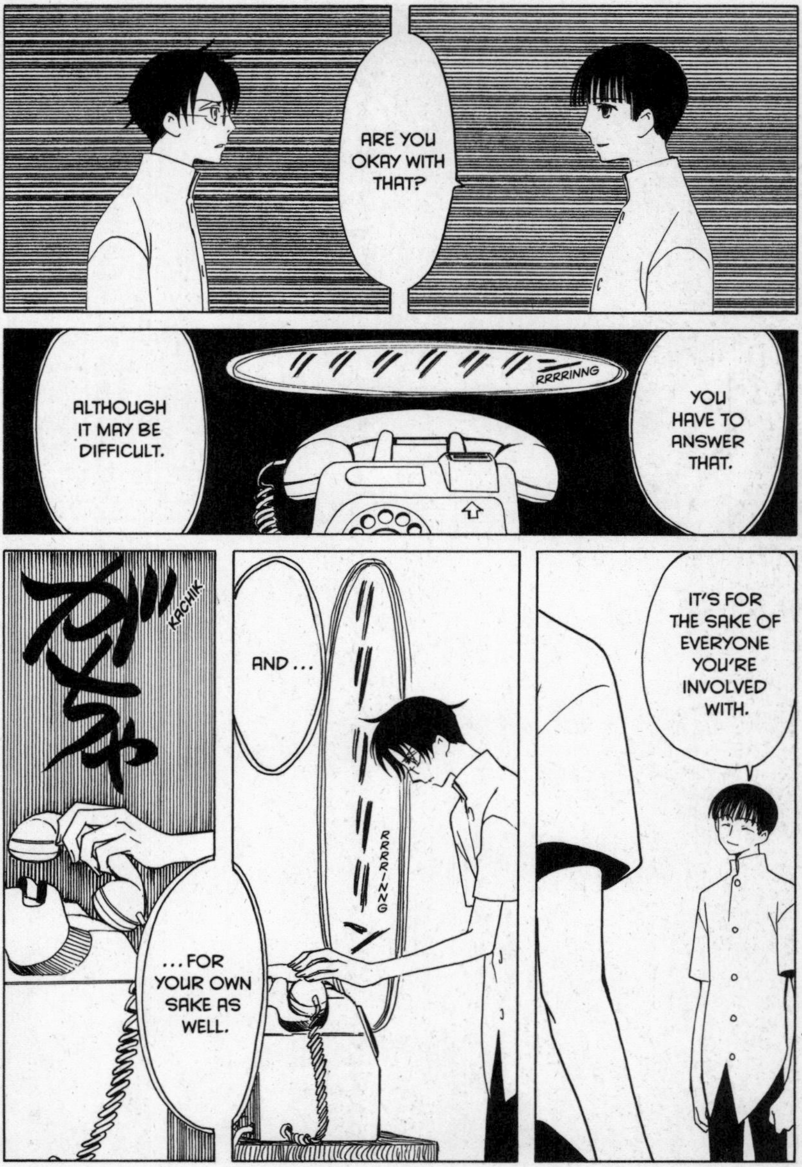
ARE YOU OKAY WITH THAT?
YOU HAVE TO ANSWER THAT.
RRRRINNG
ALTHOUGH IT MAY BE DIFFICULT.
IT'S FOR THE SAKE OF EVERYONE YOU'RE INVOLVED WITH.
AND...
RRRRINNG
...FOR YOUR OWN SAKE AS WELL.
KACHIK

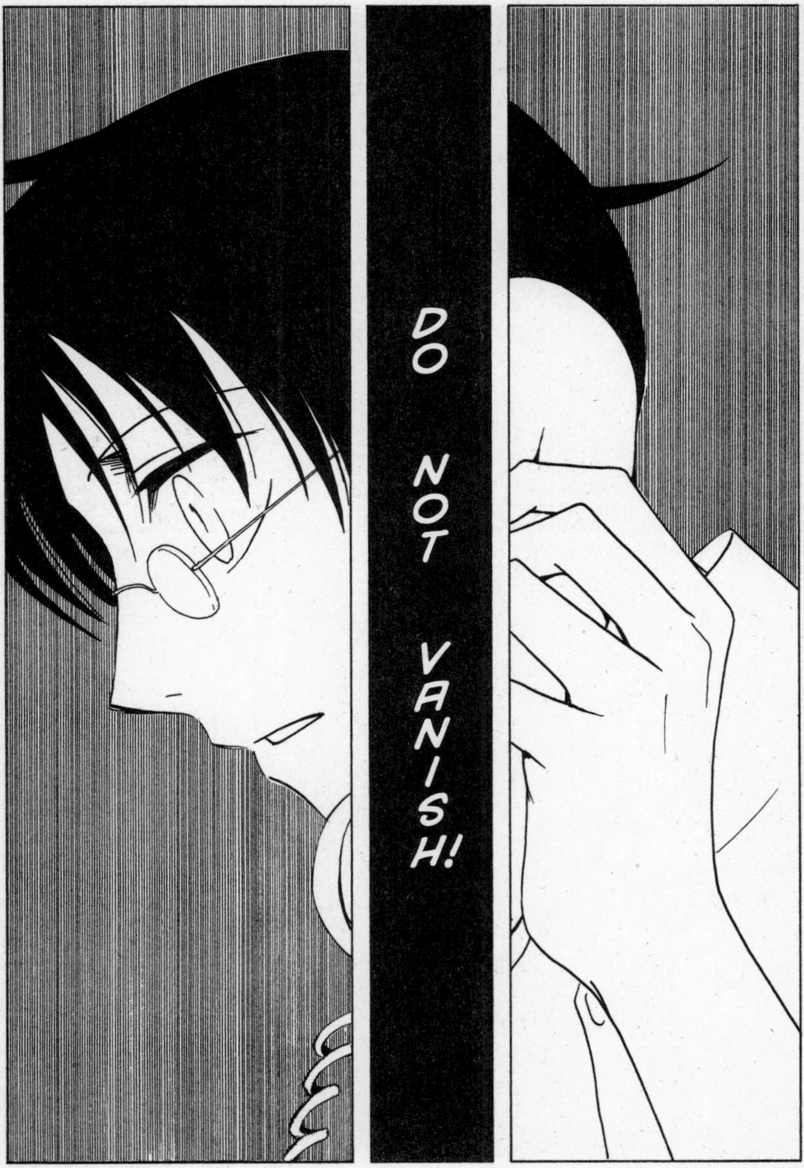
DO NOT VANISH!

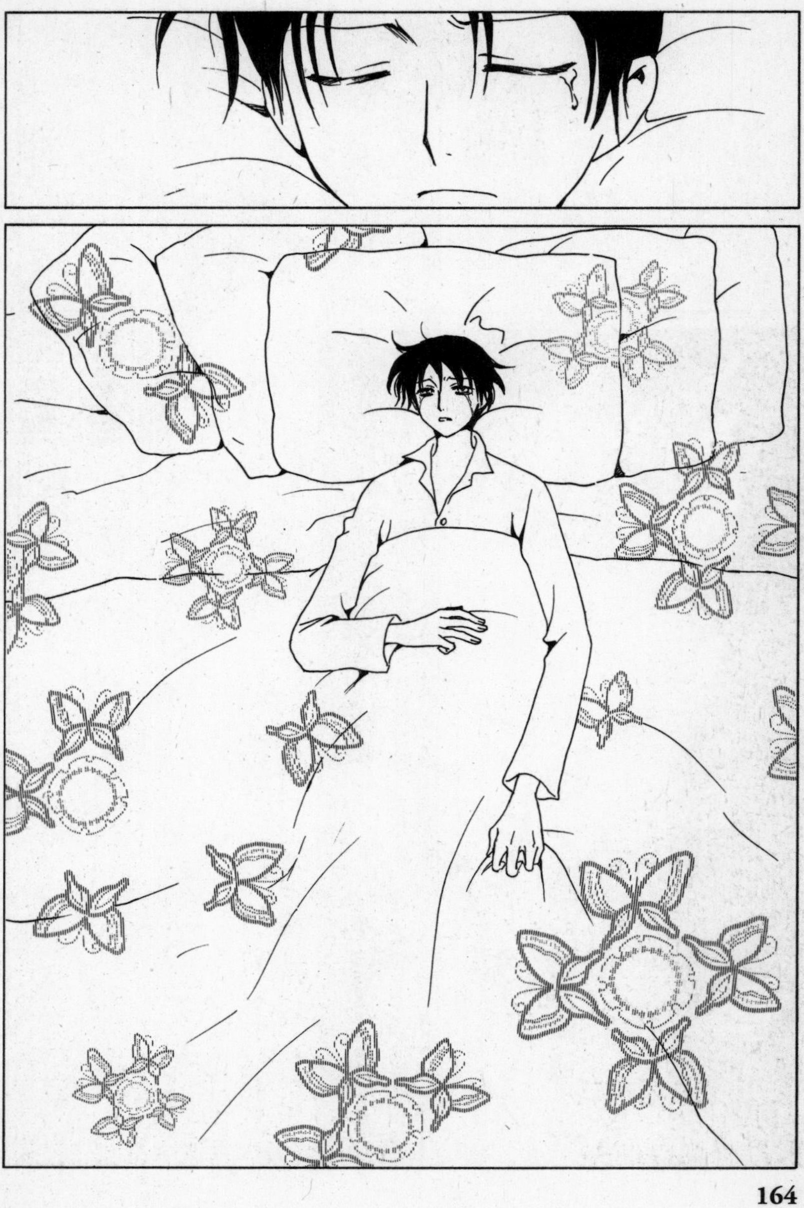

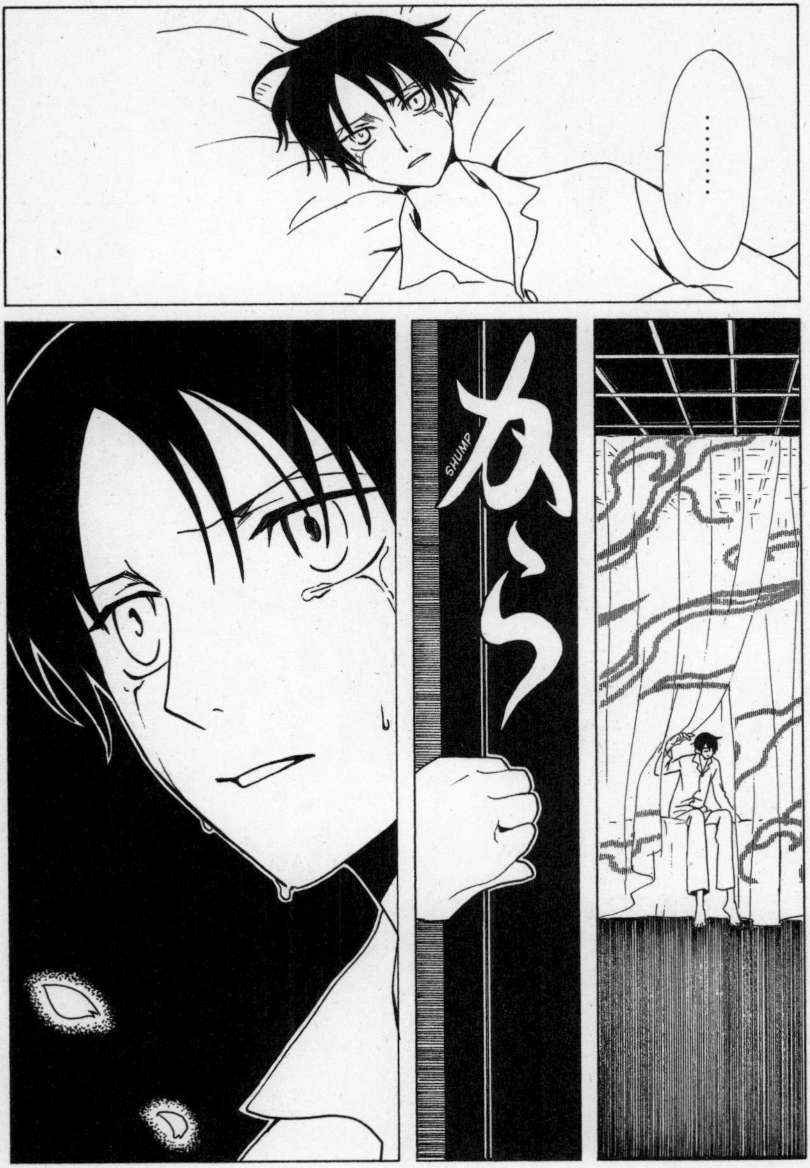
......
から
SHUMP

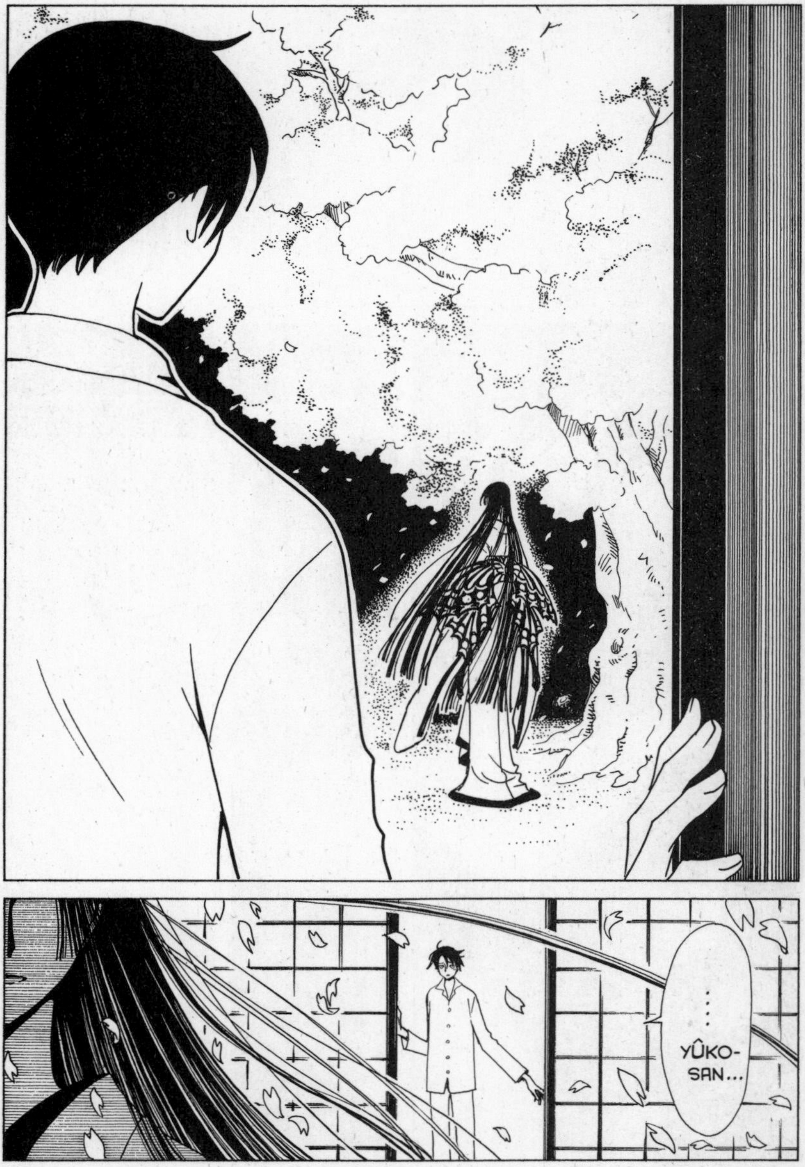
......
YÛKO-SAN...

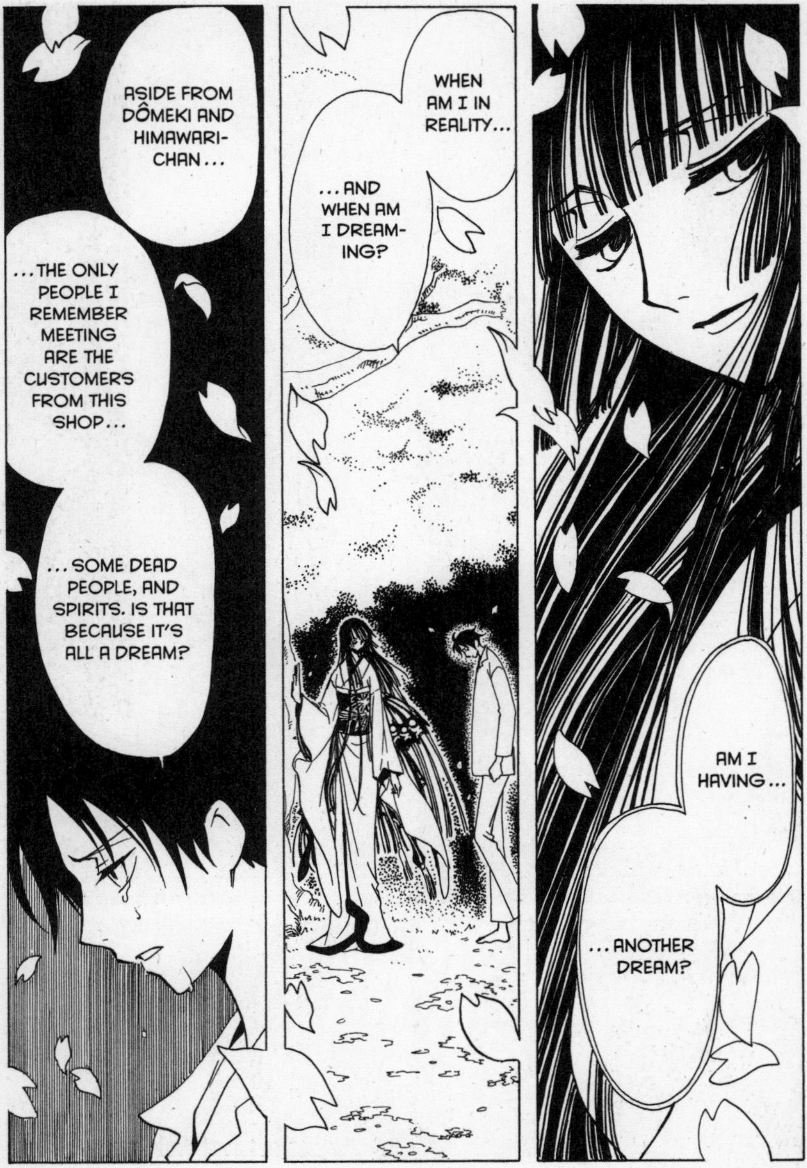
AM I HAVING...
...ANOTHER DREAM?
WHEN AM I IN REALITY...
...AND WHEN AM I DREAMING?
ASIDE FROM DÔMEKI AND HIMAWARI-CHAN...
...THE ONLY PEOPLE I REMEMBER MEETING ARE THE CUSTOMERS FROM THIS SHOP...
...SOME DEAD PEOPLE, AND SPIRITS. IS THAT BECAUSE IT'S ALL A DREAM?

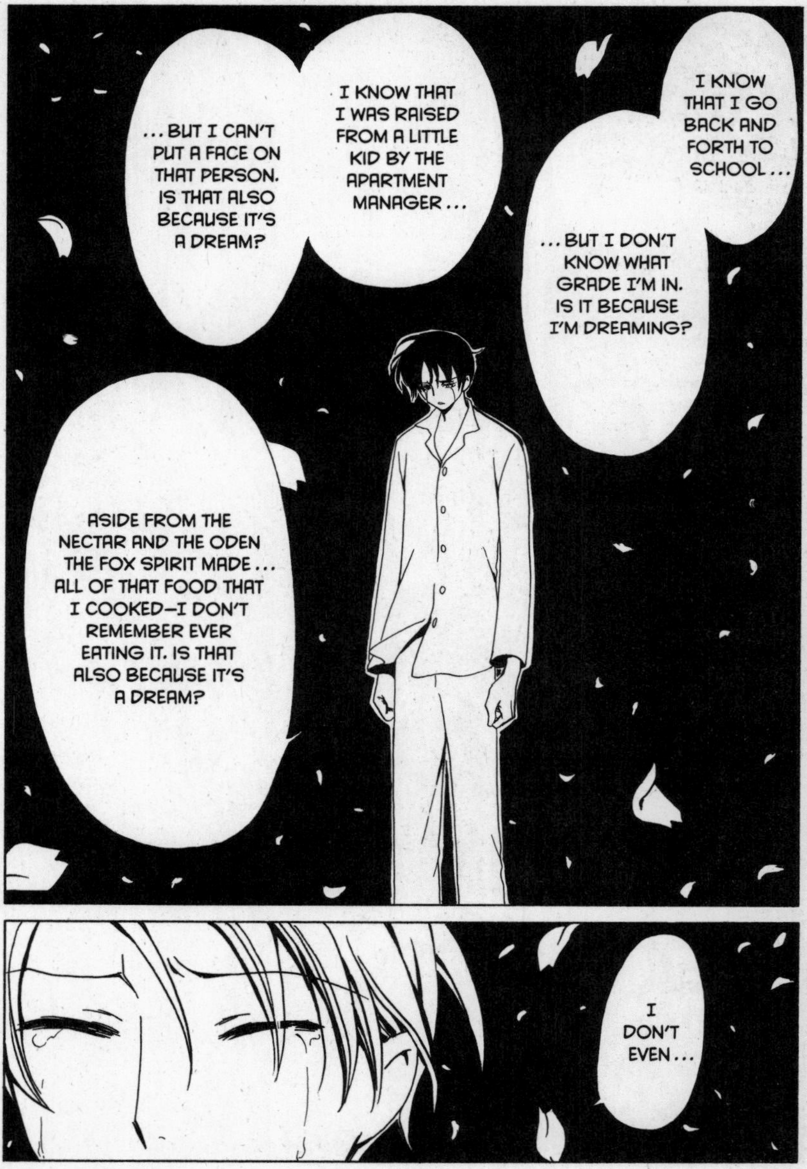
I KNOW THAT I GO BACK AND FORTH TO SCHOOL...
...BUT I DON'T KNOW WHAT GRADE I'M IN. IS IT BECAUSE I'M DREAMING?
I KNOW THAT I WAS RAISED FROM A LITTLE KID BY THE APARTMENT MANAGER...
...BUT I CAN'T PUT A FACE ON THAT PERSON. IS THAT ALSO BECAUSE IT'S A DREAM?
ASIDE FROM THE NECTAR AND THE ODEN THE FOX SPIRIT MADE... ALL OF THAT FOOD THAT I COOKED—I DON'T REMEMBER EVER EATING IT. IS THAT ALSO BECAUSE IT'S A DREAM?
I DON'T EVEN...

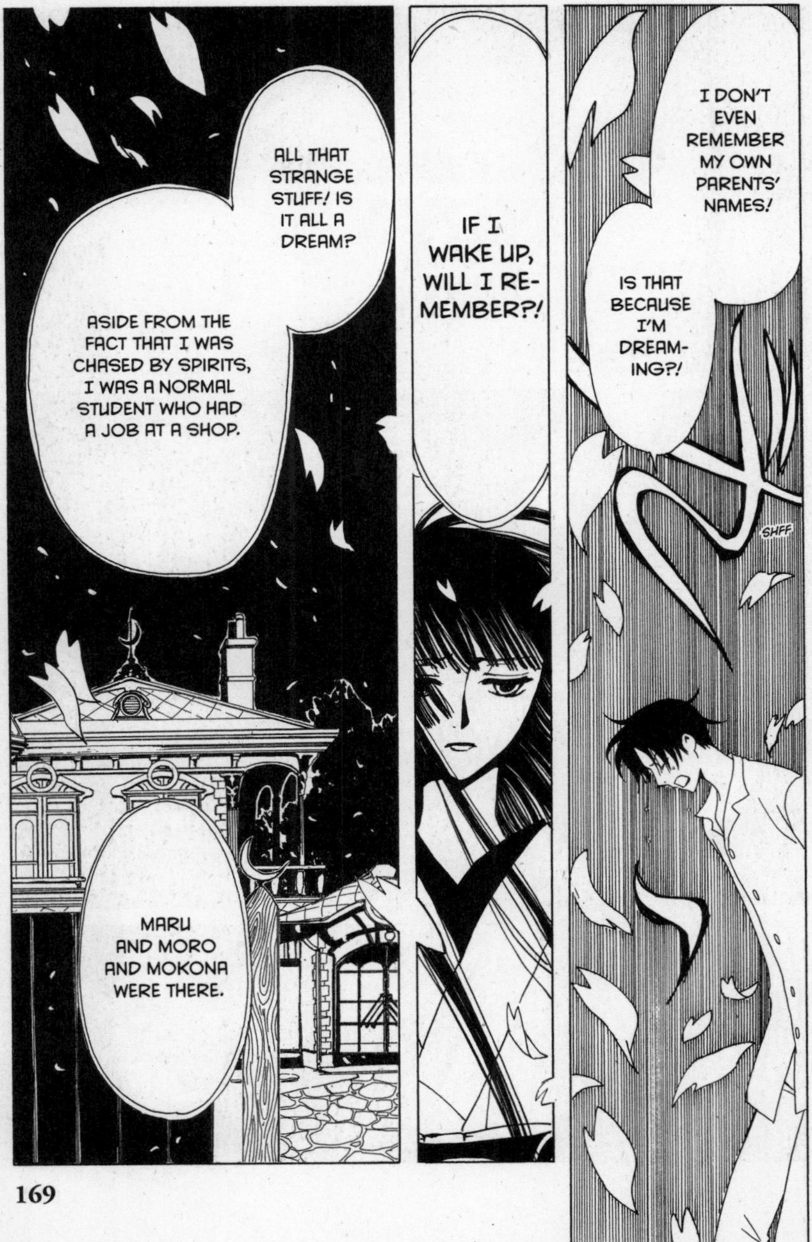
I DON'T EVEN REMEMBER MY OWN PARENTS' NAMES!
IS THAT BECAUSE I'M DREAMING?!
SHFF
IF I WAKE UP, WILL I REMEMBER?!
ALL THAT STRANGE STUFF! IS IT ALL A DREAM?
ASIDE FROM THE FACT THAT I WAS CHASED BY SPIRITS, I WAS A NORMAL STUDENT WHO HAD A JOB AT A SHOP.
MARU AND MORO AND MOKONA WERE THERE.

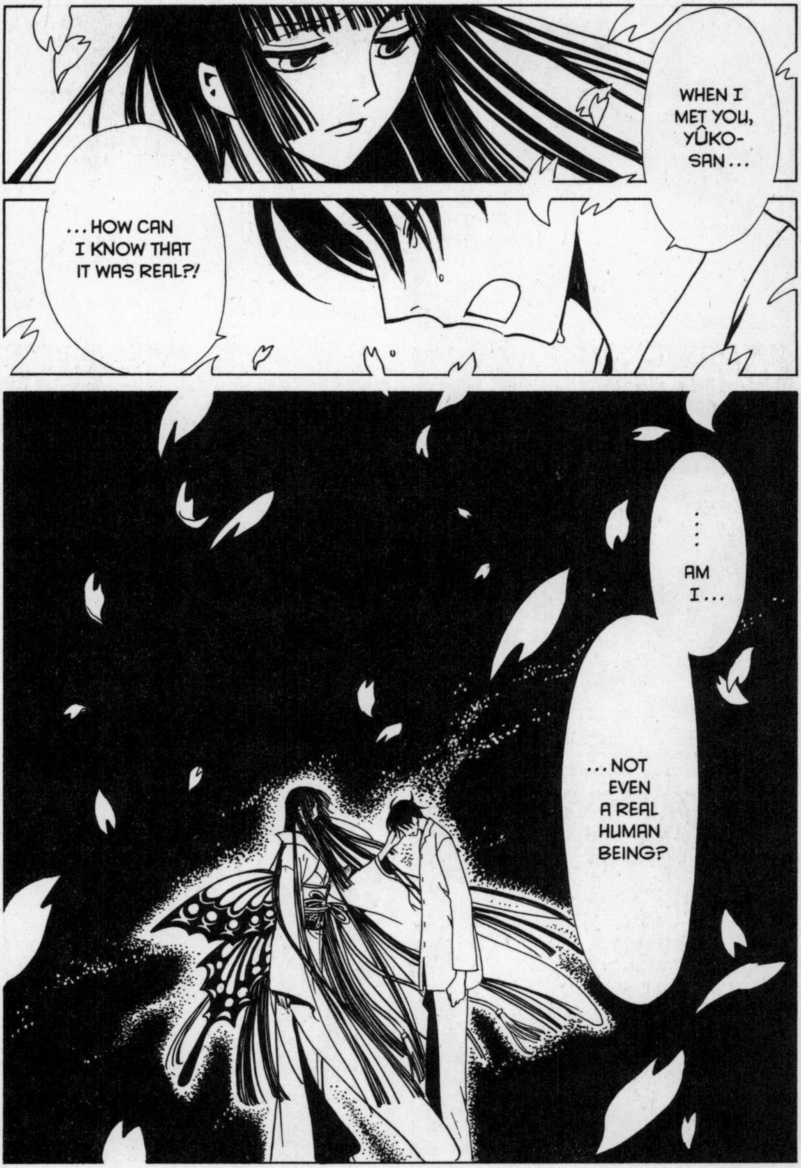
WHEN I MET YOU, YÛKO-SAN...
...HOW CAN I KNOW THAT IT WAS REAL?!
... AM I...
...NOT EVEN A REAL HUMAN BEING?

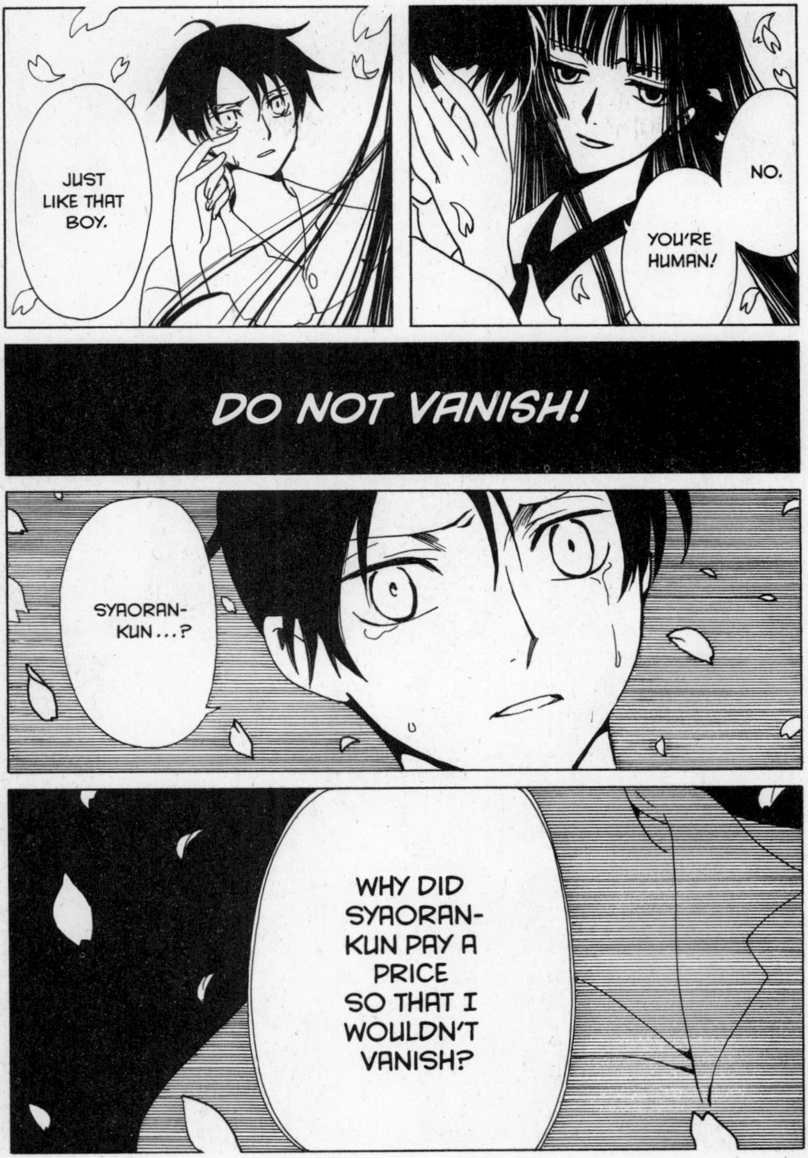
NO.
YOU'RE HUMAN!
JUST LIKE THAT BOY.
DO NOT VANISH!
SYAORAN-KUN...?
WHY DID SYAORAN-KUN PAY A PRICE SO THAT I WOULDN'T VANISH?

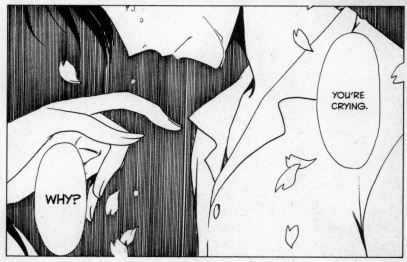

172

JUST LIKE THAT BOY.

NO. YOU'RE HUMAN!

DO NOT VANISH!

SYAORAN-KUN...?

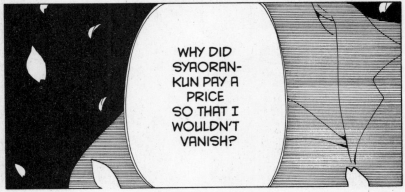

WHY DID SYAORAN-KUN PAY A PRICE SO THAT I WOULDN'T VANISH?

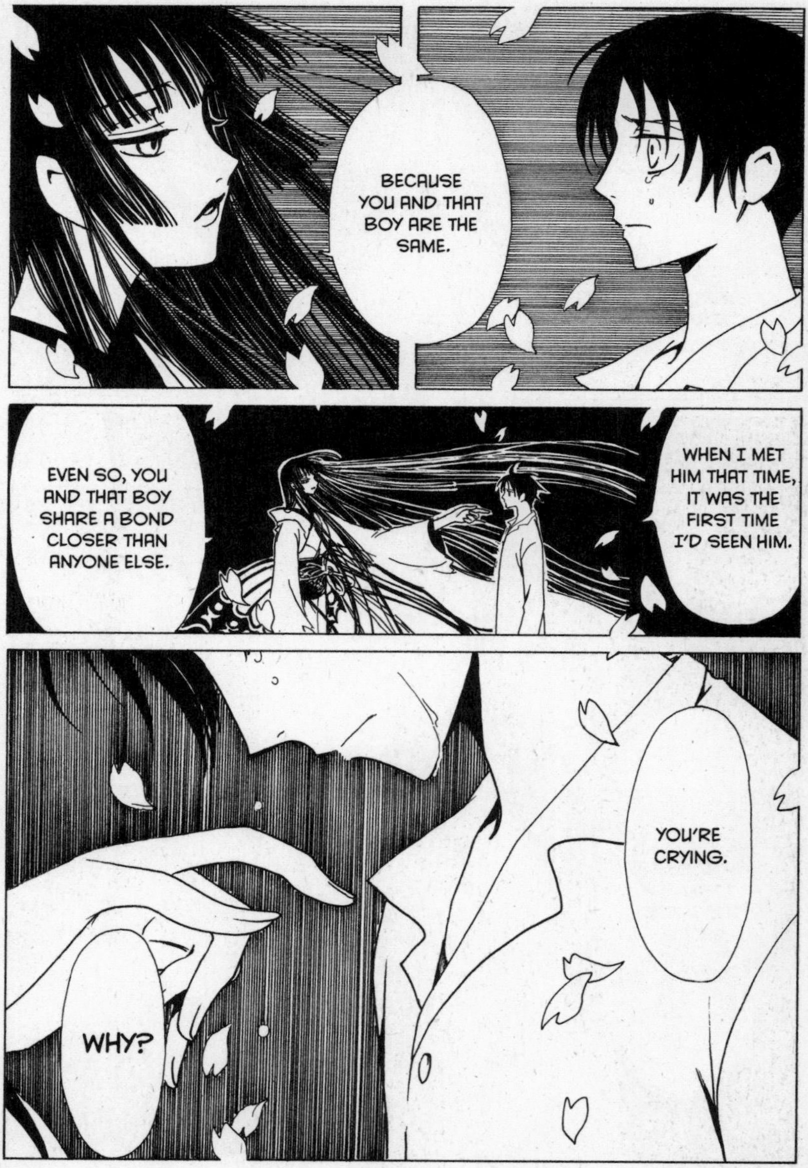
BECAUSE YOU AND THAT BOY ARE THE SAME.
WHEN I MET HIM THAT TIME, IT WAS THE FIRST TIME I'D SEEN HIM.
EVEN SO, YOU AND THAT BOY SHARE A BOND CLOSER THAN ANYONE ELSE.
YOU'RE CRYING.
WHY?

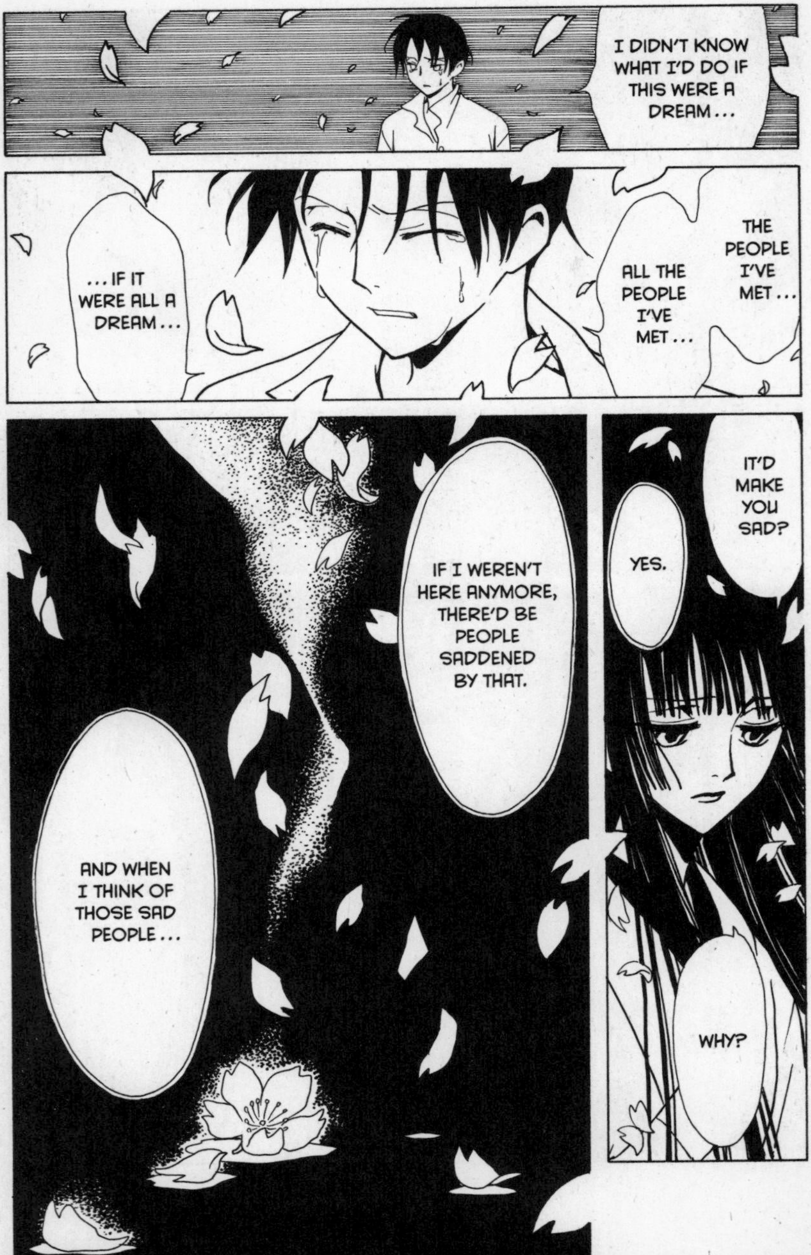
I DIDN'T KNOW WHAT I'D DO IF THIS WERE A DREAM...
THE PEOPLE I'VE MET...
ALL THE PEOPLE I'VE MET...
...IF IT WERE ALL A DREAM...
IT'D MAKE YOU SAD?
YES.
WHY?
IF I WEREN'T HERE ANYMORE, THERE'D BE PEOPLE SADDENED BY THAT.
AND WHEN I THINK OF THOSE SAD PEOPLE...

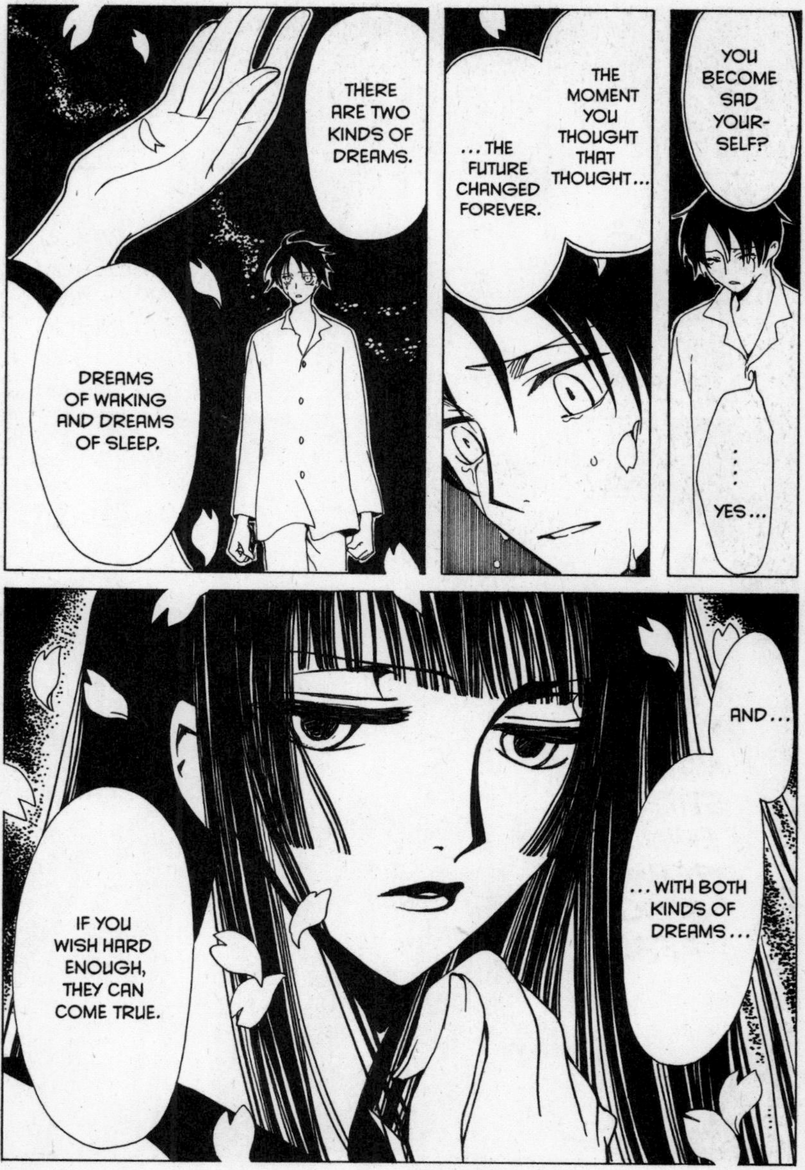
YOU BECOME SAD YOUR-SELF?
...YES...
THE MOMENT YOU THOUGHT THAT THOUGHT...
...THE FUTURE CHANGED FOREVER.
THERE ARE TWO KINDS OF DREAMS.
DREAMS OF WAKING AND DREAMS OF SLEEP.
AND...
...WITH BOTH KINDS OF DREAMS...
IF YOU WISH HARD ENOUGH, THEY CAN COME TRUE.

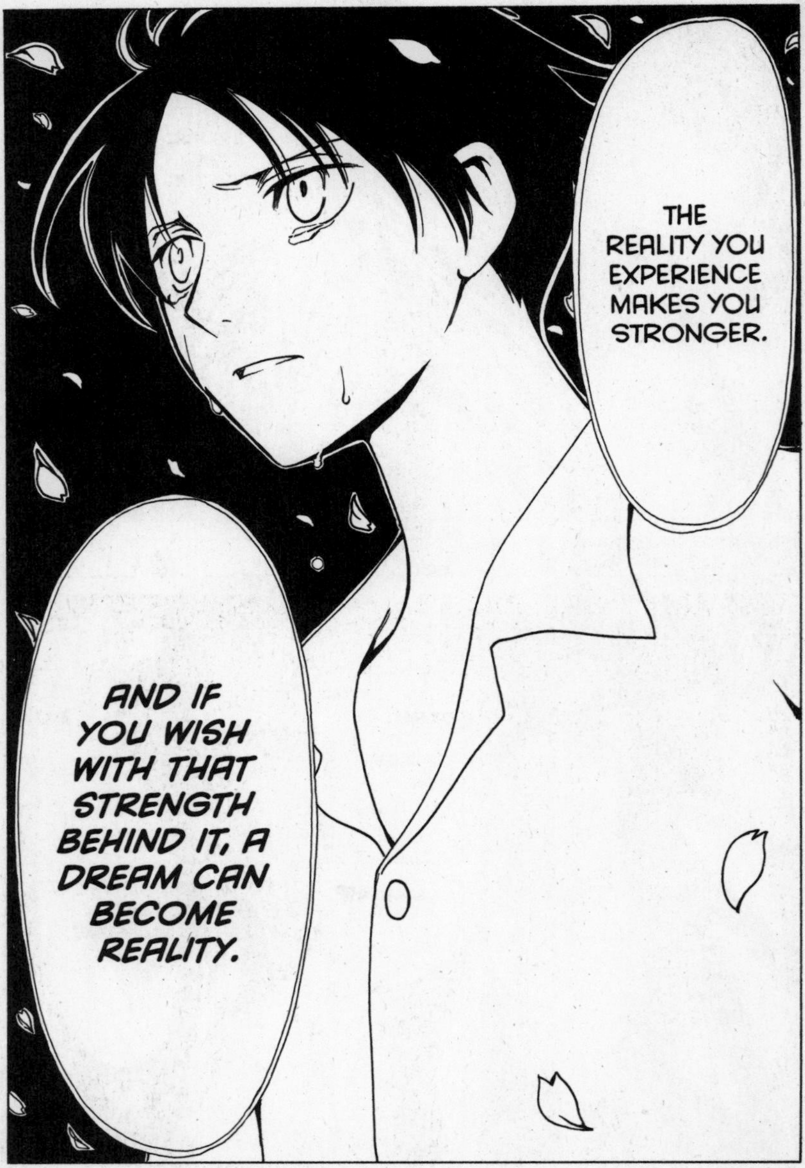
THE REALITY YOU EXPERIENCE MAKES YOU STRONGER.
AND IF YOU WISH WITH THAT STRENGTH BEHIND IT, A DREAM CAN BECOME REALITY.

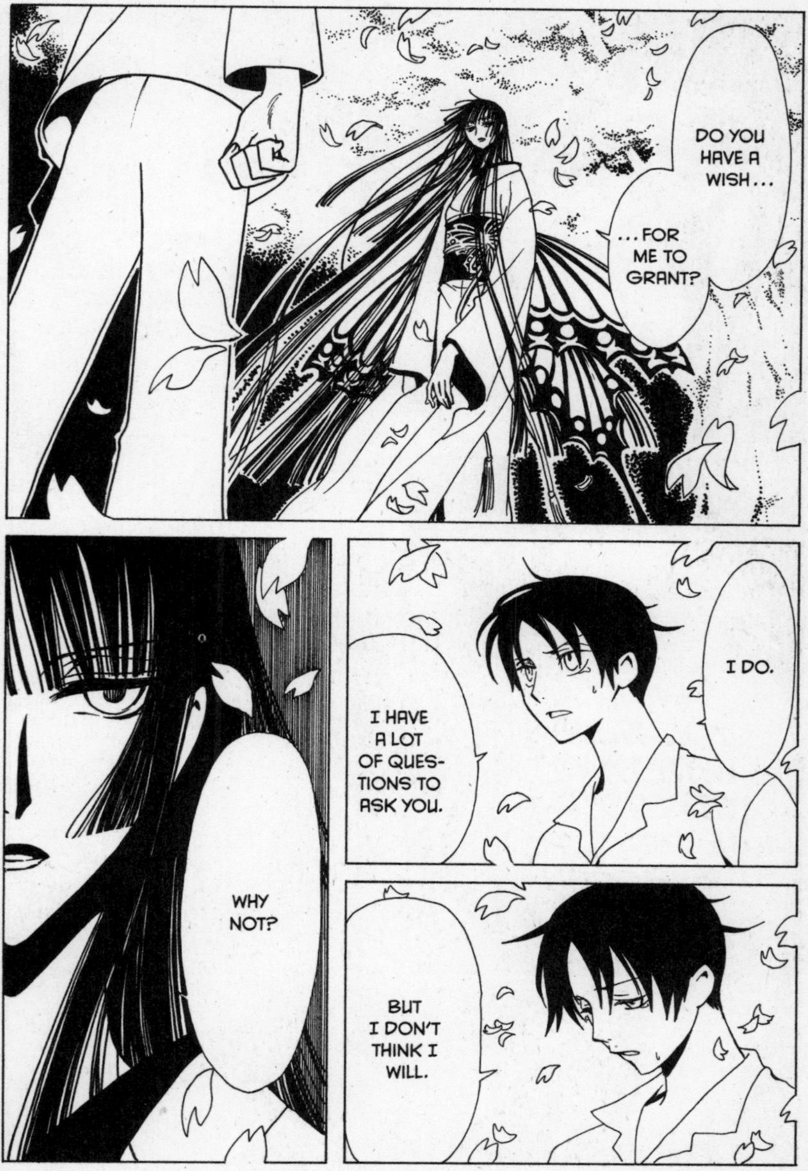
DO YOU HAVE A WISH...
...FOR ME TO GRANT?
I DO.
I HAVE A LOT OF QUES-TIONS TO ASK YOU.
BUT I DON'T THINK I WILL.
WHY NOT?

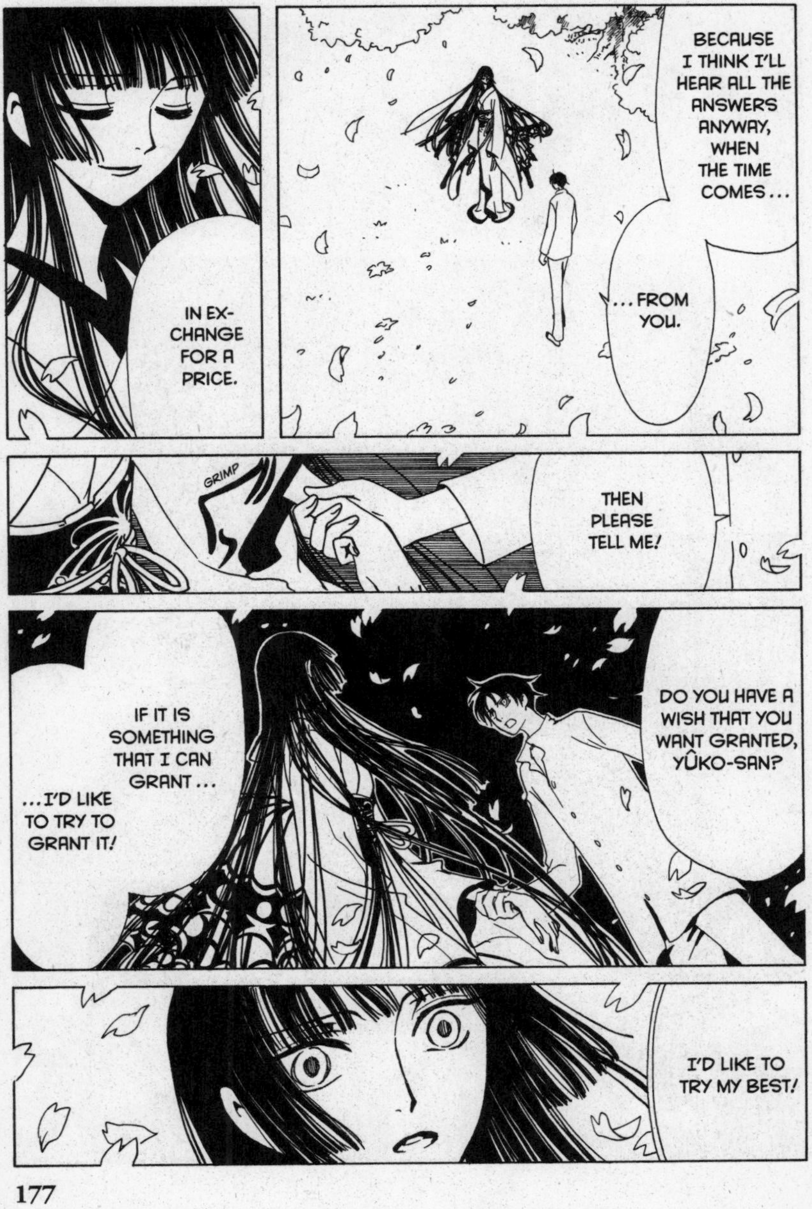
BECAUSE I THINK I'LL HEAR ALL THE ANSWERS ANYWAY, WHEN THE TIME COMES...
...FROM YOU.
IN EX-CHANGE FOR A PRICE.
THEN PLEASE TELL ME!
GRIMP
DO YOU HAVE A WISH THAT YOU WANT GRANTED, YÛKO-SAN?
IF IT IS SOMETHING THAT I CAN GRANT...
...I'D LIKE TO TRY TO GRANT IT!
I'D LIKE TO TRY MY BEST!

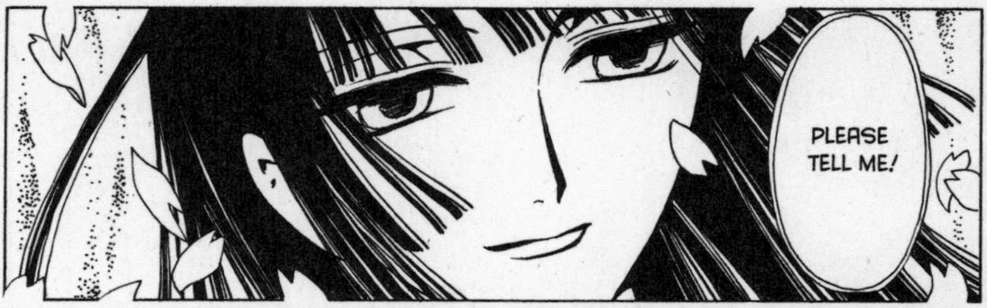
PLEASE TELL ME!
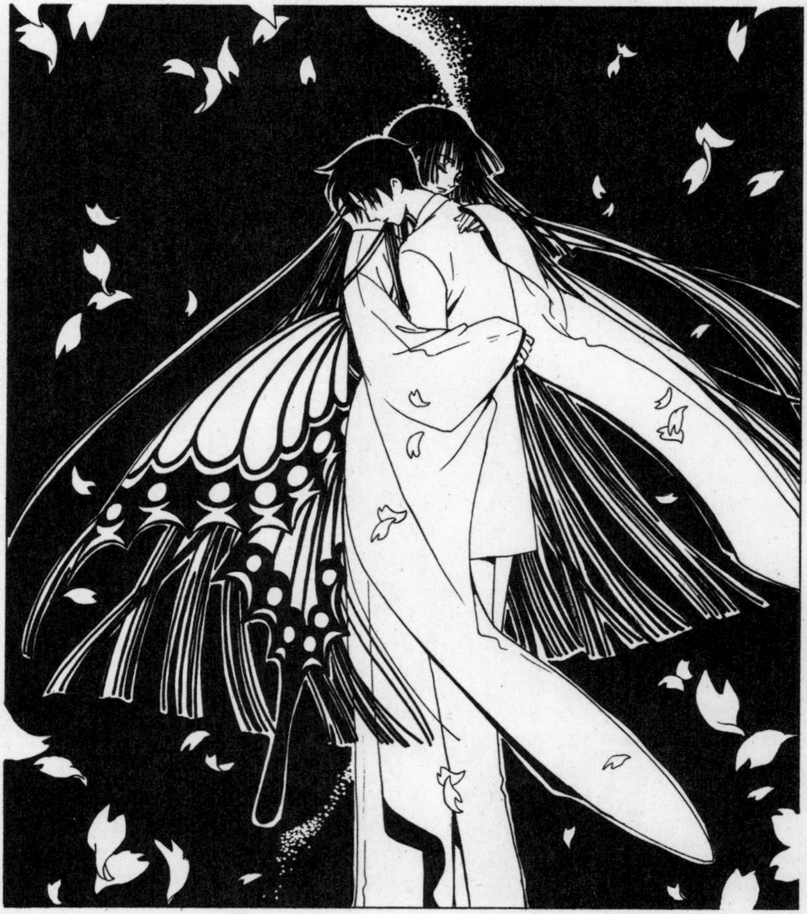

⤜ Continued ⤐

in xxxHOLiC, volume 13

About the Creators

CLAMP is a group of four women who have become the most popular manga artists in America—Satsuki Igarashi, Tsubaki Nekoi, Mokona, and Nanase Ohkawa. They started out as *doujinshi* (fan comics) creators, but their skill and craft brought them to the attention of publishers very quickly. Their first work from a major publisher was RG Veda, but their first mass success was with *Magic Knight Rayearth*. From there, they went on to write many series, including Cardcaptor Sakura and Chobits, two of the most popular manga in the United States. Like many Japanese manga artists, they prefer to avoid the spotlight, and little is known about them personally.

CLAMP is currently publishing three series in Japan: Tsubasa and xxxHOLiC with Kodansha and Gohou Drug with Kadokawa.

Translation Notes

Japanese is a tricky language for most Westerners, and translation is often more art than science. For your edification and reading pleasure, here are notes on some of the places where we could have gone in a different direction or where a Japanese cultural reference is used.

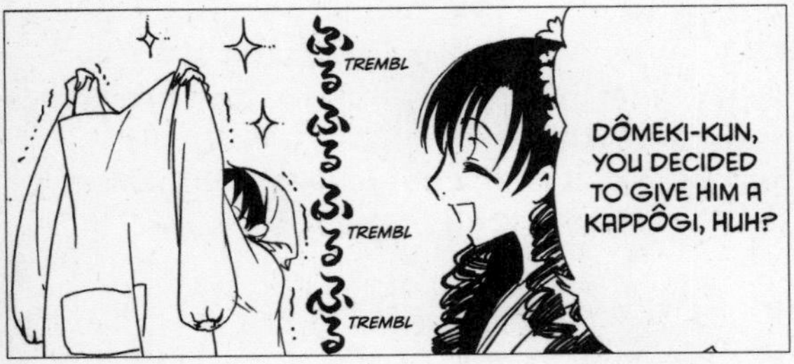
DÔMEKI-KUN, YOU DECIDED TO GIVE HIM A KAPPÔGI, HUH?
TREMBL
TREMBL
TREMBL

Page 10, *Kappôgi*
Also called a Mama-san apron, this was a cloth covering that was originally intended to be worn over a kimono. It is useful in that it covers the entire top half of the body (unlike western aprons that only cover the front). *Kappôgi* can be plain linen garments or sport bright colors, prints, and embroidery.

Page 11, *Chu*
In Japanese the onomatopoeia most commonly used to indicate a kiss is *chu*, much like "smak" or "mwah" might be used in English. But the onomatopoeia has become so common in Japanese speech that *chu* is often substituted for the actual Japanese words for kiss: *kuchizuke* or the English loan word *kisu*.

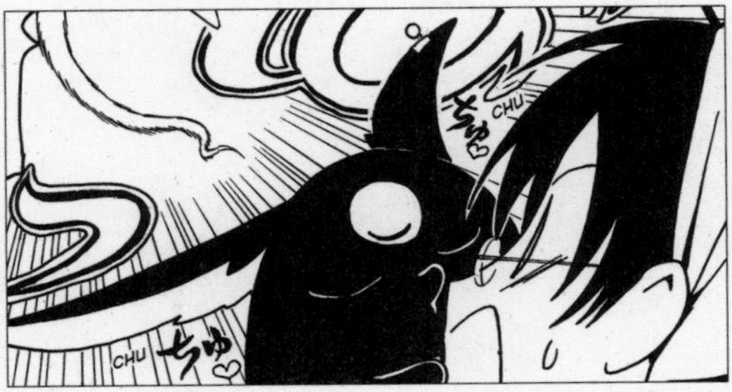
CHU
CHU

Page 20, Princess Sakura

Fans of Tsubasa Reservoir Chronicle will know Princess Sakura, and xxxHOLiC readers might recall her unconscious form from the first chapter in volume 2 of this series. For the curious, the events that lead her to appear in dreams can be found in volumes 18 and 19 of Tsubasa. However, as always, it is not necessary to pick up any Tsubasa volume to follow the events in xxxHOLiC.

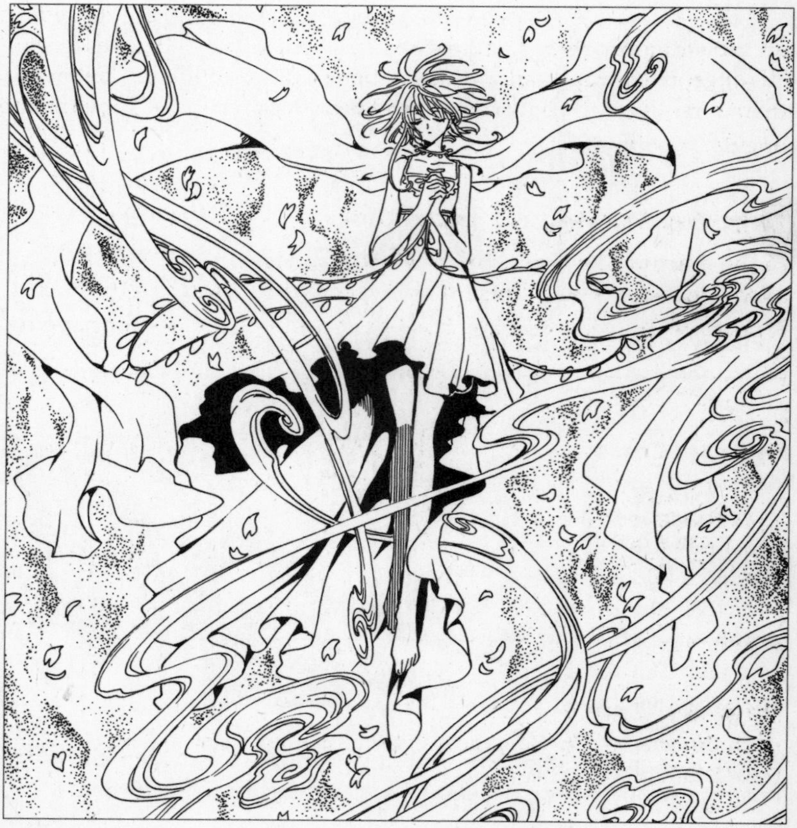

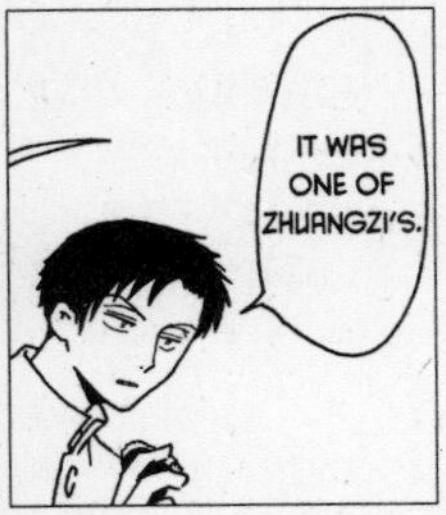
IT WAS ONE OF ZHUANGZI'S.

Page 36, Zhuangzi

The story that Haruka Dômeki told is a paraphrased retelling from a book by the ancient Chinese philosopher Zhuangzi (also known as Chuang Tzu, 369–286 BC), who is considered to be one of the two greatest philosophers of Daoism. While Confucianism was based on self-sacrifice and conformity, the Daoism of Zhuangzi was the opposite, based on individual freedoms and escape from society and its pressures. Zhuangzi encouraged spontaneous behavior and thought, believing them a reaction to reality as it truly is and rising above societal and linguistic limitations.

Page 64, Putting on your shoes

In the entrance hall (*genkan*) of most Japanese homes, there is a short step where one takes off one's shoes when entering, or puts them on again when leaving. It is not considered a place for napping.

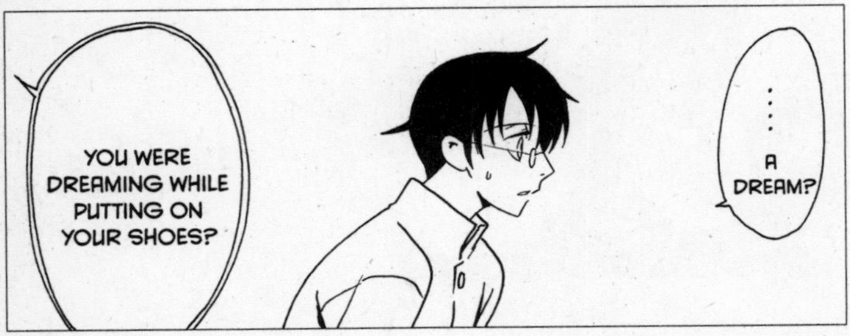
.....
A DREAM?
YOU WERE DREAMING WHILE PUTTING ON YOUR SHOES?

Page 67, *Bentô*

As mentioned in previous notes, *bentô* is a Japanese boxed lunch.

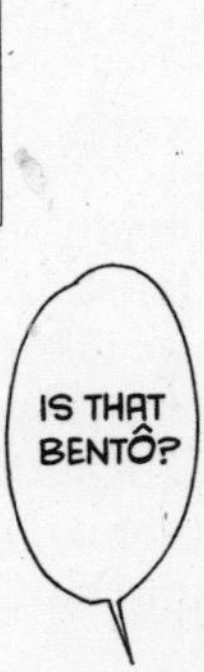
IS THAT BENTÔ?

Page 68, *Hanazushi*

Hanazushi is rolled sushi that in one way or another looks like flowers. Find more about *hanazushi* in the notes for volume 11.

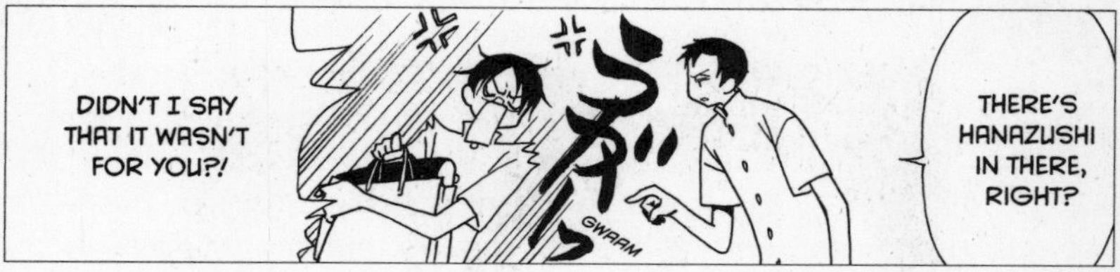
THERE'S HANAZUSHI IN THERE, RIGHT?
GWAAM
DIDN'T I SAY THAT IT WASN'T FOR YOU?!

Page 72, *Dashimaki Tamago*

Dashimaki tamago is an omelet-like fried egg dish spiced with soup stock and rolled into a thick cake. See the notes in volume 10 for more details.

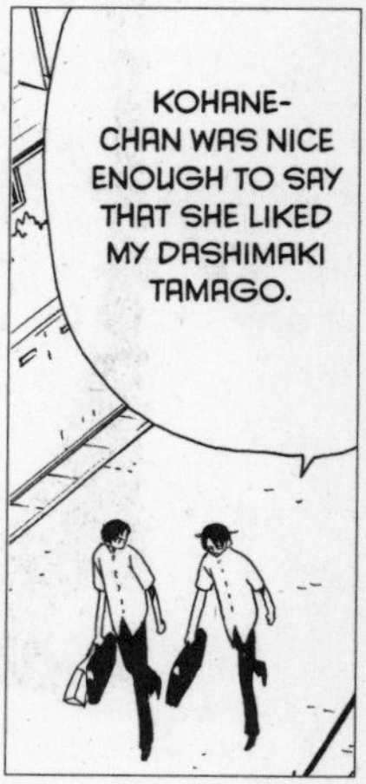
KOHANE-CHAN WAS NICE ENOUGH TO SAY THAT SHE LIKED MY DASHIMAKI TAMAGO.

Page 133, *Ongaeshi*

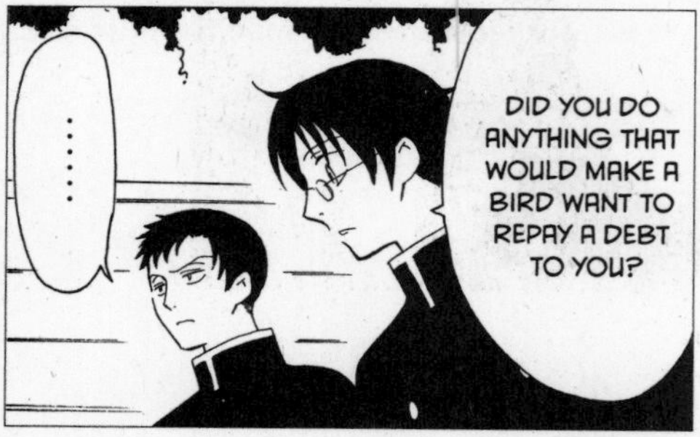
DID YOU DO ANYTHING THAT WOULD MAKE A BIRD WANT TO REPAY A DEBT TO YOU?
......

Repaying one's debt, especially for a life-saving act, is a staple of Japanese fantasy and fairy tales. The most famous fairy tale of this sort is *Tsuru no Ongaeshi* (The Crane Repays Her Debt), in which a man rescues a crane that has been pierced by an arrow, and later a beautiful woman suddenly appears to be his wife. Of course, the woman is the crane, repaying the man's kindness. The popular anime *The Cat Returns* (*Neko no Ongaeshi*) is also based on this idea.

Page 168, Nectar

The nectar that Kimihiro is talking about was given to him by the treelike plant at the end of the nearly disastrous *Hyakki Yakô* march of spirits that took place in volume 6 of this series.

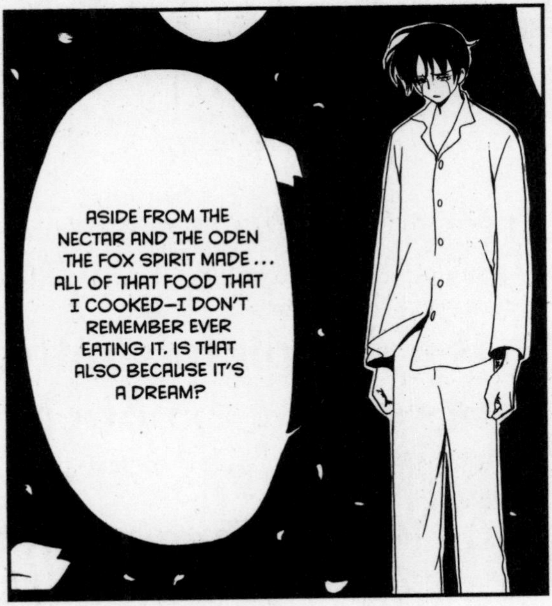
ASIDE FROM THE NECTAR AND THE ODEN THE FOX SPIRIT MADE... ALL OF THAT FOOD THAT I COOKED—I DON'T REMEMBER EVER EATING IT. IS THAT ALSO BECAUSE IT'S A DREAM?

TOMARE!

[STOP!]

You're going the wrong way!

Manga is a completely different type of reading experience.

To start at the *beginning*, go to the *end*!

That's right! Authentic manga is read the traditional Japanese way—from right to left. Exactly the *opposite* of how American books are read. It's easy to follow: Just go to the other end of the book, and read each page—and each panel—from right side to left side, starting at the top right. Now you're experiencing manga as it was meant to be!